Friends,

Writers,

and

Other Countrymen

Friends,

Writers,

and

Other Countrymen

—A Memoir—

SIDNEY OFFIT

Thomas Dunne Books
St. Martin's Press 🔠 New York

THOMAS DUNNE BOOKS.
An imprint of St. Martin's Press.

A version of chapter two, "Baker, Barth, and a Sanskrit Scholar," appeared in *Johns Hopkins Magazine,* November 1977.

"Lines Fraught with Naught but Thought," by Ogden Nash. Copyright © 1960 by Ogden Nash. Reprinted by permission of Curtis Brown, Ltd.

"Art," from *Different Hours* by Stephen Dunn. Copyright © 2000 by Stephen Dunn. Used by permission of W. W. Norton & Company, Inc.

"Ode to Maize," by Pablo Neruda, translated by Margaret Sayers Peden, from *Selected Odes of Pablo Neruda.* Used by permission of the University of California Press.

"Tell Me," from *The Collected Poems of Langston Hughes* by Langston Hughes, edited by Arnold Rampersad with David Roessel, associate editor, copyright © 1994 by The Estate of Langston Hughes. Used by permission of Alfred A. Knopf, a division of Random House.

"The Poem as Mask," reprinted by permission of International Creative Management, Inc. Copyright © 1968 by Muriel Rukeyser, from *The Collected Poems of Muriel Rukeyser,* University of Pittsburgh Press, 2005.

www.thomasdunnebooks.com
www.stmartins.com

Book design by Sarah Maya Gubkin

Library of Congress Cataloging-in-Publication Data

Offit, Sidney.
    Friends, writers, other countrymen / by Sidney Offit.—1st Thomas Dunne Books ed.
      p. cm.
    ISBN-13: 978-0-312-37522-5 (alk. paper)
    ISBN-10: 0-312-37522-0 (alk. paper)
   1. Offit, Sidney. 2. Authors, American—20th century—Biography. 3. Editors—United States—20th century—Biography. 4. Baltimore (Md.)—Social life and customs.
5. New York (N.Y.)—Social life and customs. I. Title.
    PS3565.F385Z46   2008
    813'.54—dc22
    [B]

                        2008009997

First Edition: July 2008

10 9 8 7 6 5 4 3 2 1

To Avi, Ken, and Mike,
who encouraged me to talk, listen, and write

Contents

VI. *Book—ends: Twenty-first Century*

Introduction

About five years ago our elder son, Ken, suggested I follow up my *Memoir of the Bookie's Son* with a collection of stories about people I've met: "You've told me how you smoked one of your first cigars with H. L. Mencken and received a box of cigars from Che Guevara. There must be lots more tales where they came from. Write 'em up!"

Friendships and encounters were not an approach to writing about my life experiences that I'd ever considered before. I suppose I was inhibited by hesitations about dropping names or hurting feelings. Among the lessons of my father that made a strong impression on me was his reluctance to mention names, the royalty of the racing world with whom he shared tips, wagers, and seats in the breeder's box. My wife, Avi, too, as a practicing psychiatrist, guards the names of her patients.

My life is different. My revelations don't influence the odds for the morning line nor do they violate the Hippocratic oath.

The more I thought about it the clearer it became to me that people are the adventure of my life, the collaborators and guides to my engagements with jobs, books, ideas, good deeds, and *carpe diem*! So I take the liberty of writing these scenes and experiences. The composition and structure contradict aspects of the craft of the memoir I have been teaching for forty years:

Number one: Don't apologize. No excuses. Tell your story, write your essay, and let the reader determine its compromises and failures.

Number two: Decide what your memoir is about—the premise or theme. Define it with a sentence or two. It's not necessary to remind the reader, but the theme directs the development of the narrative.

Number three: Don't jump around in time too often. A flashback now and then is comprehensible to the reader, but too many time-acrobatics tend to exhaust a reader's patience.

Chronology is as often a quest as an obvious sequence for authors of memoirs. Some place their lives in the order defined by school attendance and the psychology of aging. Others hop, skip, and jump to freely associative ramblings, resembling a cocktail of Sterne and Joyce, with a shaving of Proust. My life is more defined by activities: involvements in family, organizations, publications. Therefore, the chronology is often sequential through each activity or association, but not from the beginning of the book to the end. I've made an effort to locate the kickoffs and final bells and put them in some order that may amuse more than bewilder the patient reader.

In my seventy-ninth year of scribbling and mischief I break some of my rules to get it down—the names and games, day jobs and night thoughts. My sources include journals, diaries, board minutes, and photographs, but most of all my memory of spontaneous conversations. I just hope I didn't leave out too many friends, writers, and other countrymen whose goodwill lives after them.

A truly intelligent man is always light-hearted.

—H. L. Mencken

I

Random Encounters from JHU to NYC: 1940s and 1950s

1

H. L. Mencken: Lessons in Smoking and First-Edition Best Bets

Circa 1946

I learned about smoking and collecting from H. L. Mencken by way of Ellen Glasgow. When I returned to Baltimore from Wayne, Pennsylvania, during the years I attended the Valley Forge Military Academy, 1942 to 1946, I had few friends and, with the exception of my kid brother Benson, no one with whom to share enthusiasms. One of my classmates had mentioned the novels of a Virginian friend of his family—Ellen Glasgow. John Copley Travis, whom I considered the most literary and sophisticated of my chums, spoke about his father's collection of first editions. These slight references were all the inspiration I needed at the age of sixteen to become a collector of Ellen Glasgow first editions.

This hobby mystified both my mother, who loved books but saw no particular virtue in the rarity of the edition, and my dad, whose reading was restricted to the racing form and the local papers. Nonetheless, my mother didn't discourage me and my father bankrolled my passion with a modest investment.

I would walk from our family's apartment on Lake Drive past the islands of grass on Park Avenue, across the busy intersection at North Avenue. Then I'd cut over the railroad bridge to Charles Street and continue on to the Peabody Book Shop, where it was not only possible to search through used books but also to sit in a pleasant atrium and feast on bratwurst, knockwurst, German potato salad, and a mug of local beer.

It was at Smith's Books on Howard Street, however, that I began my Glasgow collection and often encountered Henry L. Mencken. I recall a portly, shining face, hair parted in the middle, mouth engaged with a corncob pipe or cigar as he chatted with Mr. Smith.

I recognized Mr. Mencken from my childhood. In the thirties my father was one of Baltimore's most successful bookmakers. Although his professional talents were unknown to me at the time, I was aware that on our Sunday outings we visited the best restaurants and hotel dining rooms in town. My father seemed to be known by everyone. Bartenders, headwaiters, the best-dressed guests, and certainly every man smoking a cigar greeted him. Although there was little conversation, I detected an unmistakable respect, even reverence in their regards.

Not exactly so with Mr. Mencken. As we made our way to the main dining room of the Rennert Hotel, he would be sitting at the bar with a cigar over a drink and as we passed he would acknowledge my father with a vaguely amused nod of the head or a chipper "How do you do?" My mother always identified him: "That's H. L. Mencken. He's a newspaper man."

I had heard that my father sold newspapers on the streets of Baltimore when he was eight years old and made enough money to contribute to the support of his five brothers and sister. My dad, too, smoked cigars from time to time, so I assumed H. L. Mencken, like my dad, stood on street corners hustling papers.

That impression was so indelible it remained even after my mother later expressed admiration for the magazines *Smart Set* and *American Mercury,* or quoted two of the more famous wrap-ups to his "The Free Lance" columns in *The Baltimore Sun*—"Swat the fly . . . Boil your drinking water."

I felt sufficiently comfortable with this vague but "historic" connection that I began to mimic the "Sage of Bawlamer" by plunking a cigar in my mouth when visiting Smith's. I'm not sure if Mr. Mencken was in the shop when I purchased my first edition of Glasgow's *In This Our Life,* but I do recall he celebrated my acquisition of *Vein of Iron* by passing along to me a free cigar and the advice, "Never relight a stogie once it dies on you, my boy. Read the message from above and treat yourself to another blessing from below."

That was not all I learned. After I lit up, he suggested with a voice that remains in my memory a blend of W. C. Fields and Winston Churchill, "You'd be better advised to collect Willa Cather."

2

Baker, Barth, and a Sanskrit Scholar

1946–1950

I was eighteen years old and had completed three years at the Valley Forge Military Academy with sufficient credits to qualify for the freshman class at Johns Hopkins University when I reported to orientation in the fall of 1946. To me, the war was already distant and romantic; I had trained for it and missed it. The range of my academic curiosity may be measured by my attraction to the Hopkins curriculum, where mathematics was not a prerequisite.

With the bold impulse of an adolescent I aspired to be a writer. I had read John Milton and James T. Farrell, William Makepeace Thackeray and Chester Gould, Grantland Rice and Daniel Defoe. What did I know about writing? I could not positively distinguish between composing fiction, essays, or reports, and lurking within me was the suspicion I might be a poet and dramatist. In this flush of confidence I lumped together all prose and poetry. I thought a true writer could write in any form, with a variety of styles. I could be Shakespeare.

My first semester at the Homewood campus of Johns Hopkins

University, I heard the liberal arts faculty recite the legends of Royce (Ph.D. '78, LL.D. '02), Dewey (Ph.D. '84, LL.D. '15), and Lovejoy; I heard upperclassmen boast there was no more inspired lecturer on Wordsworth at any university, anywhere, than Raymond Dexter Havens. I had seen Sidney Lanier's statue peeking over Charles Street, but the redbrick halls behind the poet's back, I found, were dedicated not to the vagaries of poetic disillusionment but to the disciplines of scholarship.

Academic standards of excellence made for little patience with an aspiring writer's experiments and failure. The writing department was buried in the cellar of Gilman Hall, and when Pulitzer Prize winner Karl Shapiro visited, the lords of the English department were heard to speculate upon his work as trivial, even self-indulgent.

A. D. Emmert (of *The Baltimore Sun*) dropped by twice a week to conduct a class in newspaper writing. That was Hopkins journalism. Or was it? In the office of the *News-Letter,* the undergraduate weekly, a clique of veterans presided over the editorial columns, solicited participation, and responded with more shock than gratitude when a freshman had the ambition to hand in a lengthy story.

The most formidable presence at the campus weekly was managing editor Russell Baker, a blond version of Gary Cooper. Baker would peer down from his lanky frame and interrogate the freshman reporters with an earnestness that belied the playful—sometimes mocking—wit that lay beneath the grim exterior.

Baker was surrounded by a group of radical philosophers. William Gresham believed, as far as I could understand, that the campus was in the grip of a fascist conspiracy, which student journalists had a sacred trust to destroy. Tom Yost was a biology major who spoke of communism in such charming and reasonable tones that it was difficult to believe Stalin was a totalitarian. The archetypal veteran, Tom Meads, on his way to Phi Beta Kappa and honors in literature, appeared to teeter on the verge of a breakdown. In his Ike jacket and worn combat boots he seemed to incarnate the combat-ravaged GI, but the suggestion was that Meads's predicament was another demonstration of the ills of capitalistic indifference.

I passed the first semester of my freshman year sharing the wisdom and ridicule of this band of iconoclasts, and I dropped Biology, flunked Spanish, and barely passed Political Economy. But my admiration was not based on verbal pyrotechnics alone: I had seen Baker at the typewriter. Pages flew from him. He filled the backs of old news stories and rejected press releases. He wrote a play and he produced copy for the paper moments before deadline. The magnum opus of his *News-Letter* days was the flow of parodies of *Time* magazine with which he covered the office walls.

When I composed a satiric piece on America's inability to confront her responsibilities as a world power, Baker suggested I write a regular column for the *News-Letter.* "Something like *The New Yorker's* talk pieces. Short paragraphs with snippets at the end." Did he say *The New Yorker?* I was sure I would have to write away for it.

To my surprise, "Doc" Manheimer, the proprietor of the premier pharmacy–soda fountain–magazine rack of our neighborhood, not only expressed admiration for *The New Yorker* but seemed eager to order a special copy for me.

Less than a week later I had my first copy, read it, and wrote what I considered a takeoff on their front-of-the-book "talk" pieces. My column was called "The American Scene" and I handed it to Russ.

Baker plugged a cigarette into the corner of his mouth and within moments rewrote the paragraphs to appear under my byline. One example: "Despite all its efforts the government has been unable to meet the farmer's demand for fertilizer, according to a report from Presidential Secretary Charles Ross. Next we'll be hearing the government will take the bull by the horns."

One afternoon, finding me downcast at the *News-Letter* office, Baker drew from me the tale of my academic woes. I could not even "absolve" freshman writing, I confessed, because the graduate student who supervised my section found my spelling and punctuation inadequate. As Baker produced copy, he awarded power. Before my freshman year was over I was copy editor of the Hopkins *News-Letter:* "We'll show them who can spell."

Baker spent less time around the *News-Letter* office during my second semester; he and Gresham worked part-time as police reporters at the *Sun*. But they returned in time to sponsor me for managing editor, and coined the slogan which has haunted me since—"On it with Offit."

When Russ Baker graduated, J. Paxton Davis became my literary mentor. A veteran of the China-India-Burma theater, Pax came to Hopkins from North Carolina and was an F. Scott Fitzgerald enthusiast. Over coffee at Levering he revealed to me the design of *The Great Gatsby*. Until that time I had not thought seriously about literary criticism, regarding analysis of technique as an obstacle course invented by literary scholars to embarrass spontaneous response. But as Pax Davis discussed the intricate triangular structure of *Gatsby,* he offered a dimension which enriched my reading without diminishing the prerogative of instinctive taste.

Pax Davis shared with me the great experience of my Hopkins undergraduate years—Earl R. Wasserman's class in the Romantic poets. Less than a dozen of us sat gathered in a room in Gilman Hall as Dr. Wasserman ('34, Ph.D. '37) would begin: "Perhaps you may recall at our last meeting we were discussing 'Ode to the West Wind.' We considered it the full exploitation of the implicitly religious character of 'Mont Blanc.' Is it not then Shelley's prayer to the Divine Power corresponding to his prayer to Intellectual Beauty?" Dr. Wasserman's classes were not all so strictly adherent to the text. In discussing Wordsworth he revealed an intimate glimpse of his own life, as he spoke of his daughter Linda's first haunting encounters with nature: "For city children, nature may be as full of fear as wonder." Along with Pax Davis, who eventually published a number of distinguished novels and a three-volume memoir, the star of the class was William Franklin Romeike. A student of varied and unique intellectual skills, Romeike was awarded a grade of H—a notch above A, for unusual distinction—in all but one of his literature courses.

By my third year at Hopkins I was spending long afternoons with Bill Romeike. We wandered through Wyman Park and the streets of

Baltimore as Bill recited passages from the *Iliad* and *Odyssey* and translated them. He could render a passage in Sanskrit, too, and there was not a poem we had read in class that was not locked in his memory and heightened by his critical faculties. Romeike was a classicist and a student of our times. He predicted a black revolution that would integrate American universities and businesses but leave a cadre of militant blacks. He foresaw the emergence of the movies as an art form and the potential of American folk singers as popular entertainers. He was the first man I knew to recognize the repression of women and to champion them as a creative, political, and intellectual force. Bill Romeike had long hair in 1947 and believed we had come too far from nature.

I lost touch with Bill soon after I graduated and moved to New York, but I shared the lament of those who knew and admired him that Bill Romeike did not complete his Ph.D. studies. The most authentic scholar among the undergraduates of my time left the university to work as an information officer for NASA. He died in 1971.

Pax Davis and Bill Romeike graduated in 1949 and I took a fiction-writing course that year, taught by Robert Jacobs. My first effort was a handwritten monologue mimicking my Uncle Ben, a Baltimore insurance man. Uncle Ben sat on his front porch, looking down the white steps, and advised his nephew on the importance of playing golf to get ahead. I read the paper in class, and my fellow students praised my comic irony and the authenticity of my dialogue.

Bob Jacobs endorsed the class's encouragement, but suggested I give more attention to developing conflict so my vignette would grow into a story. I had sufficient discipline not to challenge the teacher, but I secretly suspected my talent outreached the class. My conceit was shattered the day John Barth read from a section of what he identified as "a longer work." It was a vivid description of a Maryland village in which subtly complex characters developed and conflicted. The style was poetic, demonstrating a control of composition and language that seemed literary art. I wondered if John Barth would ever be "discovered," hidden as he was by the long shadows of scholarship and medicine that were Hopkins, circa 1950.

> *In his efforts to get to the bottom of things the laureate comes within sight of Malden but so far from arriving there, nearly falls into the stars.*

—John Barth,
The Sot-Weed Factor

3

Alger Hiss, Owen Lattimore, and My Top-Secret Clearance

1947–Circa 1994

Alger Hiss, the cold war warrior who was certified as a great American by the president of the Johns Hopkins University, Dr. Isaiah Bowman, returned to Homewood in the fall of 1946. During his undergraduate days, Hiss had been editor of the *News-Letter* and, even now after a degree from Harvard Law and a career as a policymaker in the State Department, he took the time to drop by the paper's office, where I was a member of the staff. I was impressed by Hiss's gracious manners and modesty.

Two years later, Whittaker Chambers, a *Time* magazine editor who confessed to being a communist, accused Hiss of passing along confidential government documents to the Russians. Hiss denied the charges and I believed him.

Hiss wasn't the only one under fire at Hopkins.

In January of 1949 *Newsweek* magazine featured a story naming Owen Lattimore, director of Hopkins's Walter Hines Page School of

International Relations, as holding views that "frequently paralleled the Communist Party line, in opposing the plan to spare Emperor Hirohito and to leave him in power after the peace." Before long Senator Joe McCarthy was accusing Lattimore, the author of *Solutions in Asia,* of being America's top communist.

As press baron, editor in chief of the campus weekly, I dropped in on Professor Lattimore to find out what this mess was all about. "Joe McCarthy is an irresponsible opportunist," Lattimore told me. "He knows nothing about Chinese culture or politics and is generally ignorant of the subtleties of foreign policy. I regard his accusations as moonshine."

Before I graduated I wrote an editorial defending Hiss and Lattimore and raging against the moderation of student support:

> The conviction of Alger Hiss on the good faith of a paranoiac and the solidarity of young Republicans on the Homewood campus are the microcosm of a Hopkins era. The voyaging student has wandered his legendary nine years and talked with kings and faraway men and now he will rest—in jail. . . . There has been no voice of passion in our four years at Homewood. . . . We have stood in uniform grays and black knit ties and applauded daintily for our noble Mr. Lattimore. But we have not paraded down Charles Street and shouted living issues across the Levering Lawn. . . .

I was among the few students on the campus who met and talked to both Alger Hiss and Owen Lattimore and while that seemed an historical vanity for a twenty-year-old, it certainly wasn't a recommendation for clearance in the Reserve of the U.S. Army Intelligence Corps, to which I had applied.

The only clue I have as to why I passed that test was the bemused report from my brother, who had joined me at Hopkins. Benson told me that a mysterious fellow in a narrow-brimmed hat had spoken to Ben Sankey and him at the *News-Letter* office. "He wanted to know if Ben was related to the infielder who played for the Baltimore Orioles. Then he asked if we thought there was any reason to believe you might not be a one hundred percent loyal American. I confessed that you probably held the world record for ROTC, plus three years of military school, four years at JHU, and then—to top it off—Hal Sonnenfeld convinced you to enlist in the United States Intelligence Reserve."

Hiss and Lattimore were still hot issues when, with impeccable clearance, I put in my time serving as an intelligence officer at the Brooklyn port of embarkation for soldiers shipping out for assignments in Europe. But Harry Bridges was the name that provided the organization's "loyalty test" for me. Bridges, the head of a longshoreman's union, was identified as a "communist," and it was my job to interview prospective crewmen for merchant marine ships to be sure no advocates of Karl Marx were allowed aboard. Somehow or other I always found a reason to pass on these workingmen regardless of their flirtations with the "forceful overthrow of the United States government." Bridges to Lattimore to Hiss—was a double play combination that for my money never made an out.

Decades later, after he had served his time for perjury and become the subject of a number of conflicting studies as to his guilt or innocence, I met Alger Hiss again. A mutual friend, Joe Machlis, the music scholar, celebrated Hiss's birthday with a party in the spring, another curious anomaly in the life of Hopkins's notorious alumnus. (My pal Kurt Vonnegut informed me that Alger Hiss was born on November 11, 1904, same birthday and month but not the year of Kurt's debut.)

My ritual patter reminded him that he and Donald Hiss, with Benson and me, were the only brothers to have served as editors of the *News-Letter*. With this modest bonding I took a shot at bringing up the subject of his visit in 1946. I suggested that the political situation of the time provided reasons for sympathy with the Russians and the determination of people of goodwill to work toward peace. I even went so far as to mention student dissatisfaction with President Bowman's militant position toward the Russians. Alger Hiss nodded as I spoke and clasped my hand without further comment.

Harold Taylor, the University of Chicago and Sarah Lawrence educator, presented the birthday toast. He spoke lyrically about Hiss's humor, his great dignity, and devotion to friends. Speaking to Harold later, I complimented him for waxing so eloquent. Without a quaver Taylor punctured my schoolboy illusions. "I guess I did do all right. I managed to avoid saying that Alger's historic distinction is that he's the country's most stubborn perjurer. But a good man, a good friend all the same."

Moments after Harold Taylor's "verdict," I asked Victor Navasky to snap a photograph of Alger, Harold, and me. I planned to send it to the Johns Hopkins magazine. Years later, when I discovered the snapshot I was amused by the irony—Victor Navasky, author of *Naming Names* and, perhaps, the most persistent of all those skeptical of Hiss's guilt, provided the evidence of my warm feelings for Alger Hiss. When I asked Victor if he remembered the picture, he said, "Not really. I'm not much as a photographer, but if you say so. . . ." Was he pleading the Fifth?

4

Robert Frost and My Phantom of Delight

1949

Robert Frost was no Samuel Taylor Coleridge, John Keats, or Percy Bysshe Shelley, but for my money he was the champion Romantic poet of them all because he sent Betty Belvedere flying into my arms.

In November 1947 I was invited to join Dr. Henry Carrington Lancaster, scholar of French literature and chairman of the Department of Romance Languages, at his office for a brief chat with Robert Frost prior to the poet's address to the student assembly. As an editor of the campus newspaper, it was suggested, I might evoke from the great man some lines to share with our readers.

Dr. Lancaster, a tall, heavyset gent with flowing white hair that tumbled over his shoulders, thin-rimmed glasses, and a three-piece suit that seemed to have provided a shawl for Rimbaud, Baudelaire, and Marcel Proust all at the same time, sat behind his desk. He didn't seem to mind that I'd just recently satisfied my language requirements with a C in second-semester Spanish.

Robert Frost appeared almost as old as Dr. Lancaster. His hair, too, was white but thinner, growing in a patch that sprouted across his forehead. The only one in the room who didn't look like a poet, and most wanted to be one, was me. I sat with my military school posture, trimmed hair, button-down shirt, and bow tie.

I had beefed up for the meeting by reading lots of Frost's poems and several of his commentaries. I was ready to ask him about the relationship of "Two Tramps in Mud Time" to his expressed theory on realism: "There are two types of realists—one who offers a good deal of dirt with his potato to show that it is a real one; and the one who is satisfied with the potato brushed clean. . . . To me the thing that art does for life is to clean it, to strip it to form."

I hoped to relate all this to a humdinger of a line in the last stanza of the poem, "My object in living is to unite / my avocation with vocation." I intended, too, to ask the Bard of New England if he was influenced by the Lords of the Lake District and how he thought his theories jibed with the introduction to the Lyrical Ballads.

I was raring to go, but never got started. The courtly gentleman insisted upon asking me questions. I was cast as a kind of Everyman for postwar undergraduates. What did we think about the Marshall Plan? Were we aware of the mysterious author X who wrote a piece in *Foreign Affairs* suggesting American foreign policy should be focused on containing Russian expansion? And what about television? Had many of us watched President Truman's first television broadcast to the nation?

The interview, or more appropriately my monologue, ended with a rap on the door by a member of the Student Activity Committee, who reminded us it was time to move on to the gym, where the school orchestra and a full house were waiting.

Robert Frost clapped me on the back and expressed regrets that he couldn't hear more. "Always want to know what the younger generation is thinking—and feeling." Dr. Lancaster asked me something about my plans to—did he say continue?—graduate study of French literature. I was convinced I was a case of mistaken identity. Then, as we arrived at the exit of Gilman Hall, among a cluster of Frost fans

I spotted Betty Belvedere, "the Phantom of Delight" of the evening class I was attending, Introduction to the History of Art.

Betty was several years older than I. (In those post–World War II days everyone seemed my senior.) She had long black hair pulled back in a bun and an exotic voice that sounded to me like a blend of British aristocrat and Bawlamerese. I decided she was Merle Oberon. We'd talked during class breaks and once I'd walked across Wyman Park with her. I had the impression she was going steady or was pinned or even engaged. She'd told me at the end of our walk that she thought I was "cute." That did it. Tyrone Power, Robert Taylor, Clark Gable, cute?

I'd given up my fantasy until the moment Betty Belvedere saw me with Robert Frost. She had a collection of his poems under her arm and a look of wild-eyed submission.

I said, "Mr. Frost, this is my friend Betty Belvedere."

The poet seemed as pleased by Merle Oberon as I was. He signed her book and awarded her the same pat on the shoulder he'd given me. When I insisted that she take the seat reserved for me in the front row for the Frost lecture, Betty Belvedere was all mine.

"I had no idea you knew Robert Frost. I can't wait to find out who else you'll introduce me to. . . ."

5

A Job Offer from "President-Elect"
Henry A. Wallace

Circa 1947

I was among the hundreds of local university and college students who gathered in front of the bowl on Charles Street on that October day in 1947 to hear former vice president Henry A. Wallace.

"This is not my first experience speaking to students off campus. I didn't know it could happen on the East Coast. I do know it can happen on the West Coast because it happened at Berkeley."

Later, several of us met and spoke to Wallace at his hotel suite. We wanted to know what he thought about the Hopkins administrators who kept him off campus. Wallace got even. "When Dr. Bowman says that Communism and Czarism are essentially the same, he is either exhibiting ignorance or deliberately contributing to its perpetuation. The greatest danger in the world today is not conflicting ideologies but the perpetuation of ignorance."

Although the students who hung around the *News-Letter* office overwhelmingly supported the Progressive Party candidate for president, the campus poll indicated we were a minority. Such a small minority that it would have been impossible to believe if the poll hadn't been designed by V. O. Key, the resident authority on political parties and pressure groups, and Dr. A. J. Duncan, the statistician-whiz of the Business School. So we were stuck with a sampling that indicated 63 to 70 percent of the students were for Thomas E. Dewey. (Truman 15 to 20 percent, Wallace 2 to 10 percent, and Norman Thomas, the Socialist, one and a half to 8 percent.)

Bewildered by my first experience with counterintuitive political reality, I determined to find out for myself what Henry A. Wallace was all about. When he arrived in Baltimore for a rally before the November election, I flashed my credentials and was invited to speak to him and his running mate, the banjo-playing, folk-singing United States Senator Glen Taylor. They were a party, all right. Wallace with his midwestern charm and the earnest good looks that movies prepared us for, and Taylor who actually seemed to find politics fun. We talked about a trip Taylor had made to Birmingham in the spring. He had defied a police chief named Connor by entering a public hall through the entrance marked "colored" to address a meeting of the Southern Negro Youth Congress.

"Segregation is wrong," Wallace agreed. Before our meeting was over I said a few words, too, about Negro rights, the antiwar sentiments I felt stirring among the veterans on campus, and our responsibilities to the poor nations of the world.

Wallace nodded to Taylor and said, "We must be sure not to forget this young man's name, Glen. He has exactly the kind of principles we welcome in our administration."

I was so naïve about Washington bureaucracy at the time that the very mention of a job in the president's administration conjured fantasies of no less than an appointment as undersecretary of the navy (Theodore Roosevelt, Franklin Delano Roosevelt) or ambassador to some hot spot like, say, Hungary.

My dad was sitting in his favorite rocker, puffing away on a Tareyton cigarette before dinner, when I told him about the job offer. Professionally familiar with long shots, Dad seemed amused but there was no trace of ridicule when he advised me, "Don't bet on it."

My dad also made it clear that he was going to vote for Harry Truman. "I'm a Democrat, been one all my life. Far as I'm concerned they got the best shot at helping the underdog."

A week later I was standing on the overpass, looking down at the train tracks at Baltimore's Penn Station. We'd been informed that President Truman was dropping by on the first leg of a whistle-stop tour. I was still eleven months away from qualifying as a registered voter, but it seemed to me my responsibility as a campus editor required me to take a closer look at the incumbent. Besides, my dad, whom I could not recall ever being entirely wrong, not only assured me he was voting for Truman but didn't think the campus poll was much of a morning line. "Things are going pretty good," he said. "Comes down to it, my money's on the Democrat."

There weren't more than a couple dozen of us waiting for Truman's train to arrive. Several representatives of a labor union carried signs and a group of men in suits from the local political club shuffled restlessly. Among the politicos I recognized Jack Pollack, the tall, stoop-shouldered leader of the precinct where we lived.

I introduced myself to Mr. Pollack and reminded him that I'd worked with his son Marty as a counselor at Dave Kaufman's summer camp. His expression didn't indicate he was impressed or had even heard me, but Pollack commanded one of his associates to include me in the group of people who were to shake hands with the president when he arrived.

Harry Truman gave no clue that he was disappointed by the crowd or discouraged with his campaign. He spoke briefly and offered his hand to the half dozen of us who ventured to shake the hand that shook the hand of Franklin Delano Roosevelt. I was impressed by the vitality of my dad's "best bet." He didn't seem to know that all the polls and prophets predicted that he was "going to lose"—and made no mention of a job.

6

Make Mine a Double with Ogden Nash

1950

Ogden Nash didn't have quite as much influence on the poetic muses of our time as T. S. Eliot, but he had a distinct advantage for the members of our Pi Delta Epsilon chapter of the national journalism fraternity: Ogden Nash lived in Baltimore. It may be symptomatic of the schoolboy arrogance we identified with "honorary" that we lumped poets and essayists with journalists when we selected the speaker for our June Week celebration.

Gerald Johnson and Frank Kent, stars of the editorial columns of the *Sun,* seemed too serious. Karl Shapiro, the Pulitzer Prize–winning poet, had already put in his time at a Hopkins seminar. Henry L. Mencken was suffering a debilitating illness.

And then: "How about Ogden Nash? He's writing great stuff for *The New Yorker* and he makes me laugh." That recommendation from Bill Clinger, the editor of *The Jaywalker,* the campus humor magazine, was supported by a medley of Nash lines:

> *If you thirst to know who said, "I think therefore I am,"*
> *your thirst I will quench;*

> *It was René Descartes, only what he actually said was,*
> *"Je pense, donc je suis," because he was French.*
> *He also said it in Latin, "Cogito, ergo sum,"*
> *Just to show that he was a man of culture and not a tennis tramp*
> *or a cracker barrel philosophy bum.*

And:

> *I'm mad about mustard—*
> *Even on custard*

We offered a speaker no honorarium or symbolic trophy—only drinks, dinner, and an audience. But we did entertain at the Stafford Hotel, a Baltimore institution founded around the turn of the twentieth century by Dr. William A. Maole, a member of one of the city's most ancient families.

Minutes after we'd decided by acclamation to invite Ogden Nash, Bill Clinger located his phone number and made the call, a successful exercise of his talents for diplomacy and goodwill that later served his constituents in Pennsylvania, whom he represented for a long, long time as a member of the United States Congress.

The Stafford was located a block from Mt. Vernon Place and the shadow of the Washington Monument. I arrived early to preside at the brief business meeting before dinner. Six members showed up. It didn't require a crack investigative reporter to discover it was the last day of June Week events and that only Clinger among our out-of-town members was still around. The private dining room had been set for twenty-four. We directed the manager to reduce the place settings to fourteen, and all the members except me returned to the campus to rustle up students to fill the eight empty seats.

The strategy was for me to entertain Ogden Nash at the bar, conveniently located directly to the right of the entrance. As the captive audience arrived, I had only to glance over my right shoulder to see flashing fingers posting the count.

Mr. Nash arrived right on time. The nation's master of light verse was neatly groomed, wearing a white summer jacket and striped tie.

It was easy to imagine that the briefcase he carried contained legal papers or sales reports. The moment he smiled and identified himself I felt a wave of admiration mixed with anxiety. I suggested we have a drink at the bar before "the fun begins."

Seated at the paneled bar, Mr. Nash lit a cigarette and ordered. Did he say scotch and soda? Bourbon and water? Whiskey up? Martini on the rocks? I had no idea. My drinking taste at the time was restricted to beer and an occasional adventure echoing a request for a Tom Collins, whiskey sour, or Manhattan. All I knew was that this moment called for the relaxing charms of booze. I said, "Make mine a double."

The happy hour passed in a haze of growing adoration for Ogden Nash, fingers flashing from the hall, and more drinks—for me. I suppose it was after my third refill that Mr. Nash asked if I was always such an enthusiastic imbiber or just enjoying an expense account. I never got around to answering. A not so gentle tap on the shoulder from one of our recruitment officers reminded me I'd been neglecting to check the count. We were past toast time and better move swiftly before the crab cakes turned cold.

Ogden Nash filled the room with wit, warmth, and laughter, John Ritterhoff flashed pictures for the yearbook, and no one mentioned two empty seats.

7

Jazz with Rachmaninoff's Piano, Courtesy of William Kapell

1951–1952

After graduating from Hopkins, I moved to New York. During the two years I was a bachelor in Manhattan I shared apartments with Dan Levin, a Hopkins pal who was engaged in research at Memorial Sloan-Kettering. Dan and I lived for a while at the home of William Kapell, one of the great classical pianists of the time, and later at a building owned by a modern artist whom we addressed as Mr. Romano.

Our apartment in the Kapells' house on East 94th, off Fifth, was a fourth-floor walk-up that we sublet from the Danish writer and cartoonist Piet Hein. Mr. Hein was a straightforward negotiator. He told us the Kapells were rarely at home. The house was managed by their housekeeper, and we would receive frequent visits from the Kapells' son, a toddler who made his way upstairs on all fours. It was also possible, the noble Dane informed us, that from time to time the halls might be alive with the sound of music.

Mr. Hein treated us, too, to a look at a selection of his own work—humorous drawings and sketches that even without benefit of understanding the captions we recognized as brilliant originals. We made a deal without meeting the Kapells.

Soon after we moved in, the Kapells' son climbed the three flights and entered the room overlooking 94th that Dan had adopted for his bedroom. Baby Kapell's kitchy koos and da da das were in concert when the Kapells' housekeeper arrived. We welcomed a robust lady with one of those prescient smiles that seems to be always on the verge of hilarity. We kept the baby happy with graham crackers and entertained our house manager with mimicries of the former tenant to which she responded with laughter and the gentle admonition "You bad. You bad."

I don't know how much of this was communicated to the Kapells, but when they returned from one of the maestro's concert tours William Kapell invited us to his studio. Dan was awed by two pianos back to back—one bearing a tag identifying it as an instrument that had belonged to Sergei Rachmaninoff.

Dan and William Kapell talked about Rachmaninoff compositions. Dan expressed awe for the four piano concertos. Was he hinting for a private recital? Kapell asked Dan if he played the piano. Dan couldn't have been more intimidated if Joe Louis had inquired if he boxed or if F. Scott Fitzgerald had wanted to know what he was writing.

Dan confessed he sometimes "tinkled." Kapell said he hoped to hear him play sometime. On that note of grace he offered his hand as signal of farewell to good beginning. I was more aware of handshakes than I was of Rachmaninoff compositions. At Valley Forge Military Academy we had been instructed and even had had class exercises in greetings and salutations, "Look 'em right in the eye and shake so they know you're there."

Kapell was lean and handsome. I hadn't paid much attention to his hands until that final shake. I was reminded of Kapell's hands many years later when Joe Machlis, the music historian, introduced me to Vladimir Horowitz. After Horowitz shook my hand I was surprised that the fingers of my right hand were all still there. Kapell's handshake was the strongest I had experienced at that time. Dan and I talked about it. We agreed it was remarkably firm but undemanding. We thought he was aware of his strength, trying not to show off, and would have preferred not making a guest conscious of the power of his extraordinary fingers.

We saw the Kapells rarely after that, but from time to time Dan visited the Rachmaninoff piano, just for a look. He seemed to regard it as a shrine until the Sunday afternoon that began when the bright-eyed crawler dropped in accompanied by the sounds of conversation and laughter from the floors below. It was obvious a party was going on downstairs in the housekeeper's quarters, so we improvised an upstairs version. Young Kapell was alternating between creating Play-Doh out of graham crackers, clanking like castanets the kitchen pots we'd given him, and making do with the Sunday papers spread on the floor for wee-wee pads, when one of the housekeeper's guests arrived to pick up the "landlord." He invited us down for a "cup."

The Kapell studio was filled with an assembly of friendly folks in suits and ties and neat cocktail-party dresses. Neither Dan nor I recognized a professional musician in the crowd, but it was clear from the introductions that the guests included Harlem political leaders and shopkeepers, teachers, and ministers.

I don't recall what the inspiration was that emboldened Dan to plunk down on the seat at the Rachmaninoff piano, but he did. He was encouraged to play. "Any tune makes you happy, honey, long as you have the beat."

Dan's passion for music is tempered by an ear sufficiently sophisticated for him to be a devoted audience but a reluctant performer. It may have been the wine or the moment but as the room quieted, Dan Levin, the bio major from Johns Hopkins University, class of 1949, played his version of "Stardust" on the instrument shared by two of the major musical talents of the twentieth century. From Rachmaninoff to Hoagy Carmichael, from William Kapell to Dan Levin, it was all "Eine Kleine Hausmusik" at the housekeeper's party that afternoon.

Dan's version of the haunting, romantic melody seemed right on beat until a gentleman with a wide white collar and pin-striped double-breasted suit plopped down on the facing piano. With bold but harmonious notes he fused with Dan's tinkles to jazz it up. The music hopped and flowed, bobbed and weaved, but it sang, sang, sang. I thought I recognized chords from "Georgia on My Mind" and "Skylark" as the clapping, stomping, and cheers encouraged the duet.

It's been more than fifty years since that jam session. Dan remembers it as his debut and curtain call as a musical impresario. Neither of us ever found out what William Kapell's response would have been to the celebration provided by his Rachmaninoff piano. Kapell died in an airplane crash soon after we met, but I suspect he would have approved. The Kapells, even in absentia, were gracious and generous benefactors. There was a family feeling about their house generated by the freedom with which their child roamed the premises and the liberty, bordering on possession, that characterized their housekeeper's relationship with the rooms and furnishings. For the home/ studio of a musical artist, the Kapells' was remarkably free of tension and any self-consciousness about the privacy and possessions of the great man.

After little more than a year there, Dan and I moved from East 94th Street to the Romano apartment on East 74th Street, another fourth-floor walk-up. It was located on the same block as the Mannes School of Music, but we attended no concerts there, and although Dan and I have been friends for the past five decades, I never heard him play "Stardust" again.

8

Dylan Thomas, Wally Cox,
Marlon Brando—A Village Tour with
Bon Vivant Valensi

Circa 1951

Vinnie Valensi had just returned from medical school studies at the University of Geneva when our mutual friend Len Scheer introduced him to me as "the bon vivant who will be the perfect guide for your explorations of Greenwich Village."

Vinnie's father was Italian and his mother a Spanish beauty. They lived on the Upper West Side. Vinnie seemed to think it necessary to establish his pedigree before taking me for a tour of the Village neighborhood where he lived in a small studio apartment. If Vinnie meant to impress me, he did.

Though he could speak Italian and French and was fond of quoting lines from Proust in the original (which I couldn't understand), Vinnie seemed impressed with the several published stories under my by-line that he insisted upon seeing but didn't read. *"Les hommes peuvent avoir plusieurs sortes de plaisirs. Le véritable est celui pour lequel ils quittent l'autre."* (People can have many different kinds of pleasure. The real one is that for which they will forsake all others.) He concluded that writing involved isolation and loneliness, and to compensate me for such dedication he introduced me to Village restaurants: the Jumble Shop, Chumley's, the Blue Mill.

Soon after I told him that the voice of a poet I most admired belonged to Dylan Thomas, Vinnie delivered me to the White Horse Tavern, where the Bard of Wales was stacking shot glasses, a cigarette dangling from his lips as he recited his own poetry between fits of laughter and coughing. He was surrounded by young ladies from downtown, tight skirts, and uptown, long skirts. I felt certain he could have his pick. However, it was clear from the manner in which he leered through slitted, tearing eyes that the overfueling damaged his lust.

Vinnie encouraged me to speak to the poet. I felt Thomas needed a therapist more than a fan. The rolling Welsh thunder of his language was becoming increasingly incoherent:

"A boily boy, a boily girl, boily-girly . . . When I was a gutsy man and a half . . . And a black reward for a roaring life . . ." Cough. Laugh. Cigarette ash crumbles down his shirt without a swipe. Nonetheless, just hearing Dylan Thomas's voice inspired as much poetic feeling as I had experienced while reading Wordsworth, Keats, and the entire first team of the Romantic poets. *"Parler! Hablar!"* Vinnie urged with instructions. *"Que pensez-vous de* . . . Ask him what he thinks about New York. Joe McCarthy. Another poet."

I maneuvered to Thomas's side. Even to my color-blind eyes his complexion appeared flushed so red I was sure he was about to burst. Besides, I was wearing shirt and tie and tweed jacket. Did I appear too British? Like Sir Philip Sidney's poet, Dylan Thomas seemed to be "freely ranging within the zodiac of his own wit."

I gave it a shot. "Excuse me, Mr. Thomas, I was wondering . . ." His eyes turned to me and for a moment he appeared a helpless little fat boy. "I think you are the greatest living poet." And then I said, "I wonder what you think of Robert Frost."

For a moment I thought he was going to slug me. He straightened his shoulders, lifted his head, and then raised a shot glass. "Robert Frost," he said. Not "To Robert Frost." Just "Robert Frost." The

Muses of Olympus couldn't have created more of a symphony with only a name.

Another evening Vinnie took me to the Cedar Tavern. "As close as we'll come to Paris's left bank." He knew no one and no one knew him but he was armed with a litany of names: John Ashbery, Frank O'Hara, Kenneth Koch, Larry Rivers, Jane Freilicher. He spoke, too, of Abstract Expressionism and the New York School. We didn't meet any of the poets or painters Vinnie mentioned, but the wood-paneled tavern with the long bar and a menu of bar food made such an impression on me that long after it had passed as a gathering place for avant-garde poets and painters it was my hangout on evenings when I taught at the New School or NYU.

For all his gifts of language, charm, and Belmondo good looks, Vinnie deferred to me when we met an attractive woman. I learned years later that there were reasons for that, but at the time I accepted it as Vinnie's inherent grace and generous friendship.

One of those ladies—Trudy, an unemployed actress we met at the bar of the Cedar on her day off from waitressing—led us to the East Village party where I glimpsed Wally Cox and had a front-row seat for a performance by Marlon Brando.

Trudy told us she had enrolled in an evening class to study French. Soon as she realized Vinnie "speaks French, actually speaks it just like Leslie Caron in the movies," she was determined to *parler* as much as she could. *"Êtes-vous libre ce soir?"* she wanted to know. Vinnie said we had no plans for the evening. That was all the invitation required. I was trying to remember if Leslie Caron actually spoke French in the movies. Trudy did look like her—small, graceful, dark hair hanging in bangs over her forehead.

Vinnie encouraged me to perform my mimicry of a French professor or an English don or a Baltimore Orioles batboy—any voice to distract Trudy from practicing her French and to provide reason for her to pay attention to me. Two sentences into my garbled impression of the sounds of French, Trudy was off Vinnie and on to me. By the time we arrived at the party I was less interested in my first experience with a genuine first-edition Greenwich Village classic than I was in our secondhand Leslie Caron.

The party was so jammed and "jumping" we never made it to the bar. The last I saw of Trudy she was in the warm embrace of a fellow wearing sandals, khakis, and a turtleneck, who looked like a linebacker for the Chicago Bears. Vinnie and I were the only men decked out in shirts, ties, and jackets.

I didn't know or recognize anyone. Vinnie heard the writer Leonard Bishop was in the back room, where I assumed the bar was located. Bishop had written a novel right out of Hemingway called *The Butchers*. (I remembered the title, bought the book, and admired its easy flow of action and dialogue.) Vinnie recognized Wally Cox, a stand-up comedian who was making a run as a biology teacher in a TV series, *Mr. Peepers*.

Wally Cox didn't seem to be drinking or smoking and for my money he might just as well have been a real-life biology teacher discussing nutrition. I thought I heard him talking about a meatless diet. Could he have been the first vegetarian I ever met?

Just as he had led me to the bar to talk to Dylan Thomas, Vinnie took me by the elbow and guided me through the crowd to a corner where it seemed a generator in sweatshirt and baggy khakis was electrifying the room. "Brando. Marlon Brando," a voice over my shoulder whispered. "Can you believe it. He-is-Marlon-Brando!"

Had it not been for Vinnie I would have let it go at that. I knew Marlon Brando only as the star of *A Streetcar Named Desire*. I was still locked into the matinee-idol traditions of Robert Taylor, Tyrone Power, perhaps John Garfield. But Vinnie was palpably excited by his presence and he insisted I go one-on-one with the great actor.

I was close enough to speak to Brando, but I never said a word. I heard only the last phrases of the distinctly southern accent of a young lady who was introducing herself to him. Instantly Brando assumed the voice of a southern planter (or was it a preacher?) lecturing on his impressions of New York, warning of sins and seductions. He spoke directly to the young lady. If there had been a pause, I was game to improv along with him.

Only the son of a champion bookmaker and self-anointed scholar of Montaigne (my mother), a twenty-two-year-old so loved and supported at home he had neither the guilt of ambition nor the fear of risking failure, would have presumed to play off what may have been the greatest American actor of his time. But Vinnie was encouraging me and I was "for fun." I would have done it. It may have been three minutes into the Brando oration that I was aware tears were rising in the young lady's eyes. There was no stopping him.

I stood and listened. The rolling cadences of the southern diction became so addictive, so real there was no apparent inconsistency in the character Brando was creating.

"He's reciting another Williams play—" I spotted over my shoulder the source of that misstatement: the linebacker who swept Trudy away.

Brando wasn't reciting, he was becoming another person. I was the bush leaguer observing Ted Williams at bat. I identified with the inspiration and formed a notion of the reduction of self that eventually becomes replaced by another self: a voice that becomes a character capable of speaking, thinking, even feeling, independent of the original self. It's marginal and scary and I've never risked surrender.

That evening so long ago in Greenwich Village I am certain I saw Marlon Brando do just that. I don't know how long he went on or what induced him to return to self. I'm not sure whether he was having fun, making fun of, or in control. But he defined acting for me, the kind of acting to which I momentarily aspired, creating character without a script. I wonder if such total immersion is borderline schizophrenia, the exercise of multiple personalities, or a game that—if played out as Brando was doing that night—is a dangerous addiction.

Could I disappear into another personality and sustain it for hours, even days—different voice, values, modes of feeling? It may have been the tears in the eyes of the unknown lady whom Brando was addressing that night, or my own satisfaction with being just who I am, but character creation never became more than a game to me. I've been a fan, if not an apostle, of Marlon Brando's daring ever since.

9

Joe Franklin, Down Memory Lane with "The Matchmaker"

1951–1952

In the spring of 1951, progressing in my efforts to fulfill Russ Baker's instruction that I make a pass at a career in stand-up comedy, I was introduced to Joe Franklin, the Bernard Berenson of show-business nostalgia. Joe had just completed an assignment as advisor to *The Jolson Story,* a triumph at the box office that affirmed his authority. He was putting together a proposal for a TV show that would be a video version of his WOR radio program, *Joe Franklin's Memory Lane.*

I arrived at Joe's 42nd Street office-museum by responding to a series of informal auditions and casual references that began with my meeting the owner of the Chanticlaire Night Club in Baltimore.

"I got this right," my father said when I told him I'd turned down an offer to work for the *Sun.* "You wanna be in show business." He nodded, looked grave and thoughtful for a moment, and then brightened and told me he'd set me up with a gentleman he called "Baimel" who owed him a favor.

The Chanticlaire was Baltimore's uptown nightspot, a study in pastels and crystal chandeliers that played host to the jazz stars and songbirds who didn't qualify for the stage of the Lyric Theater. Baimel told me right off he couldn't afford expensive comedians or "young talents," but he would do anything for Buckley, my father, who was "one in a million—a classy gent."

Baimel arranged to meet me in New York and escorted me to the office of Sy, the booking agent upon whom he relied for "acts." Sy's office was a small room with a cluttered desk, leather club chair, and love seat. It was a triumph of balance to navigate one's way around the room, but no one but me seemed to notice. I sat on the arm of the love seat closest to Sy and felt as if I was eavesdropping on a private conversation.

In repose Sy resembled Valdez's photograph of the beardless young Lincoln; it was easy to see why clients trusted him and the artists he represented relied upon him. No matter how disappointing the negotiation or performance turned out, Sy experienced more pain than anyone. His conversation was a litany of laments and disasters: "Jerry Lewis, ever heard of him? I could have signed him for a song. Sid Caesar? I don't even want to think about it."

I had no idea of the implications of these references but was flattered by the exchange of what I took to be confidences in my presence. The dialogue concluded with long sighs and silence. Then, Baimel introduced me. "Sid here is a college kid. The son of a very dear friend of mine. I'd move heaven and earth for Buckley. See what you can do for him."

For the next two weeks I sat around Sy's office, running errands, taking phone messages, listening to brief therapeutic monologues. I didn't know if I was guest, protégé, or ambassador-without-portfolio until the afternoon Sy turned to me as if discovering a representative of some holy order to whom he must account for his sins. I was so absorbed by the contemplation of seeing his eyes actually focus on me that when he asked me why I wanted to be in "a lousy, dog-eat-dog business," I immediately slipped into an impersonation of a frantic Cockney, mixing lines from "Gunga Din" with impressions of a London bartender.

Sy nodded through my recitation until I was thirty seconds into my second improvisation, a takeoff on a New York waiter who knew better than you did what you should order for lunch. It may have seemed too familiar. Sy held up his hand, signaling the curtain to fall. After two Tums and a sip of seltzer, he instructed me to dial a phone number and ask for Max Gordon.

I auditioned for the impresario of the Village Vanguard a few days later. It was an afternoon when the club was closed, but Mr. Gordon greeted me cordially and seemed interested in why I, a college boy with so many other opportunities, was aspiring to be a nightclub entertainer. I really didn't have much of an answer. Max Gordon hadn't heard of Russ Baker, Bill Romeike, the Tudor and Stuart Club, or the 319th Parachute Infantry Regiment, all of whom had responded to my entertainments. So I told him I thought it was something I could do.

He seemed to accept that as reason enough and led me to a large basement room crowded with tables loaded with chairs, a piano, and small stage. I made up my act as I went along—an impression of a British aristocrat in a kosher delicatessen, an aging Irishman trying to make a deal with a Negro used-car salesman, a monosyllabic hoodlum flirting with a self-absorbed college girl.

Max Gordon's failure to book me on the spot would have ended my stand-up career if he hadn't suggested I drop by one evening to watch Ronnie Graham at work and contact a booking agent for a hotel chain who might have a spot for an improv act and would certainly know where I could get more experience.

I'm not sure I would have followed through on either lead if Bob and Lyla Burns hadn't encouraged me. I knew few people in New York at the time. Robert Burns, the only straight-A student, JHU, class of 1950, was a graduate student at Columbia University. Soon after my audition with Max Gordon, Bob and his wife, Lyla, invited me to dinner at their Upper West Side apartment. They were not only the first married couple of my age to entertain me, but I was sure they were brilliant scholars and not at all reckless. So when Bob and Lyla insisted I regard Max Gordon's invitations as an opportunity, I overcame my misgiving about being rejected and considered it an excuse for a New York adventure. (Many years later I learned that Bob and Lyla's sons Ken and Ric Burns were among the outstanding documentary filmmakers of our time.)

Ronnie Graham was such a virtuoso performer that night, I had no feeling we were in the same business. Not only was he a witty monologist, but he composed and performed on the piano master-pieces of satiric song.

But the hotel booking agent was instantly responsive to my call. If I was recommended by Max Gordon that was good enough for him. He invited me to join him at an evening party at an Upper West Side duplex and "show my stuff." My reward for the perfor-mance was all the booze I could drink (I had discovered scotch by then and exploited my knowledge of the distinction between Vat 69 and Johnnie Walker Black). At the end of the evening, by default and coincidence, I was elated to escort home, in a shared taxi, a shy young lady whom everyone at the party but me seemed to know was the model for a televised brassiere ad: "You're not kidding me? You actu-ally mean it? You actually never saw me on television and you actu-ally still think I'm cute? Well, I think you're cute, too."

The next day the hotel booking agent called. "How'd you make out? What's she like—34B?" I avoided a betrayal with a fifty-second telephone improv of a Bawlamer boy so obviously from the sticks he didn't know what 34B, 36C was all about. My reward was Joe Frank-lin's telephone number.

When I called, Joe responded as if he had been waiting all his life to hear from me, and not even Ed Sullivan, Eddie Cantor, Jack Oakie, Bing Crosby, and the entire cast of Earl Carroll's *Vanities* could delay an appointment right away. "Fabulous. Great. Perfect. Let's make it Tuesday, anytime. If Lana Turner or Ginger Rogers is here, you won't mind, right? The important thing is we get together, the sooner the better."

I had no idea what I had said that inspired this response. I wasn't sure I'd even identified the reference for my call.

Joe's office on the upper floor of a 42nd Street office building, just off Broadway, was cluttered with a collection of jazz age record-ings, ballads of the '40s, films of the '30s, and posters, programs, and photographs stored in a fashion less reminiscent of the Cone sisters' stacks of paintings than the Collier brothers' trash heaps.

The maestro himself was a small, round fellow, with a high forehead, dark hair buffed to a shine, and eyes constantly moving as if observing a Ping-Pong match, dog race, and brush fire all at the same time. He wore a suit and tie, and even while sitting seemed constantly to be moving. His phone rang with the consistency of a betting parlor and he reflected neither embarrassment nor irritation over the constant interruption.

Our meetings were a series of frenetic encounters and assignments I could never explain coherently to anyone, but I do know that for a year or so Joe and I met often. I traveled with him to Queens and Brooklyn for performances he told me were benefits. "They don't pay me. I don't pay you, but we get a free meal and it's for a good cause, right?" All of Joe Franklin's bookings were defined by the acknowledgment that there would be no fee and punctuated with the rhetorical "Right?"

In addition to "benefits," Joe asked me to "look over" his TV proposal, draft a "little" script for a sitcom featuring tall girls he was considering producing for television, and write a few songs for the Eddie Cantor radio show. (But only if I wanted to. Eddie was operating with a very limited budget.) If I "had the time," but only if I "had the time," I could work along with a couple of Eastern European theatrical producers who were preparing a blockbuster Broadway celebration of the arts of Hungary, Bulgaria, and Romania that would be right up there with Ben Hecht's *A Flag Is Born.*

I was included, too, in the tape Joe prepared for a variety show that was a variation of *Down Memory Lane.* Along with nonstop gagster Joey Adams and his knockout wife, Cindy, I was "on the airwaves" for all of two minutes. I launched my career as a mime with a number I composed on the spot so as not to compete with what I perceived as the high professional comedy of the Adams duo.

It was all legit, but seemed to be leading nowhere. Joe, a Talmudic authority on show-business history, never said a bad word to or about anyone. His investments, however, were restricted to praise and hints of fortune to come. After I collaborated with my Baltimore friend Margaret Romeike to write several songs for the Eddie Cantor show, Joe put me on the phone with Eddie. Until the moment I heard the familiar voice—*"If you knew Suzie, like I know Suzie, oh, oh, oh what a girrrrl . . ."*—I suspected it was a delusion if not a hoax. But there was Eddie Cantor singing my song: *"Dancing with Molly was ever so jolly when I was a gay young blade/And in between dancing we did some romancing while sipping lemonade . . ."*

"When Eddie sings our song on the air, let me ask you something, Sid, you have a big box, a trunk?" Joe stretched his arms, his eyes glistened. "Bring it to the office to carry home all the money you'll make."

The high point of my Joe Franklin follies was the afternoon he promised me Alexander Cohen. The movie producer was flying in from Hollywood and would be visiting to hear his presentation for a movie on the life of Joe Franklin. "It's all yours, Sid. You're the greatest. Knock out a few pages, make up a story. Four—f-o-u-r—thousand dollars a week they're paying scriptwriters these days. Crazy." A shrug. "But why not you? You're the greatest!"

Five minutes and thirty seconds after Alexander Cohen entered, he left Joe's office. The genuine Hollywood smash-hit movie producer was amused but not convinced by my improvised synopsis of Joe Franklin, the kid, tracking down three rare recordings by old masters—tales of mystery, romance, and nostalgia.

But the long and tangled web of my flirtation with show business came to a happy ending. The conclusion was as ironic as it was romantic. The string of introductions and bizarre referrals concluded one afternoon at the home of Moe and Anna Fortgang, Joe's parents, who lived on upper Park Avenue. With the promise that I wouldn't stay long, Joe had brought me to their home to hear the recording of our songs.

After a brief lesson on the original block of the United States one-cent stamp that Joe's father, a renowned philatelist, was assembling, I sat over a cup of tea with Joe's parents and visiting aunt and uncle.

Abe and Carrie Komito were on their way to Brooklyn that Sunday afternoon, but the traffic was heavy and they had turned back and decided to drop in on Carrie's brother Moe and his wife, Anna.

So, there I sat with Moe, the *Who's Who* philatelist; Joe, the king of Broadway nostalgia; Abe Komito, who supervised the construction of the Brooklyn-Queens Expressway; Anna, the Park Avenue housewife; and Carrie Komito, the Catskill hotel keeper, who was determined to tell all about her daughter—a champion of the Art Students League, equestrian, dancer with the Ballet Russe de Monte Carlo, member of Phi Beta Kappa, waitress who served a station of forty guests without a busboy, and author of a prizewinning verse drama "just like Shakespeare."

Eddie Cantor never sang "Dancing with Molly" on the air. Joe's TV show launched the next year and made the *Guinness Book of Records* for its long run, but I had no association with it. Alexander Cohen went on to produce other blockbusters without a peep about the Joe Franklin story. Cindy and Joey Adams became New York classics but neither remembered me or anything at all about our joint premiere. I look back upon it all with affection and a sense of wonder. I did meet Carrie and Abe Komito's daughter, Joe Franklin's cousin. Avodah was everything her mother said she was and more. I fell in love at first sight. We eloped in 1952 and have lived just about as happily ever after as a psychiatrist and a bookmaker's son, who plunked it all down on a long shot, have a right to expect.

10

Dore Schary, Edna Ferber, Richard and Dorothy Rodgers—and Sewer Contracts

Circa 1958

Dorothy Rodgers wasn't conducting a class in creative writing or representing me as my agent when she introduced me to her husband, Richard, Dore Schary, and Edna Ferber. My friendly neighbor from around the corner was providing me with access to the registered Democrats hidden like four-leaf clovers in our Upper East Side field of Republicans.

It was Avi's idea that I join the Lexington Democratic Club in the mid-1950s. "I'm convinced you're willing to spend days and nights with me alone forever. But you need people, and I just know you'll get on with voters who adore Adlai Stevenson as much as you do." Located above Zitomer's Drug Store on Madison Avenue and 75th Street, the club meetings seemed more an Ivy League college reunion than a gathering of the job seekers and sewer contractors I associated with local political clubs.

I signed up and was soon listening to discussions of foreign policy that made me wonder if I hadn't wandered into meetings of the Council on Foreign Relations.

Once the LDC resolved its positions on control of the atom bomb, dealing with cold war tensions, and responding to the British-French advance into Egypt after Nasser seized the Suez Canal, the focus was on attacking the power of Carmine De Sapio, the Tammany boss of the city's Democratic Party. The Lexington Club was for a little-d Democratic Party. The goal was broadening the base of the party, taking control out of the hands of the bosses, and returning it to the people. That meant registering voters, distributing campaign literature, and rallying signatures for candidates' petitions.

This "grassroots" approach was dependent upon election-district captains, members of the club who were willing to cover a few blocks of densely populated city neighborhoods. It sounded like basic civics as presented by Harvard, Columbia, and Yale Law Review alumni, but when I attempted to meet the registered Democrats in my neighborhood, the fortresses on Park Avenue and East 70th and 71st Streets were not available to "solicitors," even champions of little-d democracy. "And who may I say is calling?" the uniformed doorman would want to know. And then, "Is Mr. Solinger expecting you?"

The most I could round up for our State Assembly candidate was five signatures including Avi's and mine and our first- and fourth-floor neighbors'. That dismal performance inspired the advice of Russell Hemenway that was to lead me to Dorothy Rodgers: "If you want to meet the Democrats in your district, Sid, volunteer to be a poll watcher for election day, introduce yourself, and find someone who will give you access to the big buildings."

Dorothy Rodgers, registered Democrat, 740 Park, was a lean, well-dressed woman with a thin, high-cheekboned face and a smile that suggested lots of experience with gracious rejections. The business about signing petitions was news to her as it had been to me, but she gave me her phone number and offered to "deliver" if the candidate was one she and Dick genuinely supported.

The list was in my hand and we were still talking when a bespectacled gentleman with a soft, teasing voice passed. They greeted and I was on my way to signing up Dore Schary, 30 East 70th.

It may have been the naïveté of a kid from Baltimore or my self-consciousness about enlisting Democrats but I didn't immediately associate the names with their achievements in the arts. Both Dorothy Rodgers and Dore Schary had asked me what I "did," with not unkindly expressions that suggested they expected me to define myself as a lawyer with a political identity. When I explained I was a writer just doing my bit for "the party of the little guy" (my father's phrase), they seemed amused and supportive.

The following year I made the rounds petitioning signatures for Averell Harriman's gubernatorial run. Mr. Schary invited me into his apartment. I met his wife, a pleasant woman whom he treated with great courtesy and respect and no apology for or mention of her ailments. They signed and Mr. Schary offered me a drink. We sat in a book-lined room that displayed no clue that Dore Schary was a screenwriter and the former head of one of Hollywood's major studios.

He was curious about what I wrote. I skipped the recitation of my contributions to *Thrilling Westerns, Famous Sports,* and *Inside Detective.* I said, "My wife and I sold a story to the *Saturday Evening Post* recently."

Mr. Schary seemed to find that reasonably impressive, but when I mentioned that I was working summers as the steward for my mother-in-law's Catskill hotel, he responded as if my credentials were perfect. It wasn't as neighbor, Democrat, and writer that Dore Schary was inclined to "adopt" me, but because of that bond of borscht belt alumni, who shared a unique rite of passage.

I left the Scharys' apartment not only with two signatures and an introduction to several other Democrats in his building, but unsolicited encouragement to write a novel set in the Catskills. "I came to the borscht belt by way of our family's catering business," he told me. "The world of *tummlers, gonifs,* and *fressers* wasn't as new and exotic to me as it seems to be for you. You may bring just the right degree of detachment to make it live."

I had been considering writing a novel about a season in the life of a waiter. Even though masters of comedy and theater, dance, music, and the visual arts had worked as entertainers, no one had written a novel set in a borscht belt resort. For all the compromises of my marriage that working for my in-laws involved, Dore Schary confirmed my feeling that my fascination with the hotel kitchen could provide the locomotion for my first novel.

When I met Mr. Schary the following year I was already deep into writing *Five and Three House,* a title derived from the tipping standard per guest for a week's dining at the Aladdin Hotel. After casting his vote at the polling booth at Hunter College, Mr. Schary signaled for me to join him. He was less interested in political issues than whether I was "banging away at the old novel." I told him I was, but that I wasn't quite sure where it was going. "Just get it done," he advised. "You can always revise and think about ways to make the story work a little better. Often that's serendipitous." Then, Dore Schary told me that one of the most successful films with which he'd been associated, *Bad Day at Black Rock,* was scripted and ready to shoot when at a late story conference someone mentioned that the investigator, the hero of the piece for which Spencer Tracy had signed on to play, would be a stronger character if he had an eccentricity, a characteristic that would differentiate him from the standard good guy, shoot-'em-up hero.

"We kicked it around skeptically at first. The story seemed good enough without gimmicks," Dore Schary said. "But as soon as it was suggested that maybe the hero could have one arm, we knew it was right. That deepened the plot and character. The one-armed FBI agent may be all anyone really remembers about that film."

The lesson and encouragement from Dore Schary wasn't the last of Dorothy Rodgers's gifts. She invited me to her home to meet Edna Ferber, also a resident of 740 Park. Richard Rodgers was there briefly. I had an uneasy feeling that his wife wasn't all that pleased with his running off moments after we met. There seemed to be more stirring beneath the surface of their relationship than their democratic election-district captain would be privy to. I felt a restlessness in Richard Rodgers that I suspected had something to do with me. It was as if he had no further patience for the "amateur" of either arts or politics. I accepted this as a quality familiar to people of genius who are often as compulsive as they are obsessive, as if their minds or their souls can contain only their own passions, with little space for other people's concerns.

Edna Ferber and I struck it off right away. She was a small woman with a long, lined face and narrow eyes that focused with such ferocity it seemed nothing in the world mattered to her for the moment but the person she was talking and listening to.

She stood erect with a straight back and lifted chin that reflected dignity without arrogance. With little prodding she discussed her books and experiences in film and theater. She didn't regard any one of her works as a singular masterpiece, but was not the least surprised that *Show Boat* had made it as an American classic. "It was a story uniquely American," she said, "just waiting to be told."

I was amused and surprised by her brief but summary reflection of the wit and banter of the Algonquin Round Table. "Oh, that," she said with a dismissive wave of her hand. "So much has been made of so little. We had our laughs, but I remember the long silences."

Although she didn't complain about her childhood, it was evident from her discussions of growing up as a Jewish child in a small midwestern town at the turn of the century that Ferber had been raring to take off for "fresh fields and pastures new."

When I described my satisfaction with my parents, my brother, and growing up in Baltimore, she listened politely but skeptically. I knew there was risk in reciting my tale of joy and good fortune, but I liked and trusted her and so I told her I wasn't unhappy at military school, either, and I considered my wife as perfect as I did my folks back home.

"Perfect?" Edna Ferber responded and then repeated, "Perfect?"

It didn't seem to me I had much chance of coming off as anything but shallow, sentimental, or profoundly inhibited, but I concluded, "Perfect."

"That certainly doesn't sound like the motivation to be a writer, unless, of course, you have a gift for storytelling and a responsiveness to other people's woes."

I would have liked to tell Edna Ferber that my father was a bookmaker. My dad was certainly the defining influence on my character and for reasons eventually evident to me, the motivation for my need to mimic, write, and express myself through friendship and encounter.

He was a uniquely American pragmatist who practiced neither self-pity nor self-praise. I had been guided by his brief declarations: "Every morning you get up healthy, you got a shot at it. You beat the odds. Can't do better than that. . . . I'm a bookmaker, been one all my life. I take bets on horses. It's what I wanna do. I got no complaints." Without this acknowledgment of my family, Edna Ferber only had a glimpse of who I am and why I am that way.

She never checked out my Baltimore family, but good reporter that she was, she did drop by our apartment in the brownstone on East 69th Street one afternoon and introduced herself to Avi. We had two babies and Avi was covering the beat in addition to trying to write. Of course she knew who Edna Ferber was and about my conversations with her. They sat and talked long enough for Ferber to tell me the next time we met, "You are certainly right about your wife. Avi is a most unusual and in many ways creative woman." Then she added, "It will be complicated but I'm confident you'll work it out."

Among my warmest memories of Edna Ferber is a note she sent me along with a copy of Edith Hamilton's *The Greek Way*. The note and the book suggested that she was sharing her enthusiasm not as mentor but peer, a compliment that may have been triggered by the copy of my novel she received soon after its publication. I sent only a dozen copies to family and friends with a note, "Compliments of the Author." My literary acquaintance was limited at the time, but it hadn't occurred to me to ask Edna Ferber or Dore Schary or the Rodgers for a blurb. They were, after all, my constituents and it seemed to me inappropriate to pitch for a "sewer contract."

The end of my effectiveness as the LDC's "runner" in the 35th ED was signaled by a party at the Rodgers's apartment in the early '60s. It was soon after the 1960 election. I had just met and campaigned unsuccessfully for our Democratic congressional candidate William J. vanden Heuvel, whom I considered not only a brilliant, charismatic, compassionate guy, but a good bet to go on to loftier responsibilities, perhaps president of the United States. I'd followed the vanden Heuvel debates with John Lindsay, the Republican candidate and a matinee idol in his own right, but I didn't consider the future mayor in a class with our little-d Democrats' choice.

So, there I was in the great room of America's king of Broadway musicals, Richard Rodgers. The maestro and his wife had gathered friends, all Democrats, many of whom I recognized from my beat. I stood by Edna Ferber when John Lindsay, the Republican who had just beaten my man vanden Heuvel, was introduced as a "fresh breath . . . a new wind . . . the kind of independent Republican whom we must all consider to help us put an end to the Democratic bosses' domination of New York City politics." The message was clear. John Lindsay was identified with the image of John F. Kennedy, who just defeated Richard Nixon on the same ticket that was a scratch for all the other Democratic candidates in our neighborhood.

When the speeches were over and Lindsay had said his bit, acknowledging that he would consider at some point down the line a run for mayor, Dorothy Rodgers squeezed my hand and said she hoped I would understand. Before going home Edna Ferber and I took a brief stroll up and around 72nd Street. She wanted to know what I made of it, and I had no easy answers. I'd been raised to believe in the Democrats as the party of the little guy. Perhaps I'd missed a beat, but after hearing and watching him come off as second best in his debates with Bill vanden Heuvel, it was difficult for me to believe in John Lindsay. Edna Ferber disagreed.

By 1964 the political climate in New York was changing. The LDC was in its last season as the "radical wing" of the party. And our lives were changing, too. Our son Ken was nine and Mike seven. They were both students at PS 6 and I was active in the PTA, Cub Scouts, and the 19th Precinct Community Council.

As a Cub Scout den father, I became friends with other dads willing to tie ski boots, referee King-of-the-Mat, and describe how to make a fire without matches to a battalion of Upper East Side eight- and ten-year-olds more interested in the after-meetings treats. Dan Rose and his wife, Joanna, the parents of four remarkable children who went on to outstanding careers in scholarship and public service, became among the best of our pals. Carl Spielvogel, as patient a daddy as ever made the run from Manhattan to Bear Mountain with a busload of restless, energetic PS 6ers, was sufficiently impressed with my performance as the Scheherazade storyteller delegated to keep the Scouts in their seats, that he later introduced me to his wife, Barbaralee Diamonstein, for shared cordialities that included meeting Eliot Spitzer, a true-blue Democrat who was on his way to a brief—and tragic—term as governor of New York State.

I continued to greet Democratic neighbors and exchange brief political gossip, but I rang no more doorbells after 1965 and retired from election-day poll-watching.

Perhaps the most lasting legacy of Dorothy Rodgers's generosity—as catalyst and booster—was my introduction to her daughter, Mary, a distinguished composer and writer whom I later joined on the board of the Authors League Fund. I know Mary didn't have an easy time of it with such complex parents, but I've always regarded her as their greatest achievement (and she's a little-d Democrat, too).

11

Upside Down in the Magnolia Tree with Mary Bancroft and Her Mentors? Friends? Lovers? Henry R. Luce and Allen Dulles

Circa 1962

Mary Bancroft, a relative of Boston Brahmins, was always skeptical of the motivations of the Ivy League flowers who bloomed at the Lexington Democratic Club. "All they want is enough reform for them to be judges. Judges! At the Farley Club the members are content with sewer contracts." Mary herself was more like a sunflower than the roses she distrusted. Tall, very full-figured yet angular, with a square face that surely must have been beautiful once, she captured the world as her audience with her rich, smoke-inflected voice and a twinkle in her oddly triangular blue eyes.

The author of *Upside Down in the Magnolia Tree* and *The Inseparables,* memoirs disguised as novels, Mary overwhelmed me with ten-page letters reflecting on the craft of writing: "It is so much easier for a writer to achieve the reader's suspension of disbelief with a convincing first person narrator." And political digs: "I'm from Boston. I know. Joe Kennedy will not take no for an answer. He'll buy the presidency for

Jack and you Big D, little-d liberals will just take it and lump it." Mary also persisted in reminding me of how fortunate I was to have the friendship of Bob Silberstein. "I've never seen a more devoted friend."

I didn't realize until many years later that Bob, my former room-mate, the Adonis of Valley Forge Military Academy class of '46, and the much older Mary had had a brief fling. It may have accounted for her efforts to court Avi and me. One evening during a dinner at Gino, the East Side restaurant to whose leaping zebra wallpaper she introduced us, Mary went on for more than two hours about her analysis with Carl Jung, her friendships with Allen Dulles and Henry R. Luce, and her adventures with the OSS in Switzerland during World War II. She didn't skip a name or fame, even as Avi's eyes grew misty and I exhausted my vocabulary of wrap-up lines. We couldn't escape until Avi collapsed in exhaustion and tearful headache. "I must remind her of her mother," Mary suggested as we shared the check. Not entirely off the mark. Avi requested no more "quiet eve-nings" with my political friend whom she suspected talked so much because she was "playing civics under the sheets."

Mary did eventually introduce me to Henry Luce and Allen Dulles. One evening when my dad was visiting and Avi was hard at work prepping for medical school, my old man and I set out for Voi-sin. Danny's Hideaway or the Palm would have been more our style, but this was my opportunity to test my response to "gourmet dining." I made the reservation for early in the evening. We had just entered on East 63rd, off Park, when I spied Mary and a tall, distinguished gray-haired gentleman, bald at the crown. They were drinking at a table near the bar. Dad was wearing one of his DePinna double-breasted suits, white shirt, Sulka tie.

Mary greeted us like we were Theodore S. White and John Her-sey arriving by appointment. Before I could improvise a dialogue of escape my dad, Maryland's top bookie, and I, his borscht belt novelist son, were parked next to Mr. Luce, the emperor of Time-Life, and his Madame Pompadour.

I hadn't told Mary about my father's work, but she and Mr. Luce responded instantly to some exotic chemistry. Introductions flashed and the next thing I knew Henry Luce was asking my dad what he thought about the allegations that the TV spectacular *The $64,000 Question* was rigged. Dad, whom I had rarely if ever seen in the company of strangers unfamiliar with his line of work, didn't hesitate. With his familiar Bogart-Runyon diction he said to Henry Luce, "I know nuttin' about the line on television, but if bucks are up for grabs, the fix is in."

Early the next morning Mary called to tell me, "Hank was absolutely charmed by your father. We must meet again. It's rare he meets a person whom he is confident will not call the next day to sell him an insurance policy."

My introduction to Allen Dulles was less serendipitous. It must have been Mary who arranged for us to be invited to the wedding of Barbara Hunt, an easygoing heiress who wandered into our lives on the other arm of Bob Silberstein. The black-tie wedding was in Katonah, an upstate village that in sunlight could contend for the All-American dream town. In the driving rain of that spring day, it passed as just another signpost on our way to the wedding tent.

The rain was so severe the grounds were flooded. I was content to sip champagne and practice leg-raising to keep my feet dry, but Mary insisted I meet Allen Dulles. The commissar of the CIA navigated through the flood to meet me halfway. Allen Dulles's trousers were neatly rolled up, his feet were bare, and a napkin was tied around his wrist, ideas that hadn't occurred to me. He had the flushed, jovial face of a preacher or school principal determined to make the best of it. When I offered a wry compliment about being reassured by his company before we took off on Noah's Ark, he laughed and Mary beamed like a proud parent. As soon as I returned to my table I took off my shoes and socks and later dried my feet with an embroidered napkin.

12

James Baldwin, J. D. Salinger, and VFMA Samizdat

Circa 1960

To celebrate the publication of my first novel, Isabelle Holland, the Crown publicist, invited me to the Algonquin Hotel for lunch. We were to meet Lewis Nichols, a writer for *The New York Times Book Review.* "He wouldn't ask to speak to you if he wasn't intending to write a note for his 'In and Out of Books' column."

I was familiar with the great lounge: its stuffed chairs, small tables, and scattered lamps that gave the effect of visiting a prosperous but not overly indulgent friend's living room. I arrived early. I wanted to be sure not to be late and was considering warming up with a celebratory martini. After all, novelists were supposed to drink and smoke, and if not now, when? On the other hand I wasn't quite confident enough to risk being tipsy with an interviewer. So, I stood bewitched and bewildered when a familiar voice called my name. It was Bob Mills, no longer associated with Mercury publications where I had worked as one of his editorial assistants. Bob was now in business for himself as a literary agent. He was sitting with a lean and restless, bold-eyed young writer whom I recognized as James Baldwin.

They were sitting in a remote corner of the court and when Mills waved me to join him, he made no eye contact. I looked over my shoulder to be sure it was I and not a more formidable reliefer being waved in from the bull pen.

Bob Mills was perhaps six-three, with cropped blond hair and critical eyes beneath rimless glasses that suggested he just read or was about to read a manuscript he would reject. I was familiar with Baldwin's *Go Tell It on the Mountain* and *Notes of a Native Son*. His style abandoned Strunk and White and was so defiantly poetic and self-assured he seemed an unlikely client for Bob Mills. I recalled Mills as an editor who insisted upon rationing adverbs and going "easy on the adjectives." I approached their table warily and was so uncertain that when Mills recalled our relationship, I immediately let him know I'd written a novel set in the Catskills that was not a mystery. "All novels are mysteries," James Baldwin said in a voice so deep and confident it seemed to come from the mountain.

Mills insisted I sit and join them. I mumbled something about meeting the Crown publicist and a writer for the *Times,* but when he borrowed a seat from an adjoining table I sat. As so often happened in my experience with spontaneous invitations, I remained silent for several seconds, expecting an agenda of conversation, only to be greeted by silence to which I respond by daring to get a little something going. I asked James Baldwin if he and Bob were celebrating the publication of a new book. He said he was working on a book and Bob was providing "fuel."

It seemed presumptuous but I convinced myself to volunteer intimacies about myself in the presence of a former boss and James Baldwin, whom I realized might very well be one of the major writers of our time. I sensed a tension between them that I had been invited to divert, so I mentioned the experience that provided the impetus for my novel: "I'm from Baltimore," I began, and James Baldwin immediately interrupted me. He wanted to know if I knew Rose Styron. When I told him I'd met Rose Burgunder at a dance in 1948 and she was the belle of "Bawlamer," Baldwin's eyes brightened. He was considering staying during the winter at the Styrons' guesthouse in Roxbury, Connecticut. He went on with a monologue so rhythmic and rhetorical I would have thought he'd rehearsed if there weren't specific references to me and our meeting and his advice that I enjoy every moment of publication because if I was a writer and serious about it there would be few moments to "eat, drink, and pretend you are merry."

Mills appeared relieved, even elated, that Baldwin and I had a conversation going and he poked it along, mentioning "Jimmy's" years in Paris and provoking me to discuss what it was like growing up in a city as southern as Baltimore. I dropped an old cliché with which I'd grown up: "Baltimore is the most southern of northern cities and the most northern of southern." Baldwin's eyes lowered. He was staring at his drink when he said, "All American cities are southern."

There was a playfulness about the conversation that suggested that I was being tested. Baldwin was the judge and Mills and I were barely passing. We were bumping along with our "orals" when Isabelle Holland found me.

"So, there you are, Sidney. We've been waiting in the Oak Room." I introduced Bob Mills as my old boss, but she recognized James Baldwin. As gracefully as a hostess presiding at her own party Isabelle apologized for taking me away from them. "I'm sure Sidney is having a more interesting time with you than he will with me, but promises are promises."

My early experience at Valley Forge Military Academy made me certain there would be a penalty for being late, but Isabelle Holland and Lewis Nichols provided such easy and responsive company they soon had me feeling I was a worthy center of attention. Isabelle was wearing a brimmed hat and gloves. Mr. Nichols was in a rumpled linen suit. It seemed a social conversation, much less demanding than my earlier chat with Bob Mills and James Baldwin.

When Mr. Nichols asked me if the Catskill novel was really my first, I confessed I'd written an unpublished book drawing on my experience working at at a confession magazine. I also told him I'd started to write a novel set at a military school like Valley Forge, but when I read *Catcher in the Rye* I was so awed I didn't even want to touch on a place that Salinger's early chapters identified as "Pensy Prep."

Mr. Nichols wanted to know if I knew Salinger. I said I'd met him once briefly on Madison Avenue. I'd recognized him from the photographs on his book jacket and when I introduced myself as a fellow VFMA alumnus and expressed admiration for his novel, he accepted it courteously but without encouragement for me to go on.

"I should have known better," I said, "but I really was on the verge of reciting to J. D. Salinger a verse from a class song he'd written around 1936:

> *Four years have passed in joyful ways—*
> *Wouldst stay these old times dear?*

I went on: "It inspired me to write a poem. When I read and sang that song in 1946, I knew it had been written by a cadet my age ten years earlier, 1936."

I recited to Isabelle Holland and Lewis Nichols an excerpt from the poem I'd written.

> *Two flags, a gate, a youth, he enters.*
> *A year then two, pass three and four*
> *Two flags, a gate, a man, he exits.*

"When the poem was published in the school paper, I became a hero to the two radicals on campus. Due to a typo, my last word 'exits' appeared as 'exists.'"

The Oak Room lunch crowd was gone when we wrapped up the "interview." Mr. Nichols said he supposed we should have talked a little bit about Catskill humor, but that could wait for another time.

His two paragraphs greeting the publication of *He Had It Made* linked it to another borscht belt alumnus, Moss Hart, whose *Act*

One was published that year. Lewis Nichols's concluding line was something to the effect that I'd considered writing about Valley Forge, but another writer "got there first—J. D. Salinger." I was relieved that he hadn't mentioned Salinger's song, and, following James Baldwin's advice, I "pretended to be merry."

13

Jack Paar, Moss Hart, and a Dime to Call Home

Circa 1960

Mention of my Catskill novel in the *Times* and several good reviews encouraged an old Baltimore friend, Frank Abrahams, to recommend me to Bob Shanks for an "audition." Frank, who was on the staff of *What's My Line,* was convinced that if I did my stuff, telling stories about renting rooms, dealing with dining-room *gonifs* and kitchen *meshuggenahs* while imitating the voices, Shanks would recommend me for an appearance with Jack Paar on *The Tonight Show.* "There's not much to say about a novel," Frank advised. "You have to perform."

So, Frank set up an interview that was to be my audition. I met Bob Shanks at his office, a small room at the NBC studio. Sitting at a desk with neatly stacked papers including book galleys and press releases, Shanks seemed more the editor of an Ivy League humor magazine than the talent scout for a late-night television talk show. He wore a button-down collar and thin-rimmed glasses, and seemed to have had a recent haircut. I felt comfortable and did my voices: "So you call dis a room? Let me ask you somthin, sonny, vat they give you for dis box midt a vindow?" The vegetable man wrapped it up. I performed the character, a solitary gent, peeling and chatting—to himself. And it worked.

The evening before I was to appear on the most popular TV show in the land I called my family in Baltimore—of course my parents—but also my uncles, aunts, and cousins. It seemed to me only fair. Wouldn't their feelings be hurt if a friend asked, "What relation are you to the Offit I saw on television last night?" and they didn't even know about it.

Jack Paar greeted me before the show went on the air. We stood in the hall leading to the studio, a sparsely decorated stage with a desk and several chairs for the host and his guests. The seats accommodating the audience were already filled with grateful visitors who had dared the lines of applicants for ringside seats. Avi and Frank Abrahams, my friend and "broker," had gone on to the front-row aisle seats reserved for us. Jack Paar was reassuring. "I hear you tell some very funny stories. If by any chance we don't get around to you this evening, you can be sure you'll be on the next night. Wouldn't want to miss you for the world."

"Next night?" It was a mild deflater, but I was soothed by an introduction to Moss Hart. Although he had not received the same warning, the famous playwright, too, had to wait his turn. I'd heard that Hart broke into show business at the Flagler up the road in South Fallsburg, New York. It was true, and while we waited in the wings he told me about his experience writing, directing, and performing. "There wasn't a better drama school in the land," he said. "The audiences were tough but when convinced they were getting their money's worth they celebrated like backers after a first night of rave reviews."

I was impressed by Hart's self-confidence, fascinated by his style. He dressed and carried himself like a graduate of Oxford or Cambridge to whom public performance was a lark.

On camera the chatty gentleman with whom I'd been sharing borscht belt memories moments before transformed into a theatrical presence with all the sophistication and playful wit of a character created by Oscar Wilde or—yes, Moss Hart. Jack Paar was visibly pleased to be in the presence of a guest whom he obviously admired and seemed even a mite relieved, because with Moss Hart sharing the stage he could comfortably retire to the role of straight man with confidence that the wit would flow.

They discussed the themes that had contributed to the success of *Act One,* a runaway bestseller. Poor boy makes good and enjoys if not every minute, every last cent of his deservedly acquired fortune. Paar was enraptured by Hart's candor as he expressed resolve never to ride the subway again and extolled the pleasures of custom-made accessories. The clock was moving to the last rounds—my turn—when Hart demonstrated the indulgences of his fortune and taste by removing from his back pocket a custom-made gold cigarette case. Paar couldn't have been more delighted if he'd produced the Holy Grail. The studio audience, too, was enchanted.

As time passed, I was beginning to feel twinges of compromised dignity and regret that I'd auditioned to put myself in this position.

The show was a success for everyone but me. Frank, Avi, and I made the best of it, applauding Moss Hart, honoring Jack Paar, and retreating to Schrafft's for double-dip chocolate sundaes. We explained the cancellation and reluctantly suggested to family and friends they tune in the next night, when it was likely I'd be on.

The following night Jack Paar picked up where he'd left off with Moss Hart the previous evening. There were lots of stories about theatrical legends—George Kaufman, Monty Woolley. . . . Did he say Edna Ferber? Once again the clock ran out for me. As Moss Hart stepped offstage he surprisingly put an arm around my shoulder.

"This must be difficult for you," he said matter-of-factly. "I'm sure you have lots of relatives who have been waiting to see you and now you have to call them. Where did you say you were from? Baltimore? Well, there must be one *macher* in your family—an uncle who would be flattered to do it all for you." Then he fumbled in his pocket and pulled out a handful of change. "I should be buying you a drink, but you'll be better off calling Uncle Sammy? Uncle Saul? And be sure to send them warm regards from Cousin Moss."

Moss Hart wasn't wrong about Baltimore and not too far off on the name of a fictive uncle, either. I was deflated but not bitter. It was reassuring that he acknowledged me and went so far as to identify me as a "cousin" of his showbiz family.

I was upstaged again the next night for all but the last five minutes.

After a long introduction that I was sure left me with just enough time to hold up my novel and smile, there was a break for a commercial. "You have lots of time," Jack Paar said. "Just be sure to get right to the gag line of your story." What gag line? What story? I didn't even have a pouch of pipe tobacco that conformed to the contours of my rear pocket. No mimicry. No story. I was a two-minute-and-thirty-five-second bust. But Jack Paar did hold up my novel, and I had the opportunity to confess before a national audience that I worked in a Catskill kitchen—for my mother-in-law.

Frank Abrahams and Avi joined me when I came offstage. Frank suggested we skip Schrafft's. After a night—three nights—like this, we were introduced to P. J. Clarke's, northeast corner, Third Avenue at 55th Street, where our beer flowed like borscht.

II

Other Encounters and a Good Cigar:
1960s Through 1990s

14

Lisa Howard (ABC News) Presents Eleanor Roosevelt, Adlai Stevenson, and a Box of Cigars from Che Guevara

1958–1967

"Lisa Calls at Midnight," the fantasy title of an unwritten memoir, provides the clue to the histrionic flare of Lisa Howard, the Cleopatra of the Lexington Democratic Club, who in 1963 became the first woman to have her own national news show. And she looked the part—large brown eyes, inquisitively mobile features in a face so classic that it distracted one's attention from the thinning hair and the curious absence of empathetic expression. Mary Bancroft, Lucy Geringer, Bob Silberstein, Lisa, and I comprised a self-appointed committee of five who rendezvoused after meetings for drinks and smokes, gossip and prophecy. Our political "power" was assessed by mutual agreement as "a committee of five who, when we stretched and exerted all our influence, sometimes rallied as many as eight."

Unlike Mary, who required a social engagement for her monologues, or Lucy, who seemed to have a fulfilling life outside the club,

Lisa's bursts of enthusiasm and anger were driven by a passion or ambition so intense she was indifferent to place, company, or time.

When Lisa called at midnight, I would sigh to the slumbering medical student in my arms, and say "It's Lisa," release her, stumble down the hall, and pick up the extension phone outside our children's room.

It was most frequently a political event or encounter that inspired Lisa's calls. When she learned that Nikita Khrushchev was visiting the UN, Lisa called at midnight to describe her plan to hide in the hallway of the Russian consulate on Park Avenue and 68th Street to meet him. "I have a press pass, but it's right in your neighborhood. Want to join me?" I didn't, but when I described the reason for Lisa's call to Avi the next morning, I realized I might have responded differently if she hadn't seemed a visitation in a dream. Lisa did waylay the Soviet premier and enchanted him sufficiently for Khrushchev to agree to an interview that went on for 108 minutes, including philosophical speeches by Lisa and Khrushchev's response to one Howard stunner: "I cannot enunciate the whole of Karl Marx's *Das Kapital* in five minutes." It was, I assume, cut and edited for her ABC news show.

Newsweek described Lisa as "startlingly good-looking . . . still has her curves," but on the phone at midnight all I was aware of was the textured, dramatic voice that—after all the speeches and philosophy—often got around to inviting me to come along for the ride. Sometimes I joined the "rides" more out of courtesy than conviction. In 1964, when Lisa signed me up to protest Robert Kennedy's run to unseat Kenneth Keating, the Republican senator from New York, I was much less concerned than she that Kennedy could be considered a carpetbagger. Later, when I met Kennedy at a debate Lisa had arranged, I confessed I thought Robert Kennedy was as good, probably better, than any Democrat (with the exception of Bill vanden Heuvel) that our party could nominate for any office. "Maybe Kennedy should be running for president," I quietly suggested to Lisa. That modest rebellion was dismissed with raised eyebrows and the stage-center announcement: "I'm sure when you reconsider, you'll change your mind."

Going along with Lisa, I met Eleanor Roosevelt at a rally for the organization of an alliance of reform clubs. But first I had to shake hands with former governor and senator Herbert Lehman, who seemed so tired and exhausted he rested his hand in mine as if relieved of the weight. (I was not surprised when he died a few months later.)

After Lisa brushed her way past other admirers and stood face-to-face with the former first lady, Mrs. Roosevelt smiled and said warmly, "How nice to see you again, Lisa." I didn't know whether to make a speech or sing a song when Lisa introduced me. Her bio notes were so exaggerated, it didn't seem enough to just say "How do you do?" I stretched it a line and told Mrs. Roosevelt, "You are an inspiration for all of us." With a flinch she replied, repeating my name, "You young Democrats of the reform clubs are the inspiration for *us,* Mr. Offit. It is such important work you are doing to broaden the base of our party. . . ." It reads as a political salutation but in that great hall, with Lisa beaming her million-dollar smile, Eleanor Roosevelt's remarks seemed a benediction of pure poetry.

Lisa introduced me to Adlai Stevenson during the time when he was the U.S. ambassador to the United Nations. Although Stevenson had been defeated twice as a candidate for president and had been turned down in his delayed bid for the nomination in 1960, he reigned as the patron saint of reform Democrats. It was his erudition, wit, and talent for articulating ideals of government that rallied a generation of World War II veterans and college-educated, left-leaning Democrats to grassroots participation in the party.

Lisa had invited me to join her and her husband, Walter Lowendahl, to a party celebrating Russell Hemenway at which Stevenson was the featured speaker. Russ, escorting Eleanor Roosevelt, had joined Stevenson at the podium when Eugene McCarthy nominated Stevenson for a third go at the White House. As Mary Bancroft predicted, the fix was already in and the Golden Boy of the liberals was retired to the rooting section for the Kid from Camelot. But Stevenson hadn't forgotten Russell Hemenway or his other supporters. He spoke with such grace that evening of our honoree's contribution to the vitality of the party and "the good of the nation," that I, among others, was left with a nostalgic pang.

As soon as Stevenson returned to his seat, Lisa was on her feet, tugging at my sleeve. "You must meet Adlai."

A voice was still chanting from the dais when Lisa brought me to Stevenson's table. A small man, with a bald head and earnest, twinkling eyes, Stevenson had that rare gift, with a brief nod and light touch, of making you feel he cared. He stood to greet Lisa, and though obviously distracted when she introduced me, he tapped my hand—good boy, good boy—and tried to return to his seat.

Lisa's whisper was a husky seduction. She was telling the Liberal of Liberals about my novel *The Other Side of the Street,* the story of a Baltimore bookmaker. The presentation was swift and dramatic. I was so flushed with embarrassment, I don't recall how she made the transition, but by the time the last speaker had retired and a crowd was beginning to collect about the star of the evening, Lisa Howard was dictating a blurb for my novel, and Adlai Stevenson, eyes twitching but pen secure, was transcribing.

Adlai Stevenson and I were rescued when Lisa was distracted by another friend. I managed to get us both off the hook by thanking the UN ambassador and assuring him it was best for both of us if he didn't endorse a book he hadn't read.

He agreed and assured me that if Lisa was "an enthusiast" my novel was certain to have "lots of attention anyway."

Later, when I thought about that moment—not without the regret that Lisa predicted ("People are endorsing books all the time that they haven't read")—I wondered what it revealed about our hero. Was he spontaneously generous and supportive or just easily bullied by beautiful women?

Prior to a telephone message inviting me to meet Che Guevara, I knew that Lisa had scored a journalistic coup by arranging with Alex Quaison-Sackey, the Ghanaian ambassador to Cuba and the UN, to get her a visa so she could travel to Cuba and visit Fidel Castro. After four weeks of pelting Castro with requests, she got Castro to agree.

They passed eight hours talking privately and recording a forty-minute interview.

I didn't even know Che Guevara was in town when I arrived home from a Cub Scout meeting with Ken and Mike. Avi told me Lisa had called insisting I not miss the opportunity to meet the notorious communist guerrilla leader.

Twenty minutes after abandoning my blue-uniformed Cub Scout team without a bedtime story, I had made the cut by the barricade and special police detail and was sitting in Lisa and Walter's 75th Street living room with the green-uniformed, cigar-puffing pinup boy of world radicals.

The high-ceilinged town house, furnished with the intimate possessions of two people who seemed to have led separate lives, was crowded with Tom Wolfe's cast of the radical chic. I sat in the rear on a comfortable Queen Anne chair, sipping a scotch that went right to my head. Tony Akers, a PT-109 buddy of J.F.K. and two-time congressional candidate in our district, was by my side. I was confident enough of my friendship with Tony to ask him, after several minutes of translated questions and answers, if there was anything to eat. He passed the peanuts.

Just coming off two hours of engaging sixty-eight ten-year-olds with close-order drills (the legacy of my years at Valley Forge Military Academy), games (learned as a Camp Ha-Wa-Ya counselor; Harrison, Maine, 1949) and stories (books for young readers), it was difficult to focus on meditations about capitalist injustice and the inevitable world revolution.

I was more charmed by the migrant waves of cigar smoke emanating from what I perceived to be nothing less than an eight-inch stogie that Mr. Guevara was puffing with less chomp than Winston Churchill but more lip contact than George Burns. With another scotch and encouragement from Tony Akers, I joined the question-answer exchange. I chipped in with a question about how Mr. Guevara felt about leaving his wife and children and what responsibilities, if any, he felt to them.

From the front of the room, where a semicircle of cashmeres and furs sat at the feet of the Cuban revolutionary, I heard more than a solo of snickers and groans. But Guevara answered without any sign of resentment. He said it was a good question. He had thought about it and there was no doubt in his mind that he was compromising his responsibilities to his own wife and children. He was not pleased by that, but he did it willingly because he was committed to a more important responsibility—making the world a better place for the tens of millions of other people's children who were exploited by world capitalism.

There was a ripple of applause and then silence, as if a dialogue were in progress, so I went on. I asked Guevara what he thought about the possibilities of the resumption of trade between the United States and Cuba.

After producing a perfect coil of gray-white smoke that trembled as a halo, Guevara answered that trade was up to us. Cuba was willing, but would not be intimidated by American power. I was out of peanuts and another scotch was risky, so I made the leap. "Would you consider a nonprofit trade with me, Mr. Guevara?" I asked. The translator translated and Che Guevara smiled. *"Sí. Sí."* I offered to swap two signed copies of books I had written for young readers, *The Boy Who Won the World Series* and *Soupbone*. "Baseball stories," I assured him. "Personalized signatures to your children for a box of Cuban cigars and one stogie to get me through this evening."

It was a deal. I have never experienced more envy or disdain than when the great Che Guevara, hero of world revolution, passed a hand-wrapped, perfect-leaf, genuine Cuban cigar across a room full of his fans as well as acolytes, to me. And—I lit it.

It was a great smoke but, I came to realize, an expensive one. Before the evening was over, one of Lisa's guests told me he would gladly have paid a thousand bucks for a cigar from Che Guevara.

After our exchange, the evening passed like the first movement of Haydn's Symphony No. 65 in A Major—with so many repeated fanfares it seemed we were awaiting the arrival of another major character. It was past midnight when he did, at last, arrive. Norman Mailer took over the evening. He was in the process of negotiating a trip for himself to visit Cuba when I, still puffing on my Che Guevara cigar, took off for the walk down Madison Avenue that would bring me home to my medical student, Cub Scouts, and, if my luck held out, what was left of a roast chicken in the refrigerator.

Walter Lowendahl, with his old-world charm reminiscent of European royalty, called the next morning to tell me Che had been in touch. He was sending the box of cigars to Walter for me to pick up and he was expecting signed copies of two books.

Neither Walter nor Lisa seemed to regard this as an inappropriate premium for our friendship. I shared the cigars with several writer pals and my brother Benson, who much preferred good old-fashioned Pall Malls.

I spoke rarely about the squandered treasure I'd received from the enduring hero of revolution, but I did mention it at an evening concert devoted to the works of the composer Burton Lane. When I was introduced to his widow, Lynn, by our mutual friend the writer Max Wilk, I recalled that we had met at that memorable evening at Lisa's. Sure enough, Lynn Lane told me she and her husband had been there and the composer of "That Old Devil Moon," "On a Clear Day," "Mañana," and "Everything I Have Is Yours" had also received a box of cigars from Che Guevara. "It was an extraordinary gift. Not only did Burt cherish the cigars, but we shared in the legacy of adoration for Che when we visited Cuba."

My friend Lisa Howard died several years later—a suicide. She was suffering a depression after a miscarriage and had lost her job on ABC. The last time we spoke, she called from her summer house in the Hamptons. I was working at my in-laws' resort in the Catskills. When I told Lisa I was running the kitchen, she responded with a voice that for the first time in our friendship sounded mildly critical. "Oh, I thought you'd already written your novel about that."

In retrospect, it seems to me our relationship was always warm, supportive, and full of the adventures that Lisa created, but never intimate. Even though Lisa's daughter Annie (Mushie) and our son Ken were in the same class at PS 6, we rarely spoke about our children. Several times I suspected Lisa was a breath away from discussing her encounters with other men. I discouraged her. Walter and I met a number of times, always like brothers in a family that had fun together but never analyzed or shared confidences.

Lucy Geringer and her husband, Donald Beldock, eventually became the only friends with whom to share Lisa's memory. Donald, a playwright who has written engaging dramas about Sir Walter Raleigh's execution and Christopher Marlowe's murder in a tavern brawl, didn't know Lisa. It sometimes struck me as ironic that Avi, Lucy, and I were discussing the mysteries of our friend's suicide in the company of Donald, who had been so creatively engaged in contemplation of the lives of remarkable men who died unnatural deaths.

Several years ago, shortly before he died, I met Walter Lowendahl strolling on Madison Avenue. We spoke about Lisa's suicide. Neither he nor I had strong clues that she ever planned to do herself in. Walter told me that he had never intended to marry Lisa. He was satisfied with her company and high spirits. The marriage was her idea. She had insisted upon it. "And what Lisa wanted, Lisa got."

Her connection with me was safe—free of intense sexual tension. "I think she was as pleased as I that you are so obviously married, married."

Once I got over the grief and the attempt to resolve the enigmatic riddle of why people take their own lives, I remembered Lisa not only as a catalyst for political encounters but as the first really knockout woman friend who provoked neither temptation nor jealousy even when she called at midnight.

15

Charles Bracelen Flood, James Thomas Flexner, and Betty Friedan—Graduate School at the NYPL

1959–1964

The Frederick Lewis Allen Room at the New York Public Library at 42nd Street and Fifth Avenue was one of the city's best kept secrets when I discovered it in the early 1960s. Again, it was Avi's suggestion that I "leave home," but unlike the social motivation that inspired her reasons for my joining a political club, it was to find a quiet place to work that led her to encourage me to set out for the library. The room Avi had in mind and where I banged away at the old portable for a week or so was on the second floor—furnished with a long table, wooden chairs, and offering the service of books on demand.

The Allen Room was hidden at the rear of the first floor and was available only to writers with a book contract. I found out about it when I recognized Broadus Mitchell, a former Hopkins professor, loitering by the 42nd Street entrance. I had been introduced to Professor Mitchell when he showed up on graduation day, 1950. When he heard about my editorial championing Alger Hiss and Owen Lattimore, he adopted me as a radical protégé-in-waiting. Professor Mitchell's manner was self-effacing, offering no suggestion as to the rigor of his commitments to what he considered the unfettered exchange of ideas and fair play.

"Of course I remember you, Mr. Offit," he assured me at our serendipitous reunion. He wanted to know what I was writing and on hearing that I was working in the typing room, he brought me to Mr. Camm, the administrator who served as admissions director to the Allen Room.

With Professor Mitchell as my advocate I was accepted on the spot. That same afternoon I moved my typewriter and working script to a cubicle of my very own. The Allen Room was paneled, with desks, bookshelves, ashtrays, and carpeted floors. During the two years I worked there, it became my office, social center, and graduate school. It provided, too, an opportunity to write in the company of other writers in much the same way reporters compose their stories in a city room.

If there was a presiding presence in the Allen Room, circa 1960, it was James Thomas Flexner. Jimmie was the first person Broadus Mitchell introduced me to. He cited the Johns Hopkins connection, reminding me that Jimmie's father—or was it his uncle?—had written the Flexner report that revolutionized medical education. His father and his uncle had also founded Rockefeller University and the Princeton Institute of Advanced Research.

Jimmie, a small man with graying hair that flared above his ears as if to balance the lush flow of his mustache and beard, seemed to have no warm feelings for Professor Mitchell. He accepted the brief sketch of me without comment. I was surprised and delighted when, two days after we met, Jimmie Flexner invited me to join him for lunch in the employees' cafeteria. I learned that Jimmie was writing *That Wilder Image,* a volume of art history that emphasized the importance of American art as original in inspiration and technique.

Jimmie's routine was the most disciplined of any writer in the room. He arrived promptly every weekday morning at nine, broke for lunch at twelve-thirty, tea at three-thirty, and off for home close to five. When composing, Jimmie would sometimes rise from his chair, stride around the room before returning to his cubicle to lean over his typewriter, expel what he must have thought was a silent relief of gas, and change a word of his manuscript.

Although there were a number of distinguished writers who flowed in and out of the room during my tenure there, a small group provided the life of the campus. Jimmie was most accepting and pleased with the company of several ladies: Ellen Moers, a scholar and biographer of Theodore Dreiser, and Jackie James, who was at work on a biography of her late husband, the Pulitzer laureate Marquis James.

Ellen, a formidable presence with her neat figure, laughing brown eyes, dark hair, and long cigarette holder, interrupted me at work one afternoon with a gentle tap on the shoulder and the advice, "Whatever you are writing, put it aside. You must write a book about Homer Fink."

She told me that her son Richard, who is "brilliant," remarked about the stories I'd told about a young genius named Homer Fink. "He heard you at his school assembly and came home full of praise, which for Richard is rare." Ellen was the wife of Martin Mayer, a writer whose works about the financial world and education were best-sellers. I assured myself their son had inherited good critical genes and after I finished the chapter of the novel with which I was struggling, put it aside to begin *The Adventures of Homer Fink*.

Among the men working in the Allen Room the only one who passed Jimmie Flexner's critical muster was Charles Bracelen Flood. Charlie, even younger than I, had already written a bestseller, *Love Is a Bridge*. I'd heard the story of the kid a year out of Archibald Mac-Leish's class at Harvard whose first novel was being compared to the works of F. Scott Fitzgerald and John P. Marquand. Charlie had the good looks and easy manner I associated with the best of the Roland Park gentry in Baltimore. For all his early success he presented himself with neither arrogance nor self-absorption. He was interested in all the writers in the room and only later when we were the best of friends was I privy to his searing insights and not always flattering perceptions of our colleagues. Charlie never mentioned Broadus Mitchell and to this day he seems perplexed when I tell him Professor Mitchell had recommended him to me as "an unusual young man of honor whom you can always trust."

Charlie had published two other novels since his extraordinary debut and was at work on an historical fiction focusing on the Revolutionary War battle at Monmouth. He wore an eyeshade from time to time and was second only to Jimmie Flexner in the rigidity of his schedule. Often after our group lunch breaks, Charlie and I would linger outside the Allen Room, sharing variations on the themes and impressions of the participants in our midday "seminars." It was Charlie who sent the signal for us to return to work. He insisted we approach our fictional compositions as a job with no apologies for a lack of "artistic inspiration" or excuses for other promises.

Charlie and I both suspected early on in our relationship that we would be friends for life. Our strolls up Fifth Avenue after work led to conversations about books and values, family and friends. His Catholic childhood had as much effect on Charlie as my experience with Jewish traditions. Although I was not committed to formal religion, I identified with Jewish history and told Charlie that Avi and I honored the holidays. In his years at Harvard, Charlie told me, he had never met a Jewish student who acknowledged even that modest link. Charlie reported classmates insisting that although they were born Jewish, "that's as far as it goes."

In addition to our respect, if not devotion, to organized religion, Charlie and I were both grateful for our good fortune—celebrating as gifts American freedom and opportunity, and families that were supportive. While Charlie traveled the world—writing a novel set in Korea and then a nonfiction study of the Vietnam War—I remained at home, rejoicing in the company of my wife and children. I got there first, but we both knew Charlie was on the way. He eventually met Kathy Burnam, the Kentucky belle who was to be his wife. They settled in Kentucky to raise the three children who blessed their lives. I perceived it as the achievement of an elusive balance, defying Yeats's poetic dictum: "The intellect of man is forced to choose / Perfection of the life, or of the work." For Charlie, as for me, it was "Live the life and let the mavens of the morning line predict who is making art."

Along with Jimmie, Charlie, and me, several other members of the room frequently met for lunch. We would gather around a table in the basement at the employees' cafeteria to knock off chicken or tuna fish salad sandwiches or cold platters of macaroni and cheese with tea or coffee while roaming over a range of topics before inevitably getting around to one or another's work in progress.

Peter Burchard, the matinee idol of our crowd, was a man of such sensual gifts he married four times and was never in the forty years I knew him without a woman to care for him. I often forgot that Peter stammered, but was reminded by his long silence when in company and the perpetually accepting smile that I eventually thought of as his self-produced stage role. Peter was writing a young-adult novel based on the diaries of a relative who had been a prisoner in a southern camp during the Civil War. He was also researching the life and career of Colonel Robert Gould Shaw who commanded a black regiment. Many years later, Peter's book *One Gallant Rush* provided a source for the film *Glory*. Peter, too, became an instant friend and supportive colleague. Even after he became a Guggenheim fellow he made the effort to study lacrosse so he could illustrate one of my books for young readers. He introduced me to Paul Galdone, a much-honored illustrator, who bailed me out with drawings for *Homer Fink* and later *Soupbone*.

Peter continued to produce studies of history for young readers until he was past eighty. Shortly before he died he published a book about Abraham Lincoln and slavery. Peter's most lasting contribution to our friendship was introducing me to Robert A. Caro, the champion of all historian biographers. I was enjoying my last days at the Allen Room when Bob arrived. Eventually his term expired, too, and we were both looking for working space. Peter set us up to share a desk at his studio on West 37th Street.

Betty Friedan entered the Allen Room during my second year there, in 1961. By the time she arrived, Robert Gessner, the film historian, Jeb Stuart, author of the classic pacifist novel *The Objector,* and Charles Dougherty, who was writing an introduction to anthropology for young readers, had departed. Betty Rollins was an infrequent visitor and not yet experiencing the breast cancer of which she was later to write so movingly. We had brief glimpses of Nancy Milford, still performing social curtain calls for her biography of Zelda Fitzgerald while researching a biography of Edna St. Vincent Millay, and Susan Brownmiller, warming up for her feminist history study *Against Their Will*. During my years, Betty Friedan was the most frequent woman guest at Flexner's NYPL "roundtable."

I was bowled over by Betty Friedan from the moment one of her sons knocked on the door to the Allen Room so she could escort him to the dentist. Until then I perceived her as the most intense of the writers I had met. When Betty was at work she leaned close to her manuscript, visibly lost in the trance of writing. I suppose it is not possible to write even the most elementary of sentences while thinking of something else, but writers often welcome interruption. Not Betty. Responding to clang or tap, Betty's head snapped back and she needed a moment to compose herself. She didn't look at all like Avi, but her total commitment (obsession?) to her project of the moment reminded me of my wife.

At the time that Betty's son knocked on the door, Avi was prepping for medical school, studying the science prerequisites—biology, physics, chemistry—and caring for our sons Ken, five, and Mike, three. When Avi and I married I perceived it as a partnership and felt neither threatened nor compromised, but when I heard the thesis of Betty's book *The Feminine Mystique,* I was astonished.

Only Avi knew that at the time we met I had been writing in collaboration with my friend, the classicist Bill Romeike, a series of essays mocking the popular-magazine vision of the American woman aspiring to be only a housekeeper. Bill and I concluded that women were in many ways superior to men, less apt to initiate wars, more caring, nurturing, and civilized, as well as undervalued as students, scholars, and artists. Our book, although completed, was abandoned soon after I married Avi. Offended by my acknowledgment that I would now be collaborating with my wife, Bill withdrew the script for submission to publishers and as far as I knew destroyed it.

During the years of our friendship, Betty, Avi, and I shared celebrations of housewarmings, birthdays, weddings, bar mitzvahs, and, perhaps, most coincidental of all—the graduation of Betty's daughter Emily and our son Ken from Harvard Medical School. That occasion turned out to be a serendipitous reunion. Matthew Frosch, son of our mutual pals Bill and Paula Frosch, was also on the program, ringing up a Ph.D. along with his M.D. The icing on this "small world—six degrees of separation" cake was the graduates' teacher at Harvard Medical School—none other than Mark Vonnegut, M.D., son of Kurt.

Much more recently, when I mentioned his son's reputation as a medical prof and cited the sources, Kurt, much to my surprise, revealed another dimension of Betty Friedan. Kurt told me Betty was a comfortable fisherman and right at home bouncing on small craft after big fish. Alas, an unwritten chapter of *The Feminine Mystique.*

There was no "graduation" from the Allen Room, but after two years, it was expected that the writer would pack up and make room for another scribbler. Just before my fond farewells I met Ormonde de Kay, golden boy in a field jacket, recently returned from Europe where among other adventures he had worked with the filmmaker Louis de Rochemont. Ormonde later wrote the history of the Harvard Club, but at that moment he was less into writing projects than social times. Ormonde de Kay introduced me to another option of literary society: It's rarely too early and never too late for a drink.

Charlie had taken off for Asia, Peter returned to his workshop in Rockland County, Jimmie retired to the Society Library, Betty was engaged by family responsibilities and the book that was soon to become a movement.

All those friendships endured long after the books I worked on in the Allen Room—*The Adventures of Homer Fink, The Other Side of the Street, Soupbone*—went out of print.

16

Encounters on East 69th Street—
Champions of the World Produced by
Don King and Arthur Krim

1957–2000

In the fall of 1957—before the birth of our younger son, Mike—Avi, Ken, and I moved to an apartment in a brownstone on East 69th Street between Park and Madison. During the half century we've strolled with baby carriages, parked bikes and second-hand cars, delivered groceries, and, most recently, walked Remy, our Maltese, there has been no sound in my memory—no horn or siren, cry or bark—more resonant than a salutation from our neighbor Don King, headquartered in a town house across the street, circa 1988.

"Ladies and gentle-men . . . Friends and neigh-bors . . . The Heavy-weight Champion of the Entire World . . . the One and Only En-tire World!" The voice was familiar but as it echoed up East 69th Street to where I was double-parked in front of the Austrian Embassy, I wondered to whom the announcement was addressed. It was a Saturday morning in late June. I was on my way to pick up Avi and the luggage for our retreat to a farm near the beach in Water Mill, Long Island. The only person I saw on the street was a mail carrier crossing Park and he was seemingly oblivious to the urgency of the message.

"Come and meet him. Come and meet him, one and all . . . once in a lifetime . . . the Champion of the En-tire . . . World . . ."

So, I shook the hand of Mike Tyson. A large, obviously powerful mitt that exercised no pressure—absolutely limp. "What can you do?" said the bewildered champion, who shrugged and then repeated in that high-pitched little-boy-little-girl voice that belied his speed, power, and rage. "What can you do? That's Don. That makes him happy."

A portly gent, maybe five-five in a chauffeur's uniform, opened the door to the limo, but Don King's performance was not over. As if addressing a vast audience seated in stands converted from surrounding town houses, he went on blessing "these United States, where it can happen, does happen! Only in America!"

Avi was waiting. My car was parked by a plug, but once I had volunteered to meet Mike Tyson I had no strategy for a gracious exit. Suddenly, as if picking me out of a crowd, Don King turned to me with a look of such delighted recognition that if I hadn't known better I would have thought he remembered me.

We had been introduced briefly when several of his employees recognized me as "that little man with the bow tie who fights on Channel 5," a reference to my series of televised political debates with Dr. Martin Abend presented with the ten o'clock news.

From the majestic height that the great crop of wiry hair increased, he greeted me with a broad, warm smile and asked, "And why I know you?" I told him I was his neighbor from across the street and reminded him gently that we had been introduced before. "Of course," came the booming voice and then, with a mite less volume, he said to Mike Tyson, who was fidgeting restlessly, "Mike, you gotta meet a gen-uine star of tele-vision. Shake hands with—what your name again?"

The heavyweight champion of the world and I shook hands once more and Don King was satisfied. "Nice seeing you, real nice, Sidney. . . ." The chauffeur let me know with a half smile and shrug that it was all in a day's work and the stretch limo took off.

Mike Tyson wasn't the only heavyweight titleholder with whom Don King insisted I exchange greetings. Previously Muhammad Ali had been encouraged to perform the famous Ali shuffle in front of the "promoter of promoters." Dressed handsomely in a designer suit with no visible signs of any of the ailments that were to plague him later in life, Ali delighted the assembly of King's staff, building-service workers, and me, the curious spectator. It was a generous gift as Don King reminded us, repeating "The Greatest . . . the Greatest," the prophecy of the champion himself that was converted into a benediction by the maestro of Don King Productions.

As he gracefully skipped and shuffled, without interrupting his movement, Ali shared high fives, leering at me. "Don't give my friends no trouble." The leer opened into an irresistible smile. Someone must have told Ali about my bouts—debates—with Martin Abend because the magically swift hands folded into fists and Ali said, "Let's go for the television title. . . ." Two more shuffles, a shadowbox, and I was awarded a high five.

The encounters with Larry Holmes, Roberto Duran, and Evander Holyfield in the early 1990s were less dramatic, as often distant waves from my window as closer greetings on the street. Whenever I encountered Don King in the neighborhood he was apt to ignore me but was never less than cordial when I offered the greeting. The last time we met was during the time his marble and wrought iron palace with the gold crown and signature DON was for sale.

Avi and I were on our way to a swim at the New York Health and Racquet Club on East 57th Street when we saw Don King and a good-looking lady who appeared so comfortable in his presence I thought she must be his wife or close relative. Our eyes locked and he smiled with that by now familiar expression of the person who knows you've met but needs to be reminded of the history.

I introduced Don King and "his friend" as our neighbors from across the street to Avi, who was as vaguely aware of Don King's identity as he was of ours. His lady seemed pleased to greet us. We spoke briefly about our mutual friends who serviced the houses in the neighborhood. He expressed almost as much fondness as I did for William Bridgett, and he made a real effort to recall our friend Carl Thompson, who also kept the home fires burning.

We made a slight pass at discussing the financial value of the buildings, and I was surprised at the confidence with which Don King told us of his price tag for 32 East 69th ("And not a cent less!"). When we parted it was with cordial handshakes and a burst of unexpected affection. Don King wrapped an arm around my shoulder and actually said, "I'm gonna miss you."

As we started toward the elevator to the eighth floor of the building where we would be swimming, Avi said, "That man really seems to like you. He's the sports king from the house across the street, isn't he?" Then with a wry smile she concluded, "And you're gonna miss him, too."

Before Don King presided at the house across the street, Martha Jackson had conducted an art gallery there. Farther east on our block Sherman Billingsley lived, before Arthur and Mathilde Krim took over his digs.

Mr. Billingsley and I connected as anonymous neighbors who became increasingly aware of a mutual enterprise: entertaining our children. I often observed the well-turned-out gentleman with the broad-brimmed fedora ambling up the avenue with his adoring daughter. I could tell how flattered she was by the way she beamed and clutched her daddy's hand.

My park jaunts in those days frequently involved car seats. Ken, four, and Mike, two, got a kick out of a drive around the park with a stopover, whenever a parking space was available, for a treat at the concession stand and restaurant overlooking the zoo.

After perhaps thirty-two nods, twelve "how do you dos," and four "good days," the gentleman in the fedora and I actually spoke to each

other. Two meetings later his pixieish blond daughter was enchanting
Ken and Mike from the backseat of our old Chevy while her father
sat by my side at the driver's seat and encouraged my animated tour
of the birds and squirrels of Central Park. I learned that his name was
Sherman Billingsley and by the end of that paragraph he had invited
my wife and me to be his guests "any day, any time" at the Stork
Club. "Just mention my name."

To Avi, the Stork Club was just a sophisticated version of the
Aladdin's Ali Baba Room and, besides, she was studying physics for
her pre-med requirements and so had no great interest in social adventure. I arrived solo at the line in front of the city's hottest nightspot,
mentioned Sherman Billingsley, and within seconds I was swept into a
special room and seated at the boss's table. Billingsley welcomed me
like a long-lost relative and introduced me to Walter Winchell with
the imposing invitation to tell the master of gossip and blab "all about
how we took our kids for a drive around Central Park."

A small man with puckish face and receding hairline, Walter
Winchell responded to my tour-text, complete with my impressions
of overstuffed pigeons and homeless squirrels. The scotch went right
to my head and for a while there was no stopping me. Several other
gents and smashing ladies joined the table. I became self-conscious
about too much attention and retreated into contemplations of the
radio voice from my childhood presenting himself over the air to
"Mr. and Mrs. North America and all our ships and clippers at
sea . . ."

Among the guests to whom I was introduced that evening was
the governor of Maryland and his wife. Governor Lane seemed to find
my presence at the table of the owner of the Stork Club evidence that
if you could make it in Baltimore, you could make it anywhere.

I don't remember the year Arthur and Mathilde Krim took over the
mansion up the block. But soon after they arrived, Arthur Krim and
I connected. An attorney and movie producer (United Artists and
Orion Films), Arthur was a champion fundraiser for the Democratic
Party. He, too, had a daughter who played a role in our connection.

Daphne Krim, along with Ken and Mike Offit, seemed to be the only children south of 72nd Street, between Fifth and Third, and north of 68th Street, to attend PS 6, a "private" public school coveted as the freebie available to families with the right address. It was rumored that J. D. Salinger had attended and borrowed the name Holden from one of his classmates and Caulfield from the principal at the time. Richard Avedon was among the alumni, but the distinction was not so much identified with the achievements of alumni as the superior quality of the education.

Although Arthur and I shared political loyalties, the difference in scale of our contributions to the Democratic Party couldn't have been more extreme. The originator of a program for major contributors to presidential campaigns (was it called the President's Circle?), Arthur later told me during an interview for an NYU panel on political fundraising that the premise of his appeal to big donors was not only to satisfy their needs to back up their opinions and sometimes passions with bucks but "to have access." A man sensitive to any hint of "influence peddling," he went on to define that access was most often "nothing more than the satisfactions of having your opinion heard by the president of the United States, himself." That could be arranged by phone or a word at a reception—with a photograph or perhaps a letter signed by the current tenant of the White House.

It wasn't until the taping of our seminar sponsored by NYU that I learned that access to Arthur himself was an aspiration of at least one member of NYU's film school. "Would you mind introducing me to Mr. Krim?" I was asked by a bearded young man in a turtleneck sweater. "I've always wanted to meet Woody Allen's producer. He's the chief honcho of United Artists, isn't he?"

Mr. Krim nodded graciously, acknowledging the introduction, but as far as I know nothing more came of that "access."

Krim's fundraising events—often small receptions at his town house down the block—were attended by the president, when the Democrat was crowned by the electoral college, or by the candidate when the Republicans were in power.

John F. Kennedy was the first of the Krim guests to sweep into the neighborhood with a fleet of New York City police cars and the Secret

Service, sometime after his election in 1960. I don't recall Arthur Krim being linked to J.F.K. as a fundraiser, but I do remember sharing a moment of awe—or was it mild shock?—when the dashing version of our fantasy monarch flashed his trophy smile. He acknowledged encountering me earlier and asked, "How's Lisa?" in reference to Lisa Howard, the belle of ABC correspondents, who seemed more than casually familiar with the Kennedy brothers and was notoriously energetic in supporting both Adlai Stevenson, who made a pass at blocking the J.F.K. nomination in 1960, and Kenneth Keating, the senator from New York whose seat Robert Kennedy annexed.

Lyndon Johnson's visit to the Krims in the late 1960s required cordoning the block. I was invited for a brief hello. The president arrived like a great wounded bird flying up the steps to avoid the taunts of the demonstrators behind wooden horses on the south side of our street, chanting opposition to the Vietnam War: "Hey, hey, L.B.J. How many kids did you kill today?"

The wrath of those opposed to the war was to grow in the years following, but at the moment it was a new experience for our neighborhood. I was less concerned about the issue than the insult to my friend Arthur's guest. When I returned home I rallied Ken and Mike for a diverting chant from the steps of our stoop: "Hey, hey. Ho Chi Minh. How many kids did you do in?"

That did it. The demonstrators were anxious for "debate" and moved down the block to engage us. The argument never progressed beyond the chants of couplets, but it did succeed in diverting the crowd from the Krim's reception and entertaining the captain of the 19th Precinct who knew me as the "knee-jerk" liberal president of the Community Council.

Arthur Krim entertained presidents and presidential candidates. I was most impressed by Walter Mondale, whom I considered charming, witty, warm—all qualities universally found lacking by the consensus of press and voters. "He'll schmeer Reagan," I assured friends and family. "The American people are much too smart to go for a miscast movie actor."

For all his gifts of "access" and enlightenment, I reciprocated to Arthur Krim by pulling political strings, my thin threads of cotton in contrast to his pure cashmere. When it was rumored that 72nd Street between Fifth and Third was to be the southern cutoff for PS 6, I called Alice Sachs, one of the leaders of the Lex Club, and pleaded my case. "Three, only three students that I know of will be affected by the cutoff. You can look it up." Alice did. After perhaps a dozen phone calls and 150 hours on the line, I was assured that an anonymous benefactor would see to it that the southern boundary was extended so that Daphne, Ken, and Mike could continue their education uninterrupted. The year he graduated Ken was elected president of the PS 6 student council—no fundraising but unlimited access.

Although four generations of our family at one time or another lived on East 69th between Madison and Park Avenues, the neighborhood became hometown to me when, in the 1990s, my closest cousin, Morris Offit, and his wife, Nancy, a former kid from Baltimore, moved into the co-op building on our corner at 700 Park. Morris is the son of Uncle Mike, a favorite pal of my dad's from among his five brothers. Morris and Nancy's sons, Ned and Danny, JHU graduates with more than a fair share of the family's good looks, were no longer living at home, so we didn't see much of them.

One snowy day after they'd moved in, Morris caught me shoveling the white stuff off our brownstone stoop. He was wearing boots as he walked the empty street toward Central Park. We talked, exchanging nostalgic tales about our fathers, uncles, cousins, aunts. We spoke about our cousin Morton's son, Paul Offit, a professor of pediatrics at the University of Pennsylvania School of Medicine who was writing *The Cutter Incident,* a book about how America's first polio vaccine led to a growing vaccine crisis. I brought Morris up to date on the scholarly adventures of my nephew Tom Offit, a Ph.D. in anthropology whose dissertation about the street children of Guatemala City had been accepted for publication by the University of Texas Press. Then I popped a question to Morris, without expecting an answer. "Why was it that there were so few musicians, artists, and writers among the more than one hundred descendants of our grandparents?" The founder of Offitbank and former chairman of the board of Johns Hopkins University said with a smile, "Most of us Offits, like our dads, are just not complicated people."

17

They Like Ike—Isidor I. Rabi, Harold Macmillan, and the Last Cameo by Errol Flynn

Circa 1968–1975

As far as I know, my friend Isidor Rabi and my acquaintance Harold Macmillan never met. My relationship with Rabi, the Nobel Laureate, Physics, 1944, lasted certainly over a longer period of time and was more intimate than my encounter with the former prime minister of Great Britain, 1957–1963.

Rabi and I were introduced by Detlev Bronk, a former president of John Hopkins University, who was presiding at Rockefeller University when he thrust me upon Rabi with the tag line, "Sidney writes books for children, Rabi, and he doesn't hesitate to write in classic Latin and Greek." It was an embarrassing exaggeration, but I knew Dr. Bronk meant well. We had connected when he first took over at Homewood in 1949. I was on the student committee that greeted him. A formal but friendly man with a passion for knowing and understanding what other people were up to, Dr. Bronk had adopted me as his "undergraduate" and encouraged me to send him copies of my novels. "Of course children's books, too, Sidney. There's no better way to keep up with what's influencing our younger generation."

At that first meeting with Dr. Rabi I had told him how admired Det Bronk was during his Hopkins years. I was surprised by Rabi's candor when he told me later, "Det introduced us so *you* could tell *me* what a success he had been at Hopkins, too."

My relationship with Rabi continued through many years with serendipitous encounters and two memorable declarations. When another mutual friend, Avery Fisher, told Rabi that we had discovered a shoe that required no breaking in and had relieved us both of aching corns, Rabi was curious to know where we had located such a phenomenon. That afternoon I ventured up Madison Avenue with the always chipper Nobel Prize winner to a store that featured recent models of the ECCO line. Committed to the Baconian method, Dr. Rabi exhausted every style, size, and width variation—eight and a half through nine—in pursuit of the winged foot.

When I sensed the salesman losing patience, I joined him before his final retreat to the stockroom, confided that his customer had won a Nobel Prize, and tipped him five dollars for his patience. "A Nobel Prize?" the impressed salesman responded. "For fashion?"

Alas, Dr. Rabi found no shoe that satisfied him. After a grateful thank-you to the exhausted "lab assistant," he shared with me a universal truth that may account for such a rash of shoe stores in the free world: "It is almost impossible to find a shoe that fits if you have a narrow heel." When I reported this declaration to my romantic sidekick, now Avodah Offit, M.D., she endorsed it with an exultant "Amen!"

Rabi's second pronouncement was equally memorable but perhaps a mite more historic. We had been discussing his acquaintance with various presidents of the United States before, during, and after the years he had served as a member and chairman of the general advisory board of the U.S. Atomic Energy Committee. I asked Rabi which president impressed him as being the most diligent and eager to learn about the creation and potentials of the new source of energy. With a thrust traditional to our shared heritage of Jewish rhetoric, as well as the Socratic method, Rabi answered my question with a question. "Consider presidents from Franklin Roosevelt through Richard Nixon. Who would you guess?"

I didn't hesitate. "John F. Kennedy. He impressed me as a quick study and the president most responsive to the academic."

Rabi smiled with the faintly mocking expression of a person accustomed to having the right answer that eluded others. "Roosevelt and Truman, Kennedy, Johnson, and Nixon got the point, understood the risks and priorities, but had little patience with the specifics of the science. I spent close to two hours with Eisenhower. He wanted to understand the scientific nuances as well as the political risks. I admit he surprised me, but I was impressed. We met several times and he was always a grateful and admirable student." Rabi paused and then said, "I like Ike."

Frank Upjohn quietly presided at St. Martin's Press (1962–1969) between a predecessor who had a triumph with *Anatomy of a Murder* and a formidable successor who had the wisdom to bring James Herriot's *All Things Great and Small* to hundreds of thousands of American readers. Mr. Upjohn inherited me along with a backlist of a half dozen of my books for young readers, but he treated me as a yearling fresh out of the paddock who with proper prepping could someday make a run for the roses. Even though it meant overpaying a substitute to cover the class I was teaching that evening at the New School, I responded to his invitation to a company reception.

The party was in honor of Harold Macmillan, who, I learned, was the chairman of the board of Macmillan Publishing, then the parent company of St. Martin's Press. Meeting Harold Macmillan meant nothing more to me than shaking the hand that shook the hand that lit Winston Churchill's cigars. I remembered, too, something about the tough run he had when his minister of war, John Profumo, was linked to a call girl with ties to a Soviet agent.

The reception was held in a room I recall as a loft where the staff and guests all but disappeared in the vast open space. Mr. Upjohn seemed satisfied with the turnout and determined to introduce all his constituents to his distinguished British visitor and boss. Harold Macmillan appeared a trim version of Errol Flynn with just as neat a mustache and a similar talent for transforming "How do you do?" into a condescending dismissal.

Standing in line to fulfill the assignment to swoon over Harold Macmillan, I was reminded of my brief encounter with the movie star whom I thought he resembled. My meeting with the personification of Robin Hood had been at the home of a famed pill dispenser, whose beautiful daughter was dating my school pal Bob Silberstein.

Flynn was neither tall nor lean as his movie image suggested. In person he appeared as a medium-sized broad-shouldered gent whose posture and high head carriage created the impression of stature. He was nursing a full glass of uninterrupted scotch. We connected when I mentioned that G. P. Putnam's Sons, who had published my anthology of stories from *Baseball Magazine,* was also the publisher of his memoir.

He told me his book had required no editing and expressed scorn for the rash of movie star books ghostwritten or produced by collaboration. "It's scandal and sex the publishers are after," he said. And then with a wry smile, "That was no problem for me—I've always been quite candid about sex—I would fuck a duck—and have."

His lady of the moment, a restless teenager, was standing unpossessively a half step to his side. When she caught the last phase of Flynn's anthem, she fled and didn't appear again until the party was over. My lesson for the evening was an appreciation of the etymology of the expression "in like Flynn."

Harold Macmillan, unlike the British movie star, was distracted by neither booze nor fair ladies. Even the assembly of St. Martin's charmers failed to enchant him. He was obviously putting his time in and making no effort to get a little conversation going. Once again I was cast to provide additional dialogue. Soon after H.M.'s peremptory "How do you do?" Mr. Upjohn signaled—a slight nod and come-hither hand—for me to join him. Again, my credential was a reference to *The Adventures of Homer Fink,* the story of a young classicist who dared to quote passages of classic Latin and Greek.

After a tentative smile and symphonic cluck, the former prime minister invited me to tell him about the book. "Perhaps we could sit." Settled on bridge chairs by the side of what appeared to be a failing party, I did my best with the guest of honor who seemed to accept the evening as a variation of the noblesse oblige required of politicians and corporate executives.

Nothing about Homer evoked more than a nod, punctuation for "keep trying." With a blast of desperation I switched to mention of my series of sports books set at a military school. I told the former prime minister that I'd attended the Valley Forge Military Academy and for several years a graduate of Sandhurst had been our commandant. "He was one tough number, in many ways sadistic."

Macmillan's response to that was: "Indeed. Indeed. Not much time for fun and games when there's a war on."

After a long pause he asked me, "And how are they treating you here at St. Martin's Press?" His eyes had shrunk to narrow slits, but his posture was commandingly erect and the thumping of fingers on his glass of scotch invited the inside story. I considered it an invitation to narrate my relationship with John Pope, the Harvard graduate who was editor in chief of all books published by St. Martin's.

I told the former prime minister about meeting with John over drinks at a neighboring bar before we signed the contract for *Cadet Quarterback,* the first of my series of sports books for young readers. "We became friends right out of the box," I informed him. "Both John and I were married to women we adored and wallowed in our good luck at beating the odds—John with his early connection to sixteen-year-old Anne Turner, and I off to the races with nineteen-year-old Avi Komito. Anne Pope was a Baltimore girl and her father, Thomas Turner, was the dean of the John Hopkins Medical School. It was my good fortune to have discovered the only editor in New York who recognized that 'Droodle' was Bawlamerese for Druid Hill Park, and our local 'sympathy' orchestra performed symphonic music at the Lyric Theater."

The chairman of the board didn't seem particularly impressed by the report of domestic bliss enjoyed by his top U.S. editor or the nearby author of books for young readers. Nor did he express an interest in further study of Bawlamerese. When I mentioned that

John had been responsive to *Cadet Attack,* my current lacrosse story, the publisher was not altogether pleased. "Seems like a rather limited market," I recall him saying softly. "Unless, of course, the game is far more popular here than in Europe." He went on with a tone that connoted suggestion-as-command that we would find a broader market for sports stories if I wrote about international sports—horseback riding, skiing, soccer.

I responded lamely by mentioning that Homer Fink actually played in a soccer game and Paul Galdone had illustrated his tripping adventure. I was also going to mention that Sally Richardson, the magician then in charge of St. Martin's' subsidiary rights, had sold reprint permissions for the sports series, but I had the feeling more of my inside story would just get me in deeper.

The wisdom of Harold Macmillan's marketing advice was verified for me in later years. My elder son, Ken, became a riding champion at summer camp. His wife, Emily Sonnenblick, now skis with their younger daughter, Lily.

Mike's wife, Dara Mitchell, and their daughter, Tristan, ride and jump fences at a horse farm in Bedford. Our grandson, Wyatt, plays passionate soccer when he isn't synchronizing rhythms on the drums. His dad, Mike, has been his club's golf champion more than once, but Mr. Macmillan didn't include this most international of sports on his list. I, of course, had no idea of the prophetic irony of the prime minister's remarks when we spoke forty years ago.

Deserted by the hosts and out of wind, I played the long shot and asked Harold Macmillan a question, the unimaginative and routine query, "And what are you looking forward to during your visit to the United States?" The answer was swift and expressed with the first sign of genuine enthusiasm I'd heard from him all evening. "I'm always delighted to visit my old friend Dwight Eisenhower. Actually that's the treat of my trip."

The historical connection between Eisenhower and Macmillan wasn't a subject about which I had much to say. I vaguely remembered that Macmillan had been minister of defense—or was it foreign secretary? or both?—during several of Ike's years in the White House. I wasn't an Ike fan and had never quite forgiven him for twice defeating—humiliating—our hero Adlai Stevenson. One of my room-mates at Valley Forge, Don McKee, the son and brother of West Point graduates, had been the first person to mention the name Eisenhower to me. Don told me his father, a general, was disturbed that a junior officer—Eisenhower—had been promoted, jumped, over him. "My father says remember that name Eisenhower—he's a real politician." Not much upon which to base a lifetime impression, but out of loyalty to Don and Adlai I could never get past it.

"What is it you find so interesting about Eisenhower?" I asked Harold Macmillan.

"I didn't say interesting," he answered with a tutorial voice. "Interesting is a rather shallow word, evasive of an evaluation. Ike is perhaps the most informed of the American presidents of this century. He certainly is the one who has the best understanding of Europe." After a brief pause and my encouragement that he teach me more, Macmillan said, "Neither Roosevelt nor Truman, even Hoover for all his excellent work after the First World War, had so comprehensive and intimate an experience with the realities of European politics. Ike is quite unique. And a most likeable fellow, too." He didn't say "chap."

18

What Kind of Guy Do You Think I Am, Truman Capote?

Circa 1977

The summer of 1977, soon after Lippincott published my young adult novel *What Kind of Guy Do You Think I Am?,* I dropped in to Robert Keene's bookshop on Hampton Road in Southampton with six copies in a shopping bag.

Since we first visited the Hamptons in 1968 I'd been buying and browsing at Mr. Keene's personal-library shop. The stacks of novels, histories, biographies, and travel books, some dating back three or four decades, allowed scant window space for the sprinkling of current titles that appeared to have as little to do with the proprietor's taste as the selections of the Book-of-the-Month Club.

Mr. Keene, who seemed to have staked his claim to the Meadow Club–Gin Lane identity many years before we arrived, was not a native of Southampton or New York City. His diction suggested southern origins to me, but Malcolm Rogers, the dean of neighborhood scholars, thought it more likely he was "an émigré from New England."

Whatver his geographic roots, Mr. Keene was a man absorbed in himself, with two exceptions: the social integrity of Southampton and Truman Capote.

I passed his Southampton entrance exam because I shared with him the observation that the trade edition of Boswell's *Life of Johnson* was perhaps the only biography in the history of publishing that featured on the cover a full portrait of the author and not the subject of the biography.

I'm convinced it was that totally irrelevant reference that led to Mr. Keene's invitation to bring him a half-dozen copies of *What Kind of Guy*. "We'll see if we can sell a few. I suppose someone or other of my customers has a nasty adolescent to pacify." So there I was, fulfilling the ancient tradition of my people as a "bindle bum," someone who carried belongings in a bundle.

Sitting on small chairs to the rear of the shop—a container of orange juice and a half-empty bottle of vodka between them—sat Mr. Keene, dressed in shirt and tie, a pale blue linen jacket, and gray slacks, and across from him the world-renowned caterer for *Breakfast at Tiffany's*. Truman Capote appeared just as he did in so many photographs, immediately familiar in a panama hat, silky open-necked shirt, white ducks, and scuffed buck shoes. Both held goblets in their hands.

My guess was that Mr. Keene recognized me but had only the vaguest notion of who I was or what I might be doing bringing books to his shop. Truman Capote appeared much smaller, almost dwarflike, and so much less imposing than Mr. Keene. I introduced myself to him.

"Sidney Offit," I said slowly and distinctly so Mr. Keene would begin with a clue. Then I told Truman Capote that Mr. Keene had been gracious, perhaps foolhardy, inviting me to bring him copies of a book I'd just written for sale in his shop.

"Won-der-ful," said Truman Capote somehow managing to chant that one word as benediction. Mr. Keene immediately confirmed the invitation and offered me a drink. "This young man writes children's books, Truman," he said. Then, "What is the title of your book again, Mr. Moffitt?"

I put down the shopping bag and accepted one of the stained goblets. Although it was mid-afternoon, it seemed to me I would need the fortification of a stiff drink to repeat the title. Truman Capote spared me. Playful as a child responding to an unexpected gift he asked to see a copy and pulled one from the bag. His face flushed, eyes narrowed and then opened wide with glee. *What Kind of Guy Do You Think I Am?* he repeated with a distinctive lisp and wave of the hand that was dismissal and invitation both at the same time.

Mr. Keene was less interested in the book than performing as host. Tipping the bottle of vodka to the rim of my goblet he instructed, "Say when?" I settled for just enough to satisfy the prescription and passed on the orange juice.

"So what kind of guy *are* you?" Truman Capote wanted to know. Before I could make a pass at an answer, he was examining the book and read aloud from the first chapter: "'I met Hillary Moscowitz at the beach on Long Island the summer after my father died.'" He seemed to find that opening sentence a matinee in itself. "Hillary Moscowitz. What a wonderful name. Who is your source for Hillary? I'll bet I know. I have hun-dreds of possibilities."

Mr. Keene responded to Truman Capote's random humor as endorsement. "We'll put several copies right there in the window," he said.

Truman Capote suddenly exploded. "JILL KREMENTZ! JILL KREMENTZ!" he repeated. "Well, you certainly have the au courant author's jacket photographer. Don't tell me Jill Krementz is Hillary Moscowitz?"

I explained that Jill was a friend. "She's Kurt Vonnegut's wife and Kurt and I are tennis buddies."

"Tennis buddies? Kurt Vonnegut? Robert, this is all too much. I absolutely must have another drink." Mr. Keene offered the bottle and Truman Capote treated himself.

I was woozy from Capote's verbal pyrotechnics and the sip of booze. Thanking Mr. Keene for the drink and the generous offer to sell my books, I put down the empty goblet and thrust a hand toward Truman Capote. "It's been an honor meeting you, sir," I said. "And when I run into Hillary Moscowitz I'll send her your regards."

Truman Capote passed right over my effort for a chuckle-exit. "You are not going anywhere until you sign each and every copy." He sipped, paused, and then said with vaguely sadistic pleasure, "That way Robert is obligated. They can't be returned."

I tried once more. "I'm sure if you signed them, Mr. Capote, they would have considerably more value."

"Absolutely not," he said in a voice that was declarative but not unfriendly. "What kind of guy do you think I am? If I had the answer to that it would be the story of my life."

Several years later I met Truman Capote again. He was sitting by the pool at Kurt and Jill's house in Sagaponack, a bottle of vodka and container of orange juice by his side. He was still wearing his signature panama, but he seemed to have shrunk and could hardly focus on anyone or any subject other than his own riffs and monologues. Kurt had told me that one of his neighbors had commented that he thought the voice he heard serenading from across the fence on a summer afternoon was that of an aged but beloved aunt for whom the family had infinite patience.

I was charmed and entertained by Capote's rambling discourse on the writers who lived in the neighborhood. It may have been the moment or Kurt's hospitality, but Truman Capote had only good things to say about Willie Morris and James Jones, George Plimpton and Peter Matthiessen.

When I mentioned that I'd met Willie Morris at a small dinner party at Joan Bingham's, and Willie had invited me to play in the annual East Hampton Author-Artist softball game, Truman Capote said that was "Typical Willie, all southern grace." He seemed less interested in my encounter with James Jones but only because I had difficulty making a long story short. He interrupted my tale of lunching with Jones after his long interview with Marty Gross for Gross's new project, *Book Digest*. "Gross did most of the talking," I said. "He set up the answers with the questions. He'd say, 'You must have felt guilt along with remorse when experiencing other members of your squad, your platoon killed in action.'"

Capote cut me off as if I were making the observation. "Oh, guilt again! Nonsense, guilt. Jimmie Jones wrote because he was a writer."

About George Plimpton, another of Kurt and Jill's neighbors, he was rhapsodic, reciting Plimpton's engagements with *The Paris Review,* sport, music, literature. "Where does George get all that energy?"

I was going to mention that Robert Keene's bookshop had closed after Book Hampton opened on Main Street and Mr. Keene was now writing a weekly column for the *Southampton Press,* but I was sure Truman Capote didn't remember our previous meeting. Besides, it was much more entertaining for me to provide an audience for his free associations. At the end of the visit I was surprised when Truman Capote's unceremonious farewell to me was, "Did you ever discover what kind of guy you am?" I considered, but didn't say, "Nothing cold about your blood."

19

Tuesdays at the Coffee House and Other Adventures with *The New Yorker*

1975–2007

I submitted only one story to *The New Yorker.* That was in 1947. Russ Baker had introduced me to the magazine when he suggested I write a "talk piece" for the Johns Hopkins *News-Letter.* If Russ was impressed, that was recommendation enough for me. So, soon after he rewrote my two-paragraph observations on farm subsidies and Vladimir Horowitz's concert at the Lyric Theater for our campus rag, I sent a short story for which I'd received an A- in a writing course—a takeoff on Chekhov's *The Lament.* It was returned with what I later learned was an encouraging note from Gus Lobrano, the fiction editor. "Not quite right for us, but when you write a less derivative story, we would be pleased to consider it."

The mystique of *The New Yorker* as a literary honor society, private cult, and sacred font of wit, style, and diverse genius wasn't known to me at the time. I considered the rejection embarrassing and final. I read the note in the bathroom of the campus publication's office and, as my father would process his daily betting slips, I tore the note into small pieces and flushed it down the john.

Years later, when I was carousing at Forsters on East 84th Street with members of the Lexington Democratic Club, I met Dorothy Lobrano, a congenial, straight-talking lady who had responded to a piece I wrote for the LDC bulletin about visiting the recently opened zoo for children in Central Park with Ken and Mike. "You should consider submitting talk pieces to *The New Yorker,*" Dorothy told me. Lobrano? Could she be? She was the daughter of Gus Lobrano. That was the beginning of what may well be the most extensive relationship to the *New Yorker's* staff and contributors of any writer who never progressed beyond subscribing to the weekly.

My next encounter with a *New Yorker* writer was Lillian Ross, a neighbor of Martin and Anita Gross. They lived in the same building east of Madison in the eighties. One evening at the time, Avi was plowing away at her pre-med requirements, the Grosses invited me to dinner with Ms. Ross. Just the four of us. I had read her interview with Hemingway and considered it an extraordinarily animated prose portrait.

It was easy to understand why a skeptic like Hemingway would feel comfortable performing for Lillian Ross. She totally focused on the other person, progressing easily from routine questions to establish identity to seductively phrased inquiries about what you were feeling, thinking, about even the complexities of your life.

In the company of Marty Gross, it was no challenge to keep the conversation sparkling. But Ms. Ross, who appeared a self-contained high school teacher, nudged the ideas on track like the master of a Ph.D. orals board. We were dining soon after the publication of the first issue of *Intellectual Digest* and although she offered no specific words of praise or endorsement, Lillian Ross managed with thoughtful questions and affirmative responses to give the impression of a supportive friend.

The only reservation she expressed during that long evening of conversation was a comment about Ted Solotaroff's memoir reflecting on his relationship to the fiction of his old friend Philip Roth. With his customary blast of didactic endorsement, Gross had proclaimed

Solotaroff absolutely right when he wrote that although Roth was no less critical of his background than he (Solotaroff) was, "He had not tried to abandon it, and hence had not allowed it to become a deadness inside him."

In a quiet voice as resolute as Gross's, Lillian Ross said she was not an admirer of writers who fed off the reputations of more celebrated colleagues. Her remark seemed a variation of my dad's dismissal of boasts about encounter with celebrity. "That and a nickel will get you a free bus ride." (His acquaintance with the kings of Thoroughbred racing—Whitneys, Vanderbilts—had to be pried from him. It was only late in his life, when I was poking and probing for a memoir I was writing, that Dad reluctantly told me about his experiences with Al Capone, Bugsy Siegel, and Arnold Rothstein, as well as playing golf with Bobby Jones and poker with Buzz King.)

Even though I read passages from the Hemingway interview to writing classes, it never occurred to me until thirty years later, when Lillian Ross wrote about her relationship with William Shawn, *Here But Not Here,* that she, like most of us, had needs other than the exploitive to write about such relationships.

During my visits to the Gross apartment I frequently met William Shawn either in the company of Lillian Ross or waiting in the lobby for her. He always greeted me with a tip of the hat. A small man, neatly coiffed, he reminded me of one of my mother's uncles who seemed to express a humility cultivated by centuries of persecution. "Everything about you is more important than anything about me," his manner connoted. Lillian Ross and he seemed to fit together, absorbed in each other's company with or without conversation.

At a party hosted by the Shawns celebrating the publication of one of Ved Mehta's books, I met Mr. Shawn's wife, a spirited, friendly lady, much more outgoing than her husband. She seemed to embrace Ved, with good reason. It was one thing to say we must evaluate Ved Mehta's library of Proustian memoirs, without consideration of his blindness, and another to close our eyes and consider the discipline and talent required to produce such a body of work. I enjoyed Ved's humor, his teasing, and accepted his sometimes misreading of a mood that resulted in a more wounding jest than he intended. Ms. Shawn seemed to bask in his company and achievements with maternal delight. I thought it generous and admirable.

Roger Angell and I met at meetings of the Authors Guild Council. I became a fan at first sight. Roger spoke to issues with an intense but restless candor that hit even the most elusive nail on the head. I was particularly impressed when, at a session where we were discussing the offer of a grant to the Guild to administer writing awards that would include publication as well as money for the winners, Roger said, "No. The Guild is not in the business of rating writers." Although it was true we could use the money, and we certainly encouraged publication and extra bucks for any writer, the Guild should decline any program that would require rejecting the work of our members. Roger reminded us, "In our Guild we are all equal."

His comments were so on the mark and the impression so indelible that long after the source of this wisdom was forgotten, the idea was quoted and the Guild stayed out of the award business.

I wasn't aware when we met that Roger was *The New Yorker*'s fiction editor. I'd read his *A Day in the Life of Roger Angell,* a virtuoso satiric play with prose styles. I knew, too, that he was the Thucydides, or was he the Thomas Babington Macaulay, of baseball historians? My first impression of Roger as a humorist was so indelible that I thought of him as fun long after I realized that, unlike the cartoonists Jim Stevenson, Frank Modell, and Charlie Addams, Roger Angell was not a friend with whom I could horse around.

After we appeared on a Guild panel discussing the shrinking magazine market, Roger and his wife Carol invited Avi and me to dinner and later to their annual Christmas parties on the last Friday before the holiday. Carol is beautiful, vibrant, lovable—every quality that a connoisseur of character, personality, and talent like Roger would approve. Avi was particularly impressed with Roger's engaging intimacy. He had talked to her about his relationships with his mother and father, "Not with complaint, but rather a hard-won understanding and dignity."

When Russ Baker became aware of my friendship with Roger, he wondered how that had happened. "Roger Angell is not collectible." I mentioned Russ's comment to Avi and also told her that other friends had found it curious that Roger "accepted" me as a friend. Avi remarked that *New Yorker* editors were probably cautious because soon after meeting most writers a submission was waiting on their desk. "Roger Angell is a good judge of people," Avi said. "You would never do that."

At one of the Angells' Christmas parties I exchanged comments about Richard Brown's New School film course with Woody Allen. No hello, how do you do, I admire your work, Mr. Allen (which I certainly did). I just plunged right in and mentioned the New School sell-out crowd. Woody Allen responded with that grim, pained expression that suggests he cares much too much or one false word from you and he'll collapse with a nervous breakdown. He told me he was disappointed by his experience at the New School. He thought he'd be speaking with students studying film, but the lecture hall was jammed with a "Broadway audience."

It was obvious Woody Allen wasn't comfortable at parties but was dropping in out of respect to Roger, who I suppose was the editor who introduced his pieces to *The New Yorker.* Woody Allen seemed, too, a little awed to be in Roger Angell's company. "You know he is the son of Katherine White, the stepson of E. B. White." Almost instantly after telling me that, Woody Allen seemed to have regretted saying it. He blushed with that remarkable Woody Allen self-effacing expression that is also a dismissal.

I passed him many times on the avenues after meeting him that evening, but never approached him again.

Most often at the Angells' parties I found myself wrapped in conversation with Charlie Addams, Frank Modell, or Jim Stevenson. Although different in manner, background, and style, they were just as entertaining and humorous one-on-one as the brilliance of their cartoons suggested.

We routinely met on Tuesdays for lunch at the Coffee House, a walk-up bar and dining room on East 45th Street that had been founded by Frank Crowninshield and cronies from the Knickerbocker Club. (I had been proposed for membership by Matt Clark, a *Newsweek* editor and one of the most honored medical writers in the land.) The Coffee House had one rule: no rules! There, at a long table surrounded by drawings, cartoons, and paintings contributed by members, gathered a number of *New Yorker* and *New York Times* staff for whom the club served as a company lunchroom.

Along with the cartoonists and Roger Angell, Gardner Botsford, the *New Yorker* editor whose name was sometimes mentioned as a logical successor to Mr. Shawn, was also a regular. A balding, straight-backed gent with a generous smile, Gardner had experienced less indulgent days as a combat infantry officer in World War II. Although respected as an uncompromising editor, capable of cleaning up the lines as well as getting to the heart of the piece, Gardner was a jubilantly responsive audience for one-liners, stories, and gags, and his presence always livened even this remarkable assembly.

I felt a particular bond to Gardner after I met his wife, Janet Malcolm, one of the *New Yorker*'s marquee essayists. As Jackie Onassis had reminded me of Avi in grace, Janet Malcolm gave me the feeling I was in the company of my wife's "sister." They looked vaguely alike—understated style, exotic features, as counterpoint to their all-American girl inviting smiles.

As with Avi, Janet tended to listen more than talk, but once on a subject where she had a strong opinion, she was off and running, sharing perceptions that were original and unpredictable. Janet's studies of the hassle related to the Freud archives, the Ted Hughes–Sylvia Plath marriage, and the physician accused of murdering his wife and children, as well as her personal reflections on Anton Chekhov, and most recently *Two Lives: Gertrude and Alice,* an original perspective on the lives and relationship of Alice B. Toklas and Gertrude Stein, were all presented with graceful prose, while at the same time sustaining narrative and rhetoric.

Although not by nature a committee person, in the late 1970s she was persuaded to join the Membership Committee of PEN, the writers' organization. Other members of the committee welcomed her with the expectation that she'd up the ante for quality writing. They were wrong. Janet argued that PEN was an organization of writers devoted to freedom of expression throughout the world and to supporting writers in prison. We were not a literary academy and anyone with reasonable credentials as a writer should be granted admission.

Janet wasn't the first nor the last member of the committee to express misgivings about PEN's admissions standards. Elizabeth Hardwick who, unlike Janet, didn't seem uncomfortable evaluating the quality of the candidate's book, let us know she would appreciate it if during her term as chair the committee did not consider children's "picture book *authors*," a word she managed to express as a question, editorial, and indictment all at the same time.

Bill Cole always arrived at meetings with a briefcase full of reviews and clips. Although frequently the only member of the committee who did homework, Bill accepted it with good cheer when one of his candidates was rejected. He seemed to regard our process as an incomprehensible game.

Unlike Bill Cole, who served on the Membership Committee longer than any other member in the history of PEN, or Lizzie Hardwick who departed with a teasing smile as soon as her brief term ended, Janet Malcolm called it quits as soon as it was obvious the membership-academy was continuing to grind judgmentally away.

Charles Addams had a passion for old cars, old armor, and a good cigar. I checked out the armor once briefly at his West Fifties apartment. The star of his collection was a small figure of a knight decked in armor, head to toe. He appeared not much taller than a ten-year-old. On the walls of Charlie's walk-up were crossbows. Tabletops and shelf space were decorated with creepy things he had received as gifts. The eye-catcher was a weird, kooky stuffed animal that looked alive. I recall Charlie telling me he'd received it from a Mrs. Heinz.

After Tuesday lunches, walking up Fifth Avenue, Charlie and I often stopped by the Dunhill museum-supermarket for stogies, located on a corner across the street from that other palace of devotion,

St. Patrick's Cathedral. Neither Charlie nor I had a humidor at Dunhill's, but Charlie knew several friends who did. I was always delighted when he inquired of the clerk, "How's Mr. Fontainebleau's crypt doing?"

We were merrily puffing away on our Dunhill panatelas, making a run uptown toward the fountain in front of the Plaza where we sometimes sat and watched the carriages saddle up, the afternoon we heard about Armageddon. Our informant, a gentleman who resembled Popeye the sailor after a long session with Olive Oyl, was handing out circulars on Fifth Avenue. Over his shoulders hung a large poster-board citing chapter and verse: "Rev. 16:14–16 . . . And he gathered them together into a place called in the Hebrew tongue Armageddon . . ."

Striding boldly in front of us, Popeye announced, "The end is coming. Coming. Coming. Coming."

"And when would that be?" Charlie asked, still puffing gently on his cigar.

"This week. Soon. Soon," came the urgent reply.

"Thank you," said Charlie, accepting the circular. I was expecting the street messiah to suggest salvation through spinach, when Charlie with a nod and twinkle concluded the séance. "This looks serious. We'd better tell Frank and Jim."

Charlie and I shared not only mutual friends and the same clubs, but the post office in Water Mill, Long Island. We met there frequently during the years that Charlie had his house off Cobb Road and Avi and I were renting on Flying Point. If the sun was in his grandstand seat in heaven, we'd make the turn on Old Mill Lane and walk awhile, but Charlie's summer passion was converting the local roads and paths into passageways for excursions in one of his antique cars.

Although he seemed by manner and style neither wildly imaginative nor daring, Charlie's adventures with old cars were right in there with his invention of the Addams Family as a clue to the delights of his company. He invited me one afternoon for a romp in what I recall as a two-seater gray Bugatti. He tapped the hood like a horse breeder introducing his prize Thoroughbred and told me it was a 1920s model, and he chased down parts from Italy to keep her moving. We both wore helmets and Charlie had a scarf that looked like it came right off Charles Lindbergh.

As we flashed up Flying Point, past the Burnett's Quality Farm, the summer house of our neighbors Gould and Fitzgerald, and Arnie Cooper's manse, all overlooking Mecox Bay, I wondered if Charlie was going to race right down to the beach and take off for a flight over the ocean. But he made the east turn on Flying Point and continued down the road to Burnett Cove where, unintimidated by the PRIVATE PROPERTY sign, we continued on our way until flush by Mecox Bay. There Charlie masterfully turned the Bugatti around on a dime and with scarf flying upped the speed ante for the bounce home.

I don't suppose we were moving as fast as the effect suggested. Even at twenty, thirty miles an hour it seems as if you are revving up for a takeoff into space when a car, like Charlie's Bugatti, has no windshield.

Unlike Charles Addams, Frank Modell was as at home performing as a stand-up comedian as he was composing the comic visual and prose lines that distinguished his cartoons.

The year after I became a member of the Coffee House, I attended the celebration of its founding. It was before we wised up and invited women to join. The long table, as well as the seats arranged in the barroom to accommodate the overflow crowds, filled with black-ties, gents of various ages engaged in wine and smokes and conversations about the arts, philosophy, and esoteric histories that were the signatures of celebrants at West 45th Street.

The entertainment of the evening was Frank Modell—only Frank Modell! He had agreed to speak after dinner and say "a few words about life, death, and the rituals of club life." My dinner companion was a short, well-trimmed gentleman who even in the uniform of tux and black tie managed to turn out as though tailored on Jermyn Street. His name was Monroe Wheeler, but when I met him I thought he said, "Larue something-or-other," and was probably French. If I had heard his name, I would have had no idea at the time of Monroe Wheeler's legendary status in the world of art.

It seemed clear from the first tipple of wine, which he immediately identified by vineyard and year, that he was much more interested in his own tastes and experiences than anything I might say. So I picked up on the mistaken name "Larue" and his knowledge of French wines and asked him if he had spent much time in France. Mr. Wheeler smiled indulgently, and then, with an occasional nudge, engaged me through the entire dinner with tales of his adventures fulfilling the Rockefellers' assignment that created the Museum of Modern Art.

Warming up for Frank's monologue, I heard a long and memorable critique from my neighbor. "Picasso. Of course I knew Pablo Picasso. There was no greater genius nor any artist more appreciative of his own talent and how to exploit it. . . . Oh, Gertrude Stein. Gertrude Stein. I suppose she must be credited with good taste, but she certainly had abundant funds with which to express it. Does that sound critical? I don't mean it to be. She was always very courteous to me. . . . So you are a fan of James Joyce, are you? I met Joyce in Paris many times. What can one say about James Joyce other than that he is *the* great writer of the twentieth century. But he certainly was not a nice man, anything but considerate of his family. Although I was in his company often I don't remember a single thing Jimmie Joyce ever said. It may well be because we all had so much trouble understanding him—that brogue, you know."

By the time Frank Modell was introduced, I would have given odds that Monroe Wheeler wouldn't make it through the "first act," and if he did sit through it, Frank would do no better than Picasso, Gertrude Stein, and James Joyce.

As soon as he stood to speak, Frank's clip-on bow tie fell to his feet. He picked it up without a blush and said, "Well, the tie's down but the zipper's up, so the show goes on . . ."

From there on Frank Modell was Jackie Mason with additional dialogue by Robert Benchley. He took off with a brisk impression of growing up in Philadelphia, attending art school, serving as a first sergeant in the army during World War II, and at last arriving in New York for a long run at *The New Yorker*. There was little gossip about the magazine of Ross and Shawn other than a brief tale about the difficulty of relating to James Thurber.

"Thurber liked to drink. That was no secret. And even as he was growing blind he didn't want to acknowledge it. He always seemed to be angry about something. I admired his work. I respected him. So, when I heard a thump and saw James Thurber collapsed at the bottom of a stair, I tried to help him up. Soon as Thurber was on his feet he brushed me off along with his jacket and dismissed me with a shrug of 'How dare you!' "

As he progressed to a reflection on his various adventures in New York, Frank told the story of escorting a lovely young art student through the Metropolitan Museum of Art. (Beautiful young ladies flocked to Frank Modell like helpless damsels to Lord Byron's Don Juan.)

"It was her first visit to a major museum, her first encounter with Rubens, Correggio, Rembrandt. She looked. She sighed. She nodded. But not a word. We passed through the corridors of Manet, Monet, Matisse. I talked. I plugged the masters. Couldn't encourage a complimentary word from her about the paintings or any of them."

Frank went on developing the narrative of his tour, building the tension as he teased the audience. "At last we stood in front of Rosa Bonheur's *The Horse Fair.*" He offered a vivid verbal portrait of the horses charging and panting right off the canvas. " 'Now this,' " Frank reported her commenting at the climax of his tour guide through the Met, " 'Now this,' " she said, " 'this I couldn't paint.' "

Monroe Wheeler turned to me with the first expression of absolute delight I'd experienced from him all evening. His eyes crinkled as he rephrased Frank's last line to me, "This she couldn't paint!"

The next time I encountered Monroe Wheeler at lunch at the Coffee House, thanks to my identification with Frank Modell he insisted I join him and his friend Glenway Wescott. At the recommendation of Lucy Burchard, a colleague at *Intellectual Digest,* I had read Wescott's *The Pilgrim Hawk.* The novel, published in the early 1940s, was a neglected classic, according to Lucy. I agreed, but discovered when I recommended it to writing students that *The Pilgrim Hawk* was out of print.

Glenway Wescott seemed surprised that I was aware of him or his novels. He was as shy and self-effacing as he was handsome and regal. He insisted I tell him about what I had written. There was no chance of my recounting the *bubbe meises* of a borscht belt summer to a novelist who was right in there with F. Scott Fitzgerald as a contender for champion of poetry-prose in the Jazz Age. So Glenway Wescott and I talked about PEN. He regretted he hadn't more time to devote to its Translation and Freedom to Write committees, and the Coffee House: "Monroe has always felt right at home here, but then again Monroe is at home anywhere in the world where there is an atmosphere of good taste and lively company."

I never saw Monroe Wheeler again, and only caught a glimpse of Glenway Wescott at a PEN evening. Whether an encounter will become a friendship is not easy to predict.

When I met James Stevenson I had been cutting up at the Coffee House for a while, savoring the *New Yorker* wits as well as the company of Ed Wilson, the drama critic, scholar, and playwright; Paul Greenberg, the TV news producer who was as good a Catskill mimic as I ever met south of Route 17; and Bill Ray, a photographer who could make black-and-whites resonate with living "color." Later, when women were admitted as members, Jackie Buechner, Mary D. Kierstead, and Phyllis Malamud Clark were among the belles of the ball.

Jackie was an artist and soon after she became a member one of her portraits beamed down enigmatically from the southwest wall. Mary D. Kierstead, a longtime secretary to Mr. Shawn and frequent contributor to the *New Yorker*'s "On the Avenue" columns, was the person everyone—man or woman—most wanted to sit next to. She intuitively came by that old *New Yorker* grace for deflecting gossip with wit and shared enthusiasm. Mary D.'s husband, Will Kierstead, became one of my best friends and we shared, among other values, adoration of our wives.

Phyllis, a former editor of *Newsweek* and wife of Matt Clark, my sponsor for membership in the Coffee House, soon after meeting Avi discovered my wife shared with her a passion for ballroom dance. Eventually it was Phyllis who made a major contribution to our lives. She introduced Avi to dance sessions, including the Argentine tango, at the Church of Saint Jean Baptiste, as well as to the high-stepping Pierrepont Dancers at a social club on Park Avenue.

Around this time I'd heard about James Stevenson as one of the two people on the *New Yorker* staff who could possibly produce an entire issue solo. (The other talent-for-all-seasons was John Updike.) A cover artist, cartoonist, composer of talk pieces and profiles, short stories, reviews, and humorous essays, in his spare time Jim wrote a stream of plays, musicals, and books for young readers, and eventually he originated *Lost and Found New York* for the *New York Times*'s op-ed page.

I wasn't expecting James Stevenson, who looked like a young and energetic all-around version of the genius of Henry VIII, to pick up on my confession that I was no academic student and only at home in the John Dewey school of "learn by doing." It was a lunch-hour discussion of skiing that led to that remark. Jim responded immediately. Even though he was a Yale graduate, with such a long string of successes as artist and writer, he told me he hadn't paid much attention in classes either, and was only comfortable learning on his own.

To celebrate our club-within-a-club, I performed my impression of receiving instruction on how to bend and twist the legs counterintuitively on a downhill ski slope. My mimicking of myself must have amused Jim. After that we frequently sat side by side talking about comedians—we agreed there were few stand-ups who didn't make us laugh—movies, books, and Frank Modell's social life.

Jim and I didn't discuss sex or gossip much about women. I knew he was a widower with lots of children and a great favorite with the ladies. But when I was invited to a small dinner party to celebrate his birthday about twenty years ago, I brought as a present a signed copy of Avi's *Night Thoughts: Reflections of a Sex Therapist,* recently published and already the recipient of great reviews ("Avodah Offit is the Montaigne of human sexuality . . ."—*The New Republic*).

I didn't expect more than a thank-you from Jim, but what we received was a masterpiece. Jim composed a comic takeoff on Henri Rousseau's *The Snake Charmer* that had provided the cover art for Avi's collection of essays.

Before long the walls of our New York apartment provided exhibition space for our collection of framed Stevenson originals. Among the wonders: Jim's cartoon of an unheroic gentleman approaching a tennis racket embedded in a rock—obviously the Excalibur of a hacker's dreams. I'm considering contributing the drawing to the Tennis Hall of Fame after my last double fault.

I'd first met Jim's wife, Josie Merck, at the Coffee House when we both sat at meetings of the committee that is not a committee, responsibly irresponsible for reviewing nominations that are just suggestions for membership and balancing the unbalanceable books. Josie was capable of reflecting on even the most discouraging of numbers with a pragmatist's wisdom and a romantic's enthusiasm. I hadn't realized until after she and Jim were hitched that Josie was an artist, too. When I attended her show at a gallery on Wooster Street after a New School class, I confessed all with a "remark" for the visitors' book: "I'm certifiably color-blind, but I still think your colors are great." Soon afterward, Josie ran me through a review of my color perceptions and was fascinated by what I identified as brown for green, yellow for orange, and blue for violet. "Did you ever try painting?" she said like an enchanting muse. "You should. I bet you'd be right in there with the avant of the avant."

Friendship, unlike encounter, often contributes relief, support, even a laugh during moments of despair. When Avi was recovering from a spinal operation (no spinal operation is less than serious), a number of friends came through with flying colors. Gay and Nan Talese graciously insisted I join them for dinner from time to time and always managed with empathetic sympathy to lift my spirits and eventually engage me in diverting and lively conversation. After Avi returned home Roger and Ginny Rosenblatt dropped by with a three-course dinner featuring Long Island duck seasoned with their exclusive house blend of wit, warmth, and cheer. And Jim Stevenson's cartoon takeoff on a conversation between Avi and me about liquid intake and export provided the inspiration of a humor rare on most walls but just about never seen in a convalescent's bedroom.

Through my association with the George Polk Awards and fortuitous encounters, I met William Shawn's successors as editor of *The New Yorker,* Robert Gottlieb, Tina Brown, and David Remnick.

I knew about Robert Gottlieb as the wise and responsive editor to whom Candida Donadio submitted Joe Heller's *Catch-22,* when it was identified by its original title *Catch-18.* I'd heard that story from both Joe and Candida. Later, I respected Robert Gottlieb for recognizing the genius of Robert Caro and working so diligently on his encyclopedic biographies.

Although I doubt he would recognize me, Robert Gottlieb is one of the few editors I've seen at work. There he was, poring over a Jill Krementz manuscript in the Vonneguts' kitchen when Kurt and I returned from a long lunch. "I'm not so sure about that. . . . Let's consider trying it this way, Jill." It couldn't have been an easy assignment, but I saw enough to appreciate Robert Gottlieb's talents for working with writers.

When Tina Brown took over *The New Yorker,* she had a mandate to pep it up, do things her way. I was among the skeptics. Although I didn't pry for the stories, I soon became aware that some of my friends' admirable talents were no longer welcome at their creative "home."

Henry S. F. Cooper Jr., as noble and precise a scribe as ever covered the space beat, moved out of his office on West 43rd Street and set up shop next to a room rented by Ved Mehta. Ed Fisher, who for close to three decades contributed cartoons (takeoffs on great events of ancient history with deft lines and variations of contemporary clichés), painfully admitted to me he just didn't feel welcome there anymore. "I haven't a clue as to what I might draw to please them."

Bruce and Naomi Bliven had been considered extensions of the Shawn family for most of their distinguished professional careers. Bruce, a reporter noted for his "finishing touch," and Naomi, a scholar-critic of world literature who between puffs of her "nurturing" cigarettes could make a paragraph sing, sing, sing, weren't formally dismissed but Bruce told me, "We were moved out."

I've never been consistent at bearing grudges or holding on to my seat on the heckler's bench, so before long I reluctantly appreciated that for all her callousness to major talents who had contributed so much to the reputation of the Ross-Shawn classic, Tina Brown did remain true to Roger Angell and Philip Hamburger. When I asked Roger how he felt about the new editor, he whispered, "She pays me very well." I wasn't sure if he was endorsing his most recent boss or mocking the cliché. Phil, who was already flirting with his eighth decade, shrugged and said, "I kinda like her. Why not? She likes me."

I never did find out what Tina Brown's attitude was toward Kennedy Fraser. I'd met Kennedy one evening at the Cedar Tavern where Frank Modell and I were yakking it up after one of my New School classes. I was charmed by the feisty British lady, an animated Lady Hamilton as portrayed by George Romney. Kennedy's memory of the evening as she reported to us later was: "I never got a word in edgewise."

During her run as the magazine's commentator on style and fashion, Kennedy brought a fresh and remarkable depth to her coverage. It may have been nourished by her own misgivings about shopping. "I've never quite understood why so many people 'go shopping,' just 'go shopping,'" she said to me on a rare afternoon when we were wandering up Fifth Avenue.

I don't think Kennedy was given the so-long, good-bye, so-nice-to-have-known-you farewell of my other friends among *New Yorker* writers and cartoonists, but Kennedy soon moved on to writing pieces for other Condé Nast publications.

I was disposed to withhold judgment about Tina Brown's run also because she debuted with an Ed Sorel cover. Avi and I both considered Ed Sorel and his wife, Nancy, to be among our favorite people. I met Ed in the sixties when he was a contributor to Victor Navasky's magazine *Monocle,* an inspired showcase for the Jonathan Swifts of American humor. "Victor had no money and needed an art director. I had no money and needed a place to work," was Ed's explanation for why he moved in.

My Tina grudge was also tempered when she introduced a drawing by the one and only Jules Feiffer, who understood more about the psyches of West Side neurotics than an army of Freudian-Jungian therapists. Another good friend, Arnie Roth, who wowed readers of *Punch* for several decades, was enlisted by Tina. Arnie with trumpet or pen can jazz up any joint or page.

Tina Brown's *New Yorker* ultimately hooked me when she ran a series of profiles by Michael Korda, the only writer I've known who wrote books that led the *New York Times* Best Seller List for fiction and nonfiction.

The pieces Korda wrote for *The New Yorker* were vivid sketches that characterized as they entertained: Jackie Susann ordering her husband to take the coat off his back and give it to Michael so he'd be appropriately dressed for their dinner at the Russian Tea Room; Richard Nixon referring to himself in the third person as he discussed the reasoning behind foreign policy decisions: "The president of the United States and most powerful man in the free world . . ."

Michael, to whom I was introduced by Avi when he edited and published her novel *Virtual Love,* soon became one of our friends. Along with sharing the good news of his wife Margaret's frequent victories at horse competitions, he never would, I realized, have contributed to the magazine were it not for Tina Brown's personal and persistent invitation.

I met Tina Brown and her husband, Sir Harry Evans, at a celebration for Michael's birthday at his friend Warner LeRoy's Tavern on the Green. Several months later I met her again when she hosted a PEN benefit and the next day showed up at the Roosevelt Hotel for the presentation of the George Polk Awards, highlighted by our honoring Philip Hamburger for his career achievement. Phil had charmed readers for a generation with his engaging "Mayor Watching" columns. In addition to assignments as a foreign correspondent for the magazine, Phil covered all the presidential inaugurations from Herbert Hoover through Bill Clinton.

He and his wife, Anna, were good friends with whom we shared dinners and warm company often, along with the *Times*'s perennial M.V.P. Herb Mitgang and his wise and caring wife, Shirley. So it was no surprise when Phil urged me to stand by his side when the LIU photographer arranged for a shot alongside his editor. Tina Brown was the "talk" of New York at the time and not unaccustomed to being center stage whether she wanted to be or not.

Several weeks later, when I received copies of the picture, I sent one to Tina along with a salute, a signed copy of my *Memoir of the*

Bookie's Son, quoting on the flyleaf Phil's flattering remarks about her at the luncheon: "To Tina Brown, my pal Phil Hamburger's favorite 'incumbent tornado' with warm regards . . ."

A year later my friend Len Scheer presented my Tina Brown copy to me as a gift. "A signed copy of one of your first editions." He bought it for three times the retail price from a used-book dealer. "Excellent condition."

When David Remnick's *Lenin's Tomb* was published in 1993, a blurb by Robert A. Caro appeared on the back jacket: "He has achieved a rare feat: to make the reader feel he has been present himself at a great turning point of history. It is a stunning book, moving and vivid from first page to last." With Bob's encouragement, I was among the early readers and so impressed I managed to rally support for a Polk Award. The letter accepting the award for an achievement for which he had every right to expect accolades was reminiscent of the note I'd received from William Shawn in 1989 when *he* had won a Polk Career Award.

David Remnick wrote, "It's an incredible honor, not only to win the Polk but also to have attracted your notice as a reader." The letter I received from William Shawn concluded, with similar modesty and grace, "I will be greatly honored of course to receive the award, but your cordial letter is honor enough for me."

I met Donald and Susie Newhouse four decades ago when our sons attended Temple Emanu-El Nursery School. It wasn't as hot a ticket then as it is today, and nowhere near the current tariff for tuition (then three hundred dollars).

A mutual friend, Beverly Jablon, invited Avi and me to dinner at her walk-up apartment near 72nd Street overlooking Madison Avenue. Avi was already into her pre-med drill, hitting the books every evening, and couldn't join us. Donald and Susie were just plain neighborhood folks, as far as I knew. I liked them right away.

They were aware that I wrote books for young readers and gave me the feeling it was the rarest gift in the universe. Beverly, a writer, too, was banging away at the old novel *Dance Time* that was later published to unanimous critical acclaim.

The evening that we met I ran away with myself, mimicking what people often thought of as writers of children's books—elders caught in the diction of children and obsessed by make-believe. Donald and Susie, along with the Jablons, were an audience that spoiled me and I was grateful that they didn't label me "a frustrated actor" or a guest who "drank one too many."

Later, I was invited to the Newhouses' for a dinner party. Three steps in the door and I realized the young couple I had thought of as making their way in the hard world of newspaper publishing actually were members of the family that owned a chain. It made no difference in our relationship when the Newhouses went on to buy Condé Nast and *The New Yorker.* Through the years, when we've met on the avenue or at various social events, we've always shared news about our sons and rundowns on our grandchildren.

An afternoon some years ago, while walking with our five-year-old redheaded knockout grandchild, Lily, I ran into Donald, who had just recently celebrated the birth of his second grandchild. He wore a watch with a beaming face reproduced from a photograph of the first of the Newhouses' next generation. Lily was so enchanted, I had to see what I could about doing the same to immortalize her.

My most memorable image of Donald and Susie Newhouse was observed when they were unaware, walking up Park Avenue holding hands. Holding hands! The only other long-married couple Avi and I have ever observed off guard in such tender contact is Nick Pileggi and Nora Ephron, both of whom made it gloriously on their own, though Nora may also be identified as a "contributor to *The New Yorker.*"

So long as a man rides his hobbyhorse peaceably and quietly along the King's highway, and neither compels you or me to get up behind him—pray, Sir, what have either you or I to do with it?

—Laurence Sterne,
Tristram Shandy

20

Jackie in a Corner

Circa 1992

Although I am frequently uncertain about dates and visual descriptions, my memory of a conversation is often vivid and sometimes haunting. An encounter may linger in my memory for a time out of proportion to its consequences in my life. I suppose, as for many of us, in this age of addictive celebrity, it is difficult for me to resist recalling conversations with historic figures. Yet it wasn't until I began writing this book that I shared with anyone but Avi my brief though engaging conversation with the woman often considered the most celebrated, imitated, and revered of the twentieth century.

I was introduced to Jacqueline Kennedy Onassis by our mutual friend, the dance commentator and writer Francis Mason. Francis's enthusiasm is contagious, and I respond to his passions for friendship, the arts—and ballet! Though Francis's engagements with dance included books as well as regular commentary on WQXR radio, my only credential was provided by my wife, who had danced as an extra with the Ballet Russe in New York, circa 1945.

When Francis invited me to attend a party celebrating the publication of his book about George Balanchine, I urged Avi to join me. It seemed to me justice—not poetic, but balletic—that she be rewarded for so many years with a hot-for-the-trot but off-the-beat hoofer. Avi had patients scheduled for the hour, so I arrived alone and early.

"Bob Caro has just been here," Francis greeted me. "He had another party but was his usual charming, brilliant self. I'm sorry you missed him."

I thought Francis's comment was a clue that the evening would be cast with lots of mutual friends whose links to Francis were stronger than their connection to ballet. It did occur to me that Bob's editor at Knopf, Robert Gottlieb, was a scholar-critic-fan of ballet, but as I surveyed the room from our perch on a balcony I saw no person I recognized. The room seemed filled with ballerinas curving gracefully around the drinks they held. I quickly told Francis, "I'm not staying long myself."

"Of course you are" was his instant rejoinder and then: "Jackie, dear Jackie, this is my friend Sidney who is responsible for introducing me to that wonderful room at the library where I was able to work on this book with no interruption."

I knew that Jackie Onassis was Francis's editor. He had introduced us once before. The Queen of Camelot had been sitting on the staircase steps of the McKim, Mead and White building where Francis and I so frequently hung out. That first meeting had been brief—an exchange of greetings and a tease about her increasing our club's seating capacity without more chairs.

Jackie seemed a taller version of my very own wife with a gift similar to Avi's for totally focusing on another person without restlessness or need to make a point. But had it not been for Francis's insistence, I would have let the moment pass rather than try to get something going with the reluctant contender for the most pursued and admired woman in the world.

"The Frederick Lewis Allen Room," Francis continued. "Do you know about it, Jackie? Sidney is the perfect person to tell you all about it."

The bridge defined by Jane Austen on the first page of *Pride and Prejudice* scored again: "This was invitation enough."

"It's really not all that complicated," I began. "Right there on the first floor of Forty-second and Fifth is a comfortable room where writers set up shop—typewriters, books, even smokes." As I went on describing the potential for friendships with other writers, Jackie's expression was nothing short of wonder.

"You must tell me more," she said. "And how does a writer go about applying for a seat in that wonderful room?"

As we spoke, I felt myself moving toward a corner. It was as if I were responding to an invisible choreography for avoiding interruption and maintaining intimacy. The result was that I faced the other guests but Jackie would be recognizable only to a genius for identifying people back to front.

She was a Doubleday editor attending a party to celebrate a book by one of her authors, and I was to engage her so that she didn't detract from the attention due Francis. I ran through the litany of writers I'd met through my experience in the Allen Room, and like a savvy editor familiar with author lists other than her own, Jackie suggested with a nod or brief comment that she was aware of books by Jimmie Flexner, Charlie Flood, Betty Friedan, and Bob Caro. It was obvious, too, that she had no desire to gossip about the literary marketplace and was an apostle of quality and enlightenment.

I flipped incoherently into mention of my limited roster of mutual friends. Yes, she did remember Christopher Pope, the son of my editor, John Pope, and his wife, Anne. Christopher had been a friend of her son, John, when they were students at Collegiate. She recalled they had been on a cruise together. I said that John Pope told me Chris enjoyed learning to play backgammon, instructed by Mr. Onassis.

"Oh, yes," Jackie agreed. "John considered that among his fondest memories of Ari."

I skipped back in time to George Gillet, one of the gallants of Roland Park, a tall blond tennis ace who had been my classmate at Johns Hopkins. Jackie's eyes narrowed and she seemed on the verge of a blush. "Whatever did happen to George?"

"Oh, he had a job selling ads for the Johns Hopkins magazine when I last heard of him."

The quietly suggestive rejoinder was: "George could be quite a salesman, but I'm surprised that he'd even bother."

George had a reputation for being irresistible to the ladies, and he mentioned dating Jackie when she was working for a Washington newspaper. Her comment seemed a subtle suggestion of their relationship and an appraisal of George's playboy character.

It was so easy talking to Jackie Onassis, I felt sufficiently comfortable to poke into politics. I asked her what she thought about Bill vanden Heuvel, whom I regarded as the ideal candidate for president of the United States.

"Bill? President?" she repeated with stunned curiosity. "I didn't know he was running."

"He's probably not," I admitted. "But I think you know Bill and I just wondered if you had a similar thought about him."

"Bill is just terrific" was the response and then a smile and shrug. "I've always been very fond of Bill and regard him as a good friend. But I really don't think very much about politics. I have my hands full editing books."

Jackie's back was still to the room, and no one had entered or passed who intruded upon our corner. The relaxed chatter of our conversation encouraged me to tell her about my long marriage, and my admiration for my wife as artist, scholar, friend. Then I confessed, "But Avi's just not compelled by politics. At least not the discussions generated by my experiences with the Lexington Democratic Club."

"Why do you think that is?" she asked.

I said I wasn't sure. "Perhaps because there aren't enough women involved." And then I said, "You've just told me politics isn't your favorite subject either. Do you have a clue?"

Without hesitation, Jackie Kennedy Onassis, heroine of hundreds, thousands of books integrating her with the history of her times, said, "I just find conversations about politics very, very repetitious." (An observation with which Avi absolutely agreed.)

We went on from there to a brief discussion of raising children in

New York and strategies for introducing museums as fun and not homework. I wasn't aware of the heavyset gentleman who seemed to have stepped right out of London's Savile Row until he greeted and smiled paternally to Jackie. The prearranged rendezvous was the signal that our conversation was ended, her responsibility as editor satisfied. Maurice Tempelsman escorted Jackie Kennedy Onassis from our corner.

III

Work and Other Entertainments: 1950s Through the Twenty-first Century

21

Ellery Queen and My Unsolved Crime of the Century

1953

In November 1953, a year after Avi and I were married, we realized that my half-cent-a-word income for pulp-fiction stories didn't pay the rent, utilities, grocery bills, and the price of second-balcony seats for weekend excursions to Broadway. I studied the HELP WANTED columns, and in '53 Robert Mills hired me as an editorial assistant at Mercury Publications, a magazine "empire" that retained the rights to Mencken-Nathan's *American Mercury,* along with publishing *Ellery Queen's Mystery Magazine,* the *The Magazine of Fantasy & Science Fiction,* and monthly softcover, abridged reprints of British and American mystery novels.

The staff responsible for copyediting the publications and condensing the novels consisted of two people—Gloria Levitas and me. Gloria, a good-looking, all-around genius, was a mite more subdued but had all the energy I associated with the newsroom characters of *The Front Page.* She was a swift first reader and could knock off a mountain of unsolicited manuscripts in the time it took me to recite two *brochas* and a Hail Mary before rejecting one. Gloria was also a demon line editor, never overlooking a typo or cutting a clue while whittling a two-hundred-page thriller to half its original size.

While acquiring a taste for black coffee, I was learning the craft of two genres about which I had previously known only that Ellery Queen was the pseudonym of the author-hero of a bestselling book and TV series and that H. G. Wells's *War of the Worlds* was considered science fiction.

Mills, the managing editor, was friendly but remote. His advice for revising blurbs and titles offered even fewer clues than some of the more bewildering mysteries. "Get inside it," he would say with an upward thrust of his hand, "and turn it around." He did, however, share with me a lesson learned from Anthony Boucher, the nonresident who edited *F&SF*. "The sentence in the story the reader is most willing to accept is the first," Boucher, a sage of the genre, decreed. "You don't have to build the spaceship. The reader will suspend disbelief if you begin, 'After we landed on Mars . . .'"

Fred Dannay and Manny Lee, the collaborators who created Ellery Queen, were as invisible as Boucher. We were aware that they had the last word on the selection of stories and wrote most of the blurbs and introductory paragraphs, but they had no desks at the office and I can recall in my brief run meeting them only at the Christmas party. They looked like matching bookends—short, earnest gentlemen who appeared to be busy accountants.

My experience with the magazine seemed rather vague and tentative except for our growing friendship with Gloria and her husband, Mike. They were the first New York couple of my acquaintance and I was enormously touched by the cheer and goodwill with which they adopted us as friends and colleagues. Mike, who went on to editorial posts at the *New York Post, Time,* and *The New York Times,* was working for the Voice of America when we met.

Soon after inviting us for dinner at their Bank Street apartment we learned from Gloria that it's possible to serve leg of lamb for dinner on a working day if all but the final basting and roasting is done the previous night.

Gloria's father was a chef. Mike's dad, Sol Levitas, founded and edited the biweekly political-literary review *The New Leader.* "Sid should write for *The New Leader,*" Mike suggested, and a week later Gloria escorted me to the publication office where I met the noble champion of anti-Stalin, modified socialism. Mr. Levitas teased me gently about Alger Hiss when he heard I'd been a student at Hopkins and allowed me a selection from the books stacked on his desk for possible review.

The same week I learned that Cornell Woolrich and Dashiell Hammett were associated with *Black Mask,* the archives of which were now available for reprint in *EQMM,* I was composing my own hard-boiled evaluation of Daphne du Maurier's collection *The Birds and Other Stories.* When the review appeared in *The New Leader,* I was identified as "a short-story writer and critic." Encouraged by a designation I perceived as putting me in the company of Matthew Arnold and Edmund Wilson, I determined writing a mystery novel would be a minor challenge. I'd been reading the masters for months—and the fast-paced, vernacular style of *Black Mask* seemed not that remote from the action-dialogue design of pulp-fiction magazines.

So, evenings at seven I pounded away at the old Underwood. Avi proofed and retyped, and in less than a month I was two hundred pages into a complex narrative climaxed by the murder of a Walter Winchell–like Manhattan gossip columnist. It was all there—sexual intrigue, indulgent celebrities, lots of motives, plenty of suspects. Only element lacking: the resolution. I had something in mind. At the crucial moment a brick falls from the fireplace and the murder weapon is revealed. I suspected it didn't quite work when Avi took to bed with "a headache" rather than retype the last scene.

It seemed to me not too much of an imposition to petition for a little professional counsel. All I had to do was talk to half of Ellery Queen. I was certain that with their success contriving so many crimes with resolutions, my little mystery would be no more challenging for them than resolving a traffic ticket. Bob Mills thought a long moment before allowing me Fred Dannay's number. I called and was greeted with such cordiality I was convinced Mr. Dannay knew me. But as soon as we connected on the phone I realized a verbal summary wasn't going to adequately present the problem. I'd have to ask Sir Arthur Conan Queen to read my draft. His response was immediate and a lesson in the genre. "I'll certainly read your novel, if you would like that, Mr. Offit, but I can assure you I'll be no help resolving your story. Mysteries are almost always written back to front," he informed me. "Otherwise it's pretty much like painting yourself into a corner."

My Walter Winchell murder case remains among the unsolved and unpublished crimes of the last century.

22

Jackie Robinson, Mickey Mantle,
Willie Mays, and Ted Williams—
That Ole-Time Religion

1955–1957

When Dr. Harry Edwards wrote in *Black Scholar,* circa 1972, that sports in America have assumed the rituals, saints, and leaps of faith characteristic of religion, I recognized my "church" and pew. As a boy growing up in Baltimore, from spring through early autumn when the International League Orioles were in town, my dad, brother, and I would be perched in seats slightly left of home plate. For Benson and me the seventh-inning stretch and intervals between games of the doubleheaders were celebrated with "wine and wafers," otherwise known as Coke and hot dogs.

Our pew was visited throughout the afternoon by pillars of the congregation, often wearing straw hats and rumpled seersucker suits, and puffing White Owl cigars. It was not uncommon for Dad to acknowledge the "confession" of a peripatetic parishioner with a couple bucks before the conclusion of the tale of woe or misdeeds. "A long shot who couldn't miss, Buckley. Off at ten to one. I got it right from the paddock and would you believe it, the bum is still running." This mixing of denominations—racing at the ballpark—intruded on my dad's day of rest and he would conclude the session with a quick flip from the wad of bills he always carried in his pocket.

Although the Orioles were a minor-league team, the Yankees, Giants, and Indians, among others, had "farm teams" in the league, and during the 1930s and early '40s—while we were rooting for Woody Abernathy, George Puccinelli, Howie Moss—we also were privileged to early views of the "saints" from other churches—among them, Charlie "King Kong" Keller, who went from the Newark Bears to join the outfield with DiMaggio and Heinrich for the Yankees.

My brother was so profoundly affected by these experiences that he remained a passionate sports "believer" all his life. While at Johns Hopkins, Benson turned down his first nomination to be editor of the school paper so he could remain on the sports beat. The names, averages, and won-lost percentages of major-league players were so familiar to both of us we could qualify as Talmudists on the subject.

It may have been the anthology of English poets that turned me from the "church," but by the time I graduated from college, my interest in professional sports was no more ardent than the scholarship with which I studied national politics. I continued to recognize the names of the saints but couldn't quote much scripture.

When I received the phone call from Earl Noyes, a retired Washington public relations professional, it was the winter of 1954 and I was working at Macfadden Publications. Mr. Noyes asked me if I would be interested in covering the New York teams for a magazine he was buying. *Baseball Magazine!* Scripture of our childhood! But I hadn't seen or thought about it in years. Mr. Noyes went on to tell me it was for sale, and he was buying it. He'd heard about me from my cousin's husband Colonel Mike Meritt "who, following my advice, applied and retired a brigadier general."

Mr. Noyes's presentation was more a sales pitch than an interview to establish my credentials. The job was mine if I wanted it. "I've read your stories in sports magazines, and I have no doubt your association with Macfadden will be invaluable." But my contribution to sports magazines were fifteen-hundred-word pulp fictions published during the fading years of that genre, and, as I immediately confessed, I'd only recently been hired as the managing editor of *True Experiences,* a monthly confession magazine in Macfadden's True Story group. My only relationship with *Sport* consisted of free copies and occasional lunches with Al Silverman and other members of the staff. "Fine. Perfect," said Mr. Noyes. "Ring me next time you are in Baltimore and we'll discuss business."

Within two months of my conversation with Earl Noyes I had press passes for Yankee Stadium, the Polo Grounds, and Ebbets Field, easy access to the playing field before games. All I had to produce was a story a month—three months prior to publication.

The freelance assignment along with my summer job as steward of The Aladdin, my in-laws' hotel in the Catskills, seemed a good fit. I signed off at *True Experience* and set out for the ballparks. My first story was an interview with Willie Mays, to whom Leo Durocher introduced me with the caveat: "Just don't ask him if he played baseball with his father as a kid. He's answered that one so often he's catching on that you could look it up." Until that moment it hadn't occurred to me to research what had been reported about the teams and players other than my routine readings of Jimmy Cannon in the *New York Post* and Red Smith in the *Herald-Tribune.*

I really hadn't given much thought as to what I had to say or wanted to know about major-league baseball players. I figured we'd have a conversation and I'd round it into a seven-hundred, or one-thousand-word piece that would pass for a profile.

I addressed Willie Mays as "Mr. Mays" and he seemed as confused as flattered. He was Willie to everyone. We discussed the basket catch, his variation of the traditional outfielder snaring the ball overhead with fingers outstretched to the sky.

Willie Mays said that it just came naturally to him. He didn't much think about it. How did he feel about responsibility for the winning or tying run when he was next up and a game was on the line? "Don't think about that much, either," was his reply. "Just try to figure out what the pitcher is throwing and my best chance to connect." I thought the piece routine, but by the time Mr. Noyes published it three months later, Willie Mays was on his way to becoming a star and justified my title that was a PR man's sales pitch—"Big Man Among the Giants."

Casey Stengel knew more about *Baseball Magazine* than I did. He was cordial and amused that an unknown kid was representing the magazine that he recalled publishing bylined stories by Christy Mathewson, Rogers Hornsby, Walter "Big Train" Johnson. "Didn't know them fellows could all spell their own names, 'cept of course the college boys, of which there were more than you would think if you were thinking about it at all, but there they were in black-and-white so-called writing, if you wantta believe it for your *Baseball Magazine*." He stood for a picture with me and introduced me around. After several visits to Yankee Stadium I asked Mr. Stengel if it was all right to talk to Mickey Mantle. He thought that was such a modest request from a working journalist that he called Mantle over and presented me with another incoherent but hilarious verbal essay that managed to bond us with laughter. I said, "Great to meet you, Mr. Mantle," and Mickey Mantle replied, "How d'you do, Mr. Offit." I don't think in my entire life up to that time I'd been more startled by the courtesy of a stranger.

Mickey Mantle was obviously a kid from the farm trying to adjust to the intrusion of questions—many of them repetitious—and an analysis of his game for which he had no more explanation than Willie Mays could offer for the basket catch. Once I told him this was a new beat for me, too, he seemed comfortable and willing to help me. All I had to do was come up with the questions.

The best I could do was ask him how he found adjusting to New York City and all the attention. He confessed outright that he was getting more than enough advice but he had some friends on the team—"buddies." It was clear he relied on them—Billy Martin and Whitey Ford were top of the list—for "a little fun on nights off."

I heard that Mantle had been named for Gordon Stanley Cochrane, the great catcher and later major-league manager, but the Mantles had landed on Cochrane's nickname "Mickey." What did he think of that? "Well, it's good enough for a mouse. I guess it's a lot better than Gordon for me." That was a jewel and a rare example of Mantle as a spontaneous humorist. We went on to talk about his preferences for batting right- or left-handed—a shrug indicating no choice—and how he felt about his chances of ever breaking Babe Ruth's home run record. Soon as I mentioned Ruth I knew I had gone on automatic at the wrong moment. Another shrug, this time accompanied by a shuffling of feet. He was courteous and I felt he was trying to help me, but it seemed to me enough. I said, "Thank you, Mr. Mantle." He was visibly relieved but responded, "Nice to meet you, mister."

At Ebbets Field I met Carl Erskine, Duke Snider, and Roy Campanella. Erskine was thoughtful and pleasant, with complimentary words about his teammates. Campanella seemed to me the most game-savvy of the players I'd met up to that time. I included him on a list of the ten best baseball brains in a piece I wrote for the magazine. I didn't get much going with Snider. He was weary of the verbal exchanges about his competition with Mays and Mantle and I realized so was I. My afternoon at Ebbets Field was the first time I seriously questioned what I was doing as a baseball writer. The routine analysis of statistics and predictions—(Will there ever be another Babe Ruth? Can Robin Roberts win thirty games? Who has the best shot at being the next .400 hitter?)—held little interest for me and I wasn't comfortable imposing on athletes, all of whom seemed only to want to define themselves by performances on the field.

This initial suspicion and discomfort was confirmed by two rather extraordinary conversations. I was into my second or third year covering the New York teams around 1956 when Jackie Robinson and I talked in the dugout before a game at Ebbets Field. It was an early autumn afternoon and for reasons I'm not quite sure I could explain today I was wearing a three-piece gray suit. It may have been the formality of my dress or, again, the respect for the magazine I represented, but Mr. Robinson and I had a brief but intimate conversation.

There was a rumor at the time that Jackie Robinson might be traded to the New York Giants. I supposed other reporters had asked him about his reaction to such a trade, but when I mentioned it, his face seemed gripped with an intensity on the verge of anger. He looked directly at me when he spoke and I had the momentary feeling I was responsible for the trade, not just asking about his reactions to the possibility. "It doesn't surprise me," Jackie Robinson said. "I've known long ago that all I am here is chattel." Chattel? I wasn't sure I'd heard him correctly and I recall making an attempt at softening the indictment. "That certainly doesn't apply to you. You're loved by Dodgers fans. You've already made baseball history. No trade, no management can redefine Jackie Robinson." The words came easily because I meant them. Robinson seemed to appreciate the effort. His mood softened and he addressed me as a kid, learning the business. He said it was natural for a young reporter, even one breaking in with an old magazine, to romanticize the game. He supposed that might be a help, even essential to writing the kinds of stories that please the fans. But then he reminded me that baseball was above all "a business."

He expressed appreciation to Branch Rickey for taking the risk for signing him, but that, too, he quickly explained, was primarily a business decision, a way to vitalize the franchise. Jackie Robinson spoke easily and quickly, with a voice that struck me as close to song. I was surprised and impressed when after his summary of the game as business he hadn't forgotten my original question. "They can consider me chattel," he said. "But I've had enough of it. I won't go."

That was it. My first scoop—and I didn't report a word of it. It seemed to me an exploitation of a shared intimacy, more a trust than a story. A sports photographer assigned by the magazine snapped a picture at the conclusion of our conversation. I had pen in hand but I didn't need notes to remember the lesson.

By the time I met Ted Williams, I'd collected stories from the archives of the magazine, written a brief introduction, and compiled an anthology published by Putnam's as *The Best of Baseball*. *The New York Times* reviewed my book along with Charles Einstein's *Fireside Book of Baseball* and said the relationship of the *Baseball Magazine* collection to Einstein's considerably more diverse and erudite volume was as "Dean Martin is to Jerry Lewis."

Mr. Noyes, who was now in the process of selling the magazine, was delighted with the attention. He suggested it would provide an excuse for advertising and further promotion if I could persuade a major-league star to pose with me and a copy of the anthology.

The Red Sox were in town playing the Yankees. I tucked a copy of the anthology under my arm with the intention of delivering it to Casey Stengel or, perhaps, Mickey Mantle, with whom I by now had a nodding acquaintance.

I hadn't thought about proposing this to Ted Williams until I saw him warming up in front of the visitor's dugout. I had met Ted Williams back in 1941, the year he hit .400. My dad and I were at Griffith Stadium, in Washington, D.C., for a Sunday doubleheader that day. I told Dad I'd like Ted Williams's autograph so I could send the signed scorecard to Benson, who was away at camp. He arranged it with a member of the administrative staff who seemed thrilled to do something for "Buckley's kid." In the presence of the great man, I chickened into awed silence, but Ted Williams was sympathetic to a shy twelve-year-old. Even though I was frozen and couldn't ask, he volunteered and signed my card.

I recalled this incident to Ted Williams as he was rolling his shoulders, and snapping the ball back and forth with another Red Sox player. He seemed amused. The press had been all over him that season with complaints about his withdrawals and indifference to reporters and fans.

"So I wasn't such a bad guy after all," he said, and then added, "How long ago was that?"

Without another word from me Ted Williams summarized what he perceived to be the inappropriateness of the demands upon him. "Look at it this way," he said. "Baseball is a business and if this was a corporation and not a game, I'd be a CEO, at the very least a major member of the board. CEOs come and go in chauffeur-driven Continentals and arrive and depart as they please. All that matters is the profit and loss statement. The batting statistics. I know what's best for me and therefore best for the team. I don't need anyone telling me what to do and who to talk to and what to say."

I was tempted to repeat to Ted Williams the words I'd heard earlier from Jackie Robinson. He seemed to be defining the game in similar terms although with a different complaint.

But I appreciated it as a rare opportunity. We were not interrupted and Ted Williams seemed comfortable talking, not the least irritated or impatient. I asked him about hitting, a subject I knew he enjoyed discussing and always with unique authority. He repeated that the premise of his success was eye-hand coordination. "I can afford to only hit strikes." I wondered if there was a way he could further define or illustrate this, and Williams responded, "I can hit the ball out of the catcher's glove."

It must have been the fortuitous moment, but Ted Williams continued the lesson by offering to demonstrate. He led me to the batter's box, arranged for a catcher to replace the cage, and instructed me to keep my eye on the catcher's glove.

I tried. Lord knows I tried. But the whistling ball and crack of the bat were all that genuinely registered. He'd say "Good," and snap the bat around to send the ball off to the wild blue yonder. Or "No," signaling it was out of the strike zone and let it pass.

I concentrated on the catcher's glove and convinced myself that once I actually saw Ted Williams's bat connect with the ball just before it would have reached the mitt.

I thanked him with as much gratitude in my voice as I could manage, and I told him that was a lesson I'd remember all my life. Williams nodded and smiled with the approval of the teacher who didn't want too much made of it. It was all in a day's work.

Then I told him about the anthology and presented him with a copy. I wish he had been less gracious and appreciative. But the photographer was there, and I had my assignment. "Would you mind a picture of you accepting the book, Mr. Williams?"

He flinched. This pitch was just ready to hit the mitt and he could have put me away with a justifiable "So this is what it was all about." But he didn't. "Okay," he said, "let's get it over with."

The photographer snapped the picture, and I thanked Ted Williams as warmly as I could. He moved right on with an expression I suppose was not unlike his reaction to a bad call from an umpire.

Baseball Magazine featured the picture in ads for the book, but I never looked at it without embarrassment. On my way home from the ballpark that afternoon I concluded that baseball reporting was not for me. It had been a great experience, but I had no point of view to contribute to chronicles of the game. Later, when I read Roger

Angell's brilliant essays in *The New Yorker,* I felt even more comfortable with my decision. A good baseball reporter should be a student of the art and craft, as well as a fan who is fascinated by the personalities, to illuminate the scriptures.

But I did have a scrapbook of photographs of me with the greats of that era—Robinson, Mays, Mantle, Snider, Williams, Stengel, Robin Roberts. A collector of memorabilia told me the value of such a collection is determined only by how much your family is willing to pay for it.

Even as a gift to our next generation, there's not much running for me. Our granddaughters, Anna, Caroline, Tristan, and Lily, prefer skiing, horseback riding, tennis. Our grandson, Wyatt, isn't much interested in the history of baseball either. Soccer is his game.

I may try to impress Wyatt with the story of my brief conversation with the courtly gent whom I met at the Surrey Liquor Store, corner of Madison and 69th Street, years after I quit writing about baseball.

When I suggested he step to the counter to request his purchase he demurred. "No, sir, your turn. You were in line before me," said the man who led Brazil to World Cup victories in 1958, 1962, 1970. There's no picture to celebrate it, but I exchanged courtesies with the most famous soccer player in the world of his time and, perhaps, ever after—the great Pelé!

23

Martin Abend and the Heir of Ramsey Clark, Ted Sorenson, and Mayor Ed Koch

1975–1985

By the time I arrived at the Channel 5 TV studio in the spring of 1975, Dr. Martin Abend was a local celebrity. An unrelenting foe of Soviet Communism, the Ph.D. geography professor had often been the lone voice on television championing our war in Vietnam. He was an advocate of capital punishment and a strident opponent of abortion, affirmative action, and gay rights. When he wasn't sounding off with solo commentaries, this songbird of New York metropolitan area conservatives debated political, social, and economic issues with Ramsey Clark, the former attorney general; Theodore Sorenson, President Kennedy's advisor; and Victor Riesel, a veteran labor reporter who had been blinded by a vengeful thug.

Clark, Sorenson, and Riesel, for reasons not defined to me, had departed before I was invited to engage the right-wing Savonarola. Only Congressman Ed Koch remained from the "preliminary" contenders, but his airtime was restricted to weekends and periods when he wasn't running for public office.

My qualifications for the debates were defined along with the format by Joe Feurey, an NYU colleague and the program's assignment editor. "I know you're a flaming liberal who can talk without a script and say your piece in no more than forty-five seconds. Remember, Sid, you have another thirty seconds for rebuttal and / *or*—insults!"

Dr. Abend greeted me with perfunctory courtesy, a handshake and a nod. No additional dialogue. Standing with broad shoulders atop a straight back, he sized me up with a critical eye. I felt that one misstep and he might haul off and sock me. I hadn't expected an interview, but Dr. Abend wanted to know where I taught. I mentioned the New School and New York University. When I added that I was an editor of *Intellectual Digest,* his expression softened. He seemed pleased—the pleasure of sighting plump game.

Before long we were seated across from each other on backless chairs facing the cameras. An assistant producer reminded us of our time limits and promised to signal with his fingers when ten seconds remained, and to slice a silent gash across his neck when our time was up. "We're live. On the air. The subject for the evening—capital punishment. Make it right."

Dr. Abend opened with a blitz. He attacked those opposed to the death penalty as responsible for the growing murder rate and assaulted us for lack of sympathy for victims. I was surprised but managed not to be distracted by the personal venom that seemed to energize his argument. After all, we'd never discussed this issue, so I found no reason for him to be angry at me.

I improvised a brief of the reasons I was opposed to the state taking a life: possibility of error, contradiction of our constitutional prohibition against cruel and capricious punishment, no evidence that the threat of capital punishment is a deterrent.

Dr. Abend smirked, dismissing my arguments and leaning on the rightful vengeance of the victims' families. His parting shot was a demand to know what my response would be if a member of my family—a person I *loved*—was murdered. "Tell me that, Professor Offit. Are you so forgiving, you'd excuse a person who killed your own child, your own wife?"

My wife? My child? That shot caught me so off guard all I could do was ignore it. I stumbled into the standby of the beleaguered combatant and attempted a rhetorical clinch. "By what justification, Dr. Abend, do you believe the state committed to the sanctity of every human life can risk error for the spectacle of execution?"

I felt I'd lost the debate, but Joe Feurey assured me I'd done "just fine." I had wrapped it up with one take and not allowed Dr. Abend to cast me on the defensive.

That was the first of what was to become a series of close to a thousand appearances over the span of a decade on the local news show. I eventually discovered the rejoinder to the intimidating challenge as to what I would want to do to the person who killed someone dear to me. It didn't diminish the counterpoint to capital punishment to admit that I would intuitively want to execute the killer on the spot, but—the major qualifying *but*—personal anger is not the basis for a rational evaluation of capital punishment.

I'd learned that it was important to express feelings with which a viewer could identify to bridge to moral arguments. When, during a presidential debate in 1988, Michael Dukakis was tripped up by that same question ("How would you respond if a member of your family was murdered?"), I wondered if he had the misgiving I'd experienced when Dr. Abend caught me silencing my heart.

Although the debates generated a great deal of mail and more viewer response than any other feature of the news show, Dr. Abend and I were treated as kind of stepchildren by the news director. There was no contract, not even a verbal commitment that we would appear on a routine schedule. For a while it was every weekday, then three or four times a week. When the issue suggested was particularly sensitive, Ed Koch would pass the mike to me and I'd appear on weekends, too.

"So you're an advocate of legalized drugs," Dr. Abend reminded Ed Koch one memorable evening. "Now that you have William F. Buckley Jr. on your side, too, let's argue that."

With his characteristic shrug and dancing hands, Ed Koch moved away from the microphone. "I never said that, Martin . . ." They settled on a less controversial theme and my congressman willed the legalized drug platform to me.

I'd known Ed Koch before we met at the studio. When he was a leader of the Village Independent Democrats, I'd been impressed with his humor and oratorical flair, a mix of impatient teacher and borscht belt comedian. Unlike Dr. Abend, I wasn't critical of the caution related to Ed's political ambitions.

Although we never consulted, I considered Ed Koch and myself a team. When I decided after my first six months that the attention generated by the debates was too much of an intrusion on my personal life, I told Ed I was planning to join the ranks of Clark, Sorenson, and Riesel.

Ed's head moved from side to side as I spoke, his lips pouted, but his eyes were gentle and caring. "You don't want to do that, Sidney," he advised. Then the Koch shrug and conductor's hands: "How much time does it take? And you do it so easily." In a quieter voice he confided, "And let me tell you, it's unlikely there's anything you'll do in your life that will give you a greater audience. I receive more response to these TV debates than serving in Congress. It's made me a recognizable name throughout the city. You're a writer. Who knows what this kind of exposure can lead to?"

For Ed Koch the tussles with Martin Abend may have contributed to the notoriety that led to his election as mayor of New York. My fringe benefits were full classes for my fiction workshops at the New School and oversubscriptions for the Critical Thinking class I taught at NYU. I tried to answer every letter I received, even though many were overwhelmingly critical, and I dared to compose notes to temper those petitions that demanded my removal from the airwaves. During the period that the Son of Sam murders plagued the city, my rejection of capital punishment generated death threats.

But Ed Koch wasn't wrong. In 1977, when Lippincott published my young adult novel *What Kind of Guy Do You Think I Am?* ("The one must-read of the season"—*Newsweek*), the audience was standing-room-only for my appearance at a Queens reading and book signing. At the conclusion of my sonnet to the vagaries of adolescent love, I was asked, "Do you and Dr. Abend get along?" Lots of people leafed my book like a time bomb and commented on the incongruity of a "political professor" writing novels. I sold sixty copies that night.

Dr. Abend and I did get along. Although I disagreed with his politics, I knew he cared deeply. The bitterness he expressed to liberals, whom he perceived as intellectually arrogant, privileged, and self-righteous, was profoundly felt. "Those who have the most to lose are the first to sell out our national defense," he would tell me. "Their sense of justice is to interpret the Constitution as a suicide pact."

Arriving at the East 67th Street studio by subway, in dungarees and floppy jackets, with a cap pulled low over his eyes so as not to be recognized, Dr. Abend made no pretense of caring for clothes or fashion, self-indulgence, or the adulation of his considerable constituency, including champions of the IRA, Right to Life, the New York uniformed services, conservative Catholics, Orthodox Jews, and advocates of Croatian independence.

His impatience with even his fans provoked me once—and only once—to express an off-camera criticism. After he had ignored and finally admonished an adoring fan who intruded on the set of one of our rare street debates—I was for legalized prostitution and an outraged Dr. Abend was opposed—I confessed that I might not be as passionate an advocate as our debates suggested. "I'm not by nature confrontational," I told Martin Abend. "I listen attentively to the other side of an argument and whether or not I agree, I'm frequently empathetic. I argue with you, Martin, because your presentations are always so cocksure they're abrasive."

Dr. Abend responded more gently than he did on camera. He seemed just as cocky but amused. I recall him saying, "You may not realize it, Sid, but you're the most authentic liberal I've debated. Clark, Sorenson, Riesel were working out their ideologies or satisfying some personal needs. Ed Koch is running for office. But you and I, Sid, we're on opposite sides because you believe the good in human nature is more persuasive than the evil. I know it's too often the other way around. That's the difference that matters."

The rhetoric and rhythms of our debates seemed predictable to me but our spontaneity was a major source of our popularity. Avi and I had no television set in our house before my appearances, and I was slow—even a mite embarrassed—to accept my desire to see myself.

We made frequent dates for late suppers at Donohue's on Lexington Avenue, where the owner, Mike Donohue, was always accommodating and switched the dial to Channel 5 at 10 P.M. But I never did hear the parodies of our debates that were features of local radio shows.

The night after John Lennon was shot Dr. Abend asked me what I thought of the famous Beatles. I'd seen Lennon several times in the neighborhood of the Dakota, where he lived. Once, darting into the building like a pursued fox, he waved over his shoulder to admiring fans. I was fond of the Beatles and I told Martin I thought of them as twentieth-century versions of the Romantic poets.

"We have a debate," he declared.

Once on the air, Dr. Abend led with a brief disclaimer that he didn't feel pleased when anyone was murdered. Then, he flat-out condemned the Beatles as a corrupting influence, advocates of a drug culture that was destroying our young. His fury was undiminished by my tribute to John Lennon and his colleagues as poets of peace, "minstrels of sweetness and light."

Dr. Abend concluded with an intemperate remark—did I hear him say, "Good riddance"? The petitions and protests he provoked almost "good riddanced" us off the air.

Among the pile of mail for us in the newsroom one evening in January 1983, was a letter from the White House addressed to Dr. Abend. He opened the envelope, glanced at the note, and flipped it aside. "Politicking in an election year, Reagan has got the wrong patsy if he thinks he can sweet-talk me."

I picked the letter out of the wastebasket and read:

> *Dear Dr. Abend:*
> *I thought you might be interested to know how many of your listeners write to me—and send telegrams—praising your commentary.*
> *Through the years, during visits to New York when I've*

*watched you on Channel 5, I've come to appreciate your sound
approach to a wide range of topics. I am honored that you have
supported me on so many issues so often.*

*I just wanted you to know how much I appreciate having your
informed and eloquent voice speaking out on television for the goals
and ideals we share. God bless you.*

*Sincerely,
Ronald Reagan*

The letter was signed. Although Abend seemed more angered than
pleased and the newsroom response ranged from skeptical to incredulous, I insisted upon making a copy of the letter and encouraging Martin to save the original. "Bring it home for your children. Who knows,
they may be able to use it as evidence someday that their father and
Ronald Reagan were responsible for the destruction of the evil empire."
(It was a more prescient dig than I could possibly realize at the time.)

I have no idea what Martin Abend did with the letter, but I do
know he cared for his children. Along with my memories of him
fuming on the air are visions of him appearing at the studio with
two small sons and babysitting with them at his feet below camera,
as he warmed up to demand, "Will you and your liberal friends
never learn, Professor Offit?"

Among the fan letters I received during my decade championing
left-of-center positions was a mailgram from Al Goldstein, the publisher of *Screw* and later the producer of the cable show *Midnight Blue*.
I had argued that indicting Goldstein for publishing sexual material
unacceptable to the community standards of a midwestern state was
a manipulative violation of the Bill of Rights.

Al Goldstein thanked me for my "courageous defense of the First
Amendment." He went on to say, "A few more guys like you and
there may never be another Nixon or a threat to democracy." He
signed his mailgram "an admiring fan" and called a few days later to
be sure I'd received it.

I accepted the Sultan of Porn's invitation to meet him at his
apartment and have lunch with him near his office. I was curious

about what his daily routine would be like, in addition to, perhaps, being treated to a connoisseur's stable of porn queens. That didn't happen. The Goldstein apartment was simple, his wife unpretentious, and the maestro himself appeared as attentive a father as, well, Martin Abend.

The *Screw* office, too, was unremarkable—no knockout staff, exotic displays, or aspiring porno models. Goldstein did let me in on a hidden video camera that monitored his front door. "If a sensational-looking babe comes my way, I don't want to miss her."

Contrary to the image of the belligerent lecher that he so convincingly portrayed in later years, Al Goldstein was modest and mannerly with me. When he asked if he might visit one of my writing classes, I agreed. A week or so later there he was perched in the front row, taking notes with no hint of being a person who demanded center stage. He was so courtly to the middle-aged teacher sitting next to him that when he didn't appear in my class again, she asked me what had happened to that "nice man who seemed so serious about writing."

Besides Joe Feurey, who soon left Channel 5 to join the news staff of NBC, I had no close friends in the newsroom. Dr. Abend had been introduced to television by Ted Kavanau, the news director, who was credited with bringing the first camera into a newsroom. Although sachems of the den at East 67th Street frequently reacted to our debates with a mixture of ridicule and envy, there was universal reverence for Kavanau and, by proxy, reluctant acceptance of his protégé Dr. Abend as a fixture.

Gabe Pressman, whose tenure as a local reporter was as historic as Martin Abend's, served as the conscience of the newsroom. Gabe neither praised nor condescended to us. I always found him respectfully curious. To Stewart Klein, the movie and theater critic, we were drama—low-budget, off-Broadway. Abend rarely complimented, but he told me he thought John Rowland had been a good street reporter and it was too bad he became an anchor.

Feisty mob reporter John Miller, the youngest member of the staff, had so impressed Kavanau with his unsolicited filings of crime reports from New Jersey that he had been hired while still a teenager. He seemed to me an heir of *The Front Page* and right at home in this late-1970s re-creation of the Ben Hecht–Charles MacArthur stage set. It was not surprising that John "grew up" to become a crack reporter on national television and one of the few correspondents in the world to interview Osama bin Laden.

Genial Marvin Scott was the utility infielder—as competent a street reporter as a weekend anchor. Bill McCreary, who also had his own show covering the African-American beat, was frequently asked to introduce our debates and he did so with such dignity that after his flute overture we came on like bongo drums.

My most sustained conversation with a member of the news staff other than Joe Feurey and Martin Abend was with Judy Licht. We happened to be passengers on a jitney to the Hamptons after one of our late-Friday-evening taping sessions. I knew Judy only as the well-groomed, good-mannered reporter who covered the fashion and culture beat with a diplomatic grace that enabled her to just about always get her story. After our two-hour conversation I felt like an older brother rooting for his kid sister to meet the right guy who would appreciate her. Several years later Judy hit the jackpot. Today, Jerry Della Femina, advertising wizard, publisher of the *Independent,* and restaurant-food entrepreneur, married to Judy for more than fifteen years, continues to refer reverentially to his wife as "the beautiful Judy Licht."

The Channel 5 News as created by Kavanau may very well have been responsible for as many careers in television news as CBS, NBC, ABC, or the Columbia School of Journalism: Steve Powers and Rolland Smith, Christopher Jones and Dr. Max Gomez, Graciela Rogerio, Bob O'Brien, and Victor Neufield. All impressed me as a good cast to support the two and a half minutes of our "professorial" debates.

Only Andrew Heyward, recently graduated from Harvard, seemed miscast as our newsroom's first sergeant. He suffered about scheduling debates and, though courteous to me, seemed to experience an ulcer attack when agreeing to a subject for one of our evening arguments. Young, earnest Andrew, with biting wit and conspicuous familiarity with a more sophisticated culture, was ambitious for the quality of *The New York Times,* not the emotionalism of the *Post* or

Daily News that often characterized Abend's articulation of ideas and, by association, mine.

I met Andrew again many years later, when he was running CBS News—and although I had long since left Channel 5 and Andrew Hayward's only possible identification of me was as curator of the George Polk Awards—his manner suggested he was still prepared to fire Abend and me on the spot.

I encountered Ramsey Clark from time to time on 12th Street on my way to New School classes. He had only the vaguest memory of Dr. Martin Abend as a person "who never had anything right." Theodore Sorenson scoffed at the experience, wondering why he or anyone would engage that "raging reactionary."

Several weeks after it was announced that Rupert Murdoch had bought the editorially independent Channel 5 from John Kluge's Metromedia, and just before the change of management, John Parsons, the news director, called to tell me all commentaries had been suspended. I thanked John for the courtesy of the call. After I hung up, I told Avi, "A chapter of my life is over." "You mean you've been fired," the home-team translator concluded.

"Well, I wouldn't say fired," I insisted. "They've just discontinued all commentary."

"Sounds like you've been fired to me."

That's when the phone rang and from the other end of the line Martin Abend endorsed my home-team realist's conclusion. "Parsons call to tell you we're fired?" Abend asked, and then before I could answer, he said irritably, "I suppose you thanked him for the call. Not me. I told that second-rate supplicant he had it all wrong. He couldn't fire me. I quit. I wouldn't work for someone so dumb he didn't realize that debates, controversy, that's what makes a TV news show click. What does he know? They'll never learn . . ."

But "they" did learn: *60 Minutes* with a four-year run of "Point Counterpoint," featuring Shana Alexander and James J. Kilpatrick, then Molly Ivins and Stanley Crouch; *Crossfire,* featuring Tom Braden and Pat Buchanan, Michael Kinsley and John Sununu; CNN, CNBC,

Fox. . . . A debate, an argument somewhere on the dial, most of the time. Eventually the Kavanau-Abend invention graduated from local club fighter to heavyweight contender—the *No Spin Zone* with Bill O'Reilly, top ratings, big bucks for the Abend heir Marvin Kitman dubbed "the man who wouldn't shut up."

The last time I saw Martin Abend, we met for lunch, my suggestion, at Gino on Lexington Avenue, in 2004. I'd been indulging with friends in parodies of an imagined exchange between us, debating the values of George W. Bush's recent initiation of our invasion of Iraq.

Although we hadn't faced off for more than ten years, I had reason to believe Dr. Abend had heard about my making comedy of our viewpoints. So after a Merlot for me and iced tea for him, I did my takeoff: Abend fiercely defending the invasion as an imperative to punish terrorists of the Middle East, countered by my moral outrage at destroying lives, creating chaos, attempting to impose democracy as a front for securing oil.

Martin Abend listened, patiently smiling, and then with a great sigh he set me straight. "You should know better, Sid. You have me all wrong." He followed with a blast of his signature venom, this time directed at the stupidity of the Bush administration for their ignorance of geopolitics (the subject, he reminded me, he had been teaching at Jersey City State College for more than forty years). Dr. Abend predicted chaos in Iraq at enormous cost to us, with no dividends.

There I was, thinking I was the Greek, Democritus, the laughing philosopher who mocked human folly, and at our last meeting Dr. Abend usurped my role with an unpredictable but not unkindly last laugh.

"Make mine a double," with Ogden Nash, circa 1950. *(Photo by John W. Ritterhoff)*

Writers' party time with Gay Talese and Jerzy Kosinski. *(Offit Archives)*

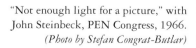

Happy birthday, Alger Hiss. Naming names with Harold Taylor. *(Photo by Victor Navasky)*

"Not enough light for a picture," with John Steinbeck, PEN Congress, 1966. *(Photo by Stefan Congrat-Butlar)*

Our "saint," Heinrich Böll, passing "the Word" to Tom Fleming and his designated PEN delegate, West Berlin, 1974. *(Offit Archives)*

Toni Morrison suggests, "You should be home writing, Sidney." *(Offit Archives)*

Vad Vashem, PEN Congress, Jerusalem, 1973, flanked by Sir V. S. Pritchett (in a yarmulke) and Heinrich Böll (in a beret). *(Photo by Sholomo Lavie)*

Interviewing Jackie Robinson for *Baseball Magazine*, 1955. *(Photo by William Jacobellis)*

"Big Man Among the Giants" Willie Mays for *Baseball Magazine*, 1955. *(Photo by William Jacobellis)*

Casey Stengel, my host at Yankee Stadium, circa 1955. *(Photo by William Jacobellis)*

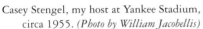

Reunion with my mentor Russell Baker, recipient of the George Polk Award for career achievements, at the Golden Jubilee celebration, 1999. *(Offit Archives)*

Isidor Feinstein, a.k.a I. F. Stone, life of the Polk Party, with Bill Moyers, 1981. *(Billie Billing)*

With Kurt Vonnegut and granddaughter Anna Offit, circa 1988. *(Offit Archives)*

A Man without a Country

FOR PROFESSOR OFFIT,
MY OFFICIAL AS WELL
AS SPIRITUAL BEST
FRIEND—

AUG. 8 2005

With Richard Gilman and Ralph Ellison at Saul and Gayfryd Steinberg's PEN reception *(Roxanne Lowit)*

Murray Kempton, winner of the Polk Career Award, and Roger Rosenblatt, recipient of the award for magazine reporting, second time around for both, 1987. *(Rodney K. Hurley)*

My guest Isidor Rabi, Nobel Prize laureate, 1944, joins Ted Koppel, winner of the Polk Award for T.V. reporting, 1995. *(Offit Archives)*

Celebrating Madeleine L'Engle's wrinkle in time with Eli Wallach, Judy Blume, Madeleine, and Herb Mitgang. *(Offit Archives)*

With novelist, teacher, publisher Barry Beckham and doer of good deeds Monica Beckham, Esq. Guess whose seventieth birthday? *(Amelia V. Panico)*

My fondest memory of little-d Democrat politics with Russ Hemenway and the people's choice, Bill vanden Heuvel. *(Amelia V. Panico)*

With Avi, celebrating every day, every year, this time in London, 1988. *(Dr. William Frosch)*

Toasting a summer in Water Mill: Bob and Ina Caro with my muse and goddess, Avi, enjoying the scene. *(Offit Archives)*

Cover of our Hall of Fame issue autographed by a genuine All-Star, Walt Frazier. *(Offit Archives)*

Visiting Al Murray, great man of letters and j-a-z-z, on his ninetieth birthday, with one of his other fans, Wynton Marsalis, 2006. *(Paul Derlin)*

One man's family, courtesy of Avi. Mike, Dara Mitchell, Ken, Emily Sonnenblick, Tristan, Caroline, Anna with Lily and Wyatt. *(Offit Archives)*

A Guggenheim fellowship reception with our poet laureate Joel Conarroe, and Michael Cunningham, man of *The Hours*. *(Offit Archives)*

At the Faculty Club, Johns Hopkins University, toasting Martin Rodbell's Nobel Prize for Medicine, 1994, and sharing reverence for our fathers working the other side of the street. *(Offit Archives)*

Five former presidents of the Authors Guild, supporting a foundation benefit: Scott Turow, Erica Jong, Mary Pope Osborne, Letty Cottin Pogrebin, and Nick Taylor. *(Authors Guild Archives)*

Morley and Jane Safer with Betty Friedan (to my left) on the Roses' lawn in East Hampton, summer 1995. *(Dan Rose)*

James Stevenson, former *New Yorker* man for all seasons, and his wife, the artist Josie Merck. *(Offit Archives)*

Mary Pope Osborne, who built the Magic Tree House, with her fans Anna, Caroline, Lily, Wyatt, and Tristan Offit, 1998. *(Offit Archives)*

Sharing a half century of memories with Ed Albee, who always had it right. *(Offit Archives)*

24

Intellectual Digest: Cutting Up with Octavio
Paz, Heinrich Böll, Jorge Luis Borges,
E. B. White, and a Table of Contents

1970–1974

"Intellectual Digest," Bill Ziff, president of Ziff-Davis Publishing Company, paused, blushed with mock embarrassment, and then went on. "It's an unfortunate title but we're stuck with it."

It was December 1973, less than a month since Davis's specialty-magazine empire had bought Martin Gross's invention from Communications Research Machines, a subsidiary of Boise Cascade. I was the last of the founders remaining on the staff, and with a spontaneous blast of candor, interrupted, "It's the title that defines this magazine. No one can suggest a better title because there isn't one."

Soon after the meeting, when the young emperor who disarmingly posed as more interested in ideas than commerce entered my office, I was sure he would fire me. It would have been neither shock nor disappointment. My reluctance to accept a nine-to-five job was an ideal that had become a conceit, a self-entrapment that committed me to continue banging away at novels and books for young readers.

Martin Gross, with whom I'd connected as cochair of a program committee of the PS 6 PTA, had insisted I join his then-new venture as associate editor in the spring of 1970. I went along, persuaded by Gross's iconoclastic humor, which I found vastly entertaining, the stock he generously thrust upon me ("Five percent, ten percent, the next thing you know, bubbala, you'll be a runner-up to DeWitt Wallace . . ."), and an infatuation with cutting essays and chapters that expressed the ideas of the Western world's leading intellectuals.

The magazine had already experienced a major transformation when Gross was bought out and the "wise men" of CRM had brought in a team from *Psychology Today* in November 1971 to conduct the search committee for his successor. It seemed to me from early conversation with publisher Jim Horton that the job was mine if I wanted it. As we say in Bawlamer: I definitely "dint."

Martin Goldman, as diplomatic a gent as ever graced an editor in chief's office of a mass-market magazine, was brought in to succeed Gross. We gradually became pals. Our bonds were strong enough for Goldman to temper the Boss after my challenging remarks at the staff meeting.

Bill Ziff didn't appear much older than I, probably mid-forties. He had that plump, comfortable look of a fellow who prefers reading by candlelight to long excursions into the great outdoors. "So you really like that title?" he asked with a touch of the incredulous. "You don't find it pretentious? An oxymoron?"

I reminded him that four hundred thousand readers who responded to the various subscription promotions didn't seem to mind it. Then I said I thought it was an inspiration. "It sure made me some money when CRM bought us out, and the past three years have been more of a graduate school than a job."

Bill Ziff repeated, "Graduate school." Then he concluded, "I kinda like that."

That was the last I ever saw or heard from Bill Ziff.

In the spring of 1970, *Intellectual Digest* had debuted with a *Reader's Digest*–size cover featuring red, naked-skulled profiles of Milovan Djilas and Herbert Marcuse facing each other above the cover line WHICH PROPHECY FOR THE 1970S? The battle was waged with selections from Marcuse's *An Essay on Liberation* and Djilas's *The Imperfect Society*. Along with the political philosophers, readers who had responded to our ad in *The New York Times Book Review* and limited newsstand distribution were presented with readings from Günter Grass, Kenneth Clark, Joseph Wood Krutch, Eric Bentley, Theodore Solotaroff, and John Canaday. My contribution to the lineup had been the selection of Susan Sontag's "A Letter from Sweden" that had appeared in *Ramparts*.

In the process of making that recommendation, I was introduced to Gross's prescription for an Olympian marquee: "If the author, title, and first or last paragraphs hook you, buy it."

"The Sweden I know is first of all a place where I've been working," Susan Sontag wrote. "More than that: the place where I've been able to do something—writing and directing a movie—that has given me more pleasure than any work I've ever done. I know the work has been good not just because of my loving my relation to it but because I've done it here, in a country whose cultural policy is so generous to the independent film-maker. . . . One is simply encouraged to do one's best and left alone. . . ."

My enthusiasm for the Sontag piece also led to my first experience negotiating with a major literary person on such tender issues as modest honorariums and excerpting.

Susan Sontag couldn't have been more gracious and professional. She agreed to the terms and accepted our guarantee that she would have the final approval on any excerpt. When I told her we planned to publish her piece in two installments, if indeed we made it to the second issue, she was amused and encouraging. "I wish you luck."

With seven thousand subscribers and the sixty thousand dollars Gross had rallied from investors, there were enough bucks in the bank for the family store to publish a second issue. Paul Goodman, whom Gross and I entertained among our guests for a PS 6 discussion on trends in education, was the cover boy for the second issue, which included pieces selected from *Partisan Review, Science, Physics Today, Annals of Internal Medicine, The Paris Review,* and *The New Society.*

Goodman looked like a tired scholar on his way to or from a nap. He identified himself as a "Neolithic conservative" but presented his views with the passions of a young radical.

The cover and excerpt from Goodman's book intrigued our contributors as well as readers. When I spoke to Arthur Koestler, whom we had tracked down at an Austrian villa to check the excerpts of his essay from *Encounter,* he expressed interest in our table of contents. So, there I was on a transatlantic call probably spending more money talking with the author of *Darkness at Noon* than we were paying him for the lines from his "Literature and the Law of Diminishing Returns." Koestler's comment as I recited our roster of authors was a series of monosyllabic acknowledgments: Gore Vidal, "Yes." John Dos Passos, "So." Kate Millett, "Who?" James MacGregor Burns, "Of course." Robert A. Nisbet, "Hummph!" Michael Harrington, "Ummm?" Thomas Szasz, "Ich." But when I mentioned Paul Goodman, Arthur Koestler wanted to know the point of his piece: ". . . what he has to say."

I took my shot by quoting to Koestler from the blurb that Gross had written: "Goodman argues that mass higher education isolates the young from society and is perhaps the chief cause of alienation. . . . Goodman recommends a cutback in extended formal schooling and return to 'incidental' learning." "Again, please," came the Hungarian-British–accented voice from across the sea.

After three readings I had memorized the blurb and was prepared to condense and paraphrase, but Koestler let me off the hook with an enigmatic laugh and the comment, "What I would have expected."

Thomas Mann and Jorge Luis Borges were cover boys for other editions of the digest-size magazine, but the issue Gross declared his greatest triumph featured Aleksandr Solzhenitsyn's prose poems and his letter to the writers union of the USSR, decrying censorship and the cruel harassment of their Soviet colleagues. Celebrating his release from the Soviet labor camps, the 1970 Nobel laureate wrote of

the simple pleasure of breathing: "I cease to hear the whirring of mo-
torcycles, the bleating of radios and record-players, the tambourining
of the loudspeakers. Under an apple tree after the rain, one may
breathe again and even live a while longer."

A reissue of Gertrude Stein's portrait of Picasso provided us with
an opportunity to inform our readers of the verbal innovations of
Stein's style—conversational free-association beyond "A rose is a rose
is a rose.":

> Well then, Picasso at nineteen years of age was in Paris,
> where, except for very rare and short visits to Spain, he had
> lived all his life.
>
> He was in Paris.
>
> His friends in Paris were writers rather than painters,
> why have painters for friends, when he could paint as he
> could paint.
>
> He needed ideas, anybody does but not ideas for painting,
> no, he had to know those who were interested in ideas, but as
> to knowing how to paint he was born knowing all that.

Simone de Beauvoir on aging, Betty Friedan's critique of sexual
politics, Dwight Macdonald revisiting Dorothy Day, Robert Penn
Warren discussing poetry in a time of crack-up, and John A. Wheeler
introducing the concept of the black hole in space were among the
features of that April 1971 issue. Dwight Macdonald told me on
the phone he was not only satisfied with the excerpt of his piece but
surprised that he was so engaged by "a magazine of reprints."

On our way uptown with an armload of copies hot off the
press, Marty, his all-around partner and caretaker wife, Anita, and
I passed a tall, graceful gentleman in flaring trousers and a
broad-brimmed felt hat. I recognized Ken and Mike's favorite New
York Knick, the magical basketball guard Walter "Clyde" Frazier.
Flushed with the pride of our "classic" magazine anthology, I introduced myself and the Grosses to the prime playmaker of Madison Square Garden.

"It's our great privilege to meet you, Mr. Frazier, on this—our night of all-stars." I held up a copy of the magazine and recited the names of several of the contributors. It occurred to me in mid-list that it was likely Walt Frazier was no more aware of Aleksandr Solzhenitsyn and Gertrude Stein than Marty and Anita Gross were of Walt Frazier and Willis Reed.

Frazier accepted a copy of the magazine graciously and when Marty asked him where he was from, he responded as if it were a routine question to inquire of the Toast of New York.

"I was born in Atlanta," he replied with the notorious Frazier cool.

"I see," Marty said, and then, "So how do you like New York?"

"Good," Walt Frazier said with no sign of impatience. "Couldn't be better when we win a championship."

I had the uneasy feeling Marty might ask, "What kind of championship?" Our encounter with the NBA Olympian concluded when I interrupted to present another copy of *Intellectual Digest* to Walt Frazier with a request that he sign it to our son Michael. He did with a modest and cheerful acknowledgment that he was pleased to be in "such good company."

Although the response to our small samplings of direct-mail lists was astonishingly positive—ranging from 11 percent to 3 percent, including a 5 percent return from the members of a major credit card company—there was not sufficient capital for additional mailings. Resting near a hot dog stand on Lexington Avenue after what seemed the last interview with a reluctant investor, Gross suggested we bring franks with sauerkraut home to his wife Anita and daughters Ellen and Amy. With a fatalistic smile punctuated by mustard at the corner of his lips, he told me, "I'm down to my last buck."

Two days later, the deus ex machina arrived. John Veronis together with his partner Nick Charney had built *Psychology Today* into one of the most successful national magazines to emerge after World War II.

For something close to twenty million dollars, Veronis had sold the concept of "the invisible university" to the giant Boise Cascade Company and was looking for publishing properties that could be identified with this premise. Less than forty-eight hours after meeting Gross, Veronis, an unequivocal decision maker, plunked down the money to clear all debts, provide funds to build the subscription list, and publish.

A massive mailing went out during the summer of 1971, a mailing of such staggering volume that on one day, we were told, freight trains were backed up at the circulation station in Boulder, Colorado. When the last freight train unloaded, more than two hundred thousand readers were waiting for Volume II, Number 1.

The new owners made two decisions with which Gross had no choice but to reluctantly agree. The digest size was converted to folio size and a designer from California introduced to the magazine the quality of graphics which had contributed to the prize-winning design of *Psychology Today.*

A painting of Saul Bellow by Robert Weaver was commissioned for the cover. Bellow's "Culture Now," a rhapsodic indictment of the contamination of literature and ideas of the new left, was the featured piece. It originally appeared in Philip Rahv's *Modern Occasions,* a journal that expressed Rahv's disenchantment with what he considered the decline in taste and vitality of his former platform, *Partisan Review.*

When I discussed the Bellow piece with Rahv, he condemned the *Partisan Review,* presided over by his successor William Phillips, as "pretentious, apologetic—polemic without a consistent idea. In brief . . ." Did I hear him say "*dreck*"? Rahv, too, was skeptical when I told him our circulation was more than two hundred thousand and growing. "Dere are obviously more vould-be intellectuals den I ever met."

Bellow's piece developed the Rahv argument by attacking, among others, Leslie Fiedler, who had written, "Almost all today's readers and writers are aware that we are living through the death throes of literary modernism and the birth pangs of postmodernism."

Bellow mocked Fiedler as calling for "more obscenity, more of the manic, the mad and the savage . . . This is amusing but it is dismal, too."

Responding to Bellow's piece in our following issue, William Phillips wrote, "It is quite common today to hide one's conservative opinions behind a liberal stance, and this is what Bellow is really doing—and not just attacking me, or Susan Sontag or Leslie Fiedler." He went on to criticize Bellow's most recent novel *Mr. Sammler's Planet* as "a projection of Bellow's fear of the young, of radicals, of blacks, of the passing of those historical landmarks that made Bellow feel at home."

Later, at the PEN International Congress in Jerusalem, I walked to the Wailing Wall with Saul Bellow. He didn't seem disturbed by the Phillips rejoinder, but he mentioned that the reprint in *ID* caused a greater "stir" than its original publication in *Modern Occasions.* He offered no speculations on why this magazine was attracting such a large audience, but he prophetically mentioned that he suspected it was a "freak" and would eventually "flop." After this endearing encouragement, I changed the subject. We were walking down a steep hill and could see an assembly of bearded, orthodox "pilgrims" in yarmulkes and prayer shawls collected in front of the wall.

I glanced at Bellow, who was wearing a suit, shirt, and tie, his freshly shaven, borderline movie star good looks and scornful eyes discouraging further conversation.

I cast him in a shawl, painted on a beard and *peyes* in my fantasy to give me the spunk to try again. I mentioned as sincerely as I could the sense of history and unity with our people this experience of approaching the ancient wall evoked. "I wonder what my grandfather, my great-grandfather would have felt."

I recall Bellow mentioning that he'd visited the wall before and summarily dismissed any feelings of identity with these people. Fortunately, I neither quoted nor retold the story. Several years later, Saul Bellow published a moving account of his visit to Israel. I recommended it, but our other editor thought it "too parochial" for *Intellectual Digest.*

Although I didn't hit it off with Saul Bellow, my experiences with Octavio Paz, Heinrich Böll, E. B. White, W. H. Auden, Jorge Luis Borges, and Harry Edwards were enriched with letters, conversations, and encounters that were never less than cordial and, with Böll and Paz, fleeting friendships. When we reprinted his interview with Rita Guibert, Paz wrote to me expressing admiration for our magazine. "I like *Intellectual Digest* very much and I used to buy it every month when I was in Cambridge." The future Nobel laureate went on to discuss *Plural,* a magazine he was publishing in Mexico, and asked if from time to time "we could reprint some of the articles you have published, translated, of course, in Spanish."

I called Paz immediately after reading his letter, to assure him that the one hundred fifty dollars he mentioned as an honorarium for reprinting our stories would more than likely satisfy the holders of the copyright. He was grateful for the reassurance. We went on to discuss the growing popularity of South American writers and the responses to their novels, poems, and essays from the American literary community. "The United States is the arbiter of literary reputations at the moment," he said. "I suppose it is a corollary of economic and military power, but for how long, how long?"

It wasn't long after that conversation that I was on the phone again with my new friend. I always insisted that I call him back when he called me, so he wouldn't be responsible for the long-distance tab. It seemed to me only fair, as we were paying so little for reprint rights. Soon we were addressing each other by first names and chatting about our families and considering a time and place where we would meet.

My conversations with Heinrich Böll began in Piran, Yugoslavia, where we were delegates at a PEN congress in August 1971. While I strolled along the banks of the Adriatic with him and his wife, Böll mentioned that Anna Maria translated American writers into German. She spoke with particular admiration about the novels and stories of J. D. Salinger. Böll mentioned his high regard for the morality expressed in the work of Kurt Vonnegut.

Although their literary styles were not similar, Böll and Vonnegut were both distrustful of political leaders. As a consequence of their experiences as combat soldiers during World War II, I think it no exaggeration to consider Heinrich Böll and Kurt Vonnegut pacifists.

Sophie Wilkins translated an excerpt from Böll's address to the PEN congress in Berlin and, soon after he was awarded the Nobel Prize, Alice Fleming interviewed him for *ID*. Böll told her, "I see everything politically, even a picture." When I was checking the excerpt and interview—both of which he approved without reservation—Böll expressed gratitude to Alice's husband, Tom Fleming, one of the most versatile and prolific of American writers. (Among Tom's most recent distinctions, he has been elected president of the Society of American Historians.) Heinrich Böll considered Tom and Charles Bracelen Flood responsible for his nomination and election as president of International PEN.

But for all his success, in that last conversation with Heinrich Böll I felt as I had on other occasions when we spoke, that he endured an incurable sadness. Even when he laughed it was as if breaking through great pain. I suspect he came as close as any person I ever met to suffering for our sins.

Jorge Luis Borges was sitting with his cane on a bench in a hall of the Council for the Americas that afternoon I came uptown to Park and 68th to meet him. Frank MacShane, the chair of the Graduate Writing Program at Columbia, had introduced me to the works of the Argentine prose poet. We'd reprinted MacShane's conversation with Borges along with a selection of six of his pieces from *The New Yorker* and *Antioch Review,* and featured Borges on our cover with a portrait. But the "portrait" that trumped the issue was Borges's ode to Shakespeare translated by Norman Thomas di Giovanni in collaboration with the author. In less than six hundred words Borges sang his song and composed a startlingly vivid sketch:

> In him there was no one. Behind his face (even in the poor paintings of the period it is unlike any other) and his words (which were swarming, fanciful, and excited) there was only a touch of coldness, a dream undreamed by anyone . . .

Norman Thomas di Giovanni, his translator and friend, was by Borges's side when we met. I was aware from the MacShane interview that Borges was blind, but the distant look about his eyes seemed to be searching for a manageable expression. I introduced myself and he greeted me as a valued patron, which I wasn't, or a fan. That I certainly was.

He insisted upon being called Borges. Not an easy address to a gentleman who presented himself with such dignity—British cut, straight back, and obviously a scholar as well as artist.

We spoke much longer than I intended about my living in the neighborhood, around the corner. Borges wanted to know about our house. He asked me to describe it and responded with delight when I mentioned the brownstone stoop. Eventually I was able to plug in a question about his reading taste. He spoke in well-constructed sentences as if translating from Spanish for print. From time to time di Giovanni interrupted to answer for Borges or wrap up an observation that seemed too discursive.

Borges said he preferred the short story to the novel. When he mentioned Rudyard Kipling among the writers whose shorter works he enjoyed (James and Poe also made his list), I dared my cockney accent and recited the opening lines of "Gunga Din."

Borges urged me to go on, but I quit before turning a snippet into a performance. MacShane had written that Borges told him, "I am never bored because I am always thinking, always existing." I felt the vitality of Borges was a discipline, not a "spontaneous response to life," as MacShane described. His writings were exquisite fusions of fantasy and realistic detail, not unlike his conversations, where he was careful not to go overboard with the reckless observation or ungrammatical sentence. Our meeting concluded with Borges signing his name on a slip of paper for me to attach to a copy of one of his books. It may have been a tribute to the universality of his appeal that it disappeared from my office soon after I'd shown it off.

When I called di Giovanni to thank him for the introduction to the great man, he told me Borges had been so pleased with our meeting he would offer as a gift another of his pieces. Soon after, I received in the mail a copy of "The Disinterested Killer Bill Harrigan." "Along about 1859, the man who would become known to terror and glory as Billy the Kid was born in a cellar room of a New York tenement. . . . He never completely matched his legend, but he kept getting closer and closer to it. Something of the New York hoodlum lived in the cowboy. . . ." It appeared in our September 1972 issue with Borges's name featured on the cover bordering Susan Lombardo's photograph of a physicist amidst a maze of coils, cables, insulators, and compactors at the Princeton Plasma Physics Laboratory.

Proud of this diverse company, I promptly sent a copy off to Borges in care of di Giovanni. Less than a week later I received an irritated call from di Giovanni inquiring as to when they would receive payment. Hesitantly I confessed that I thought he'd said the Borges piece was a gift. Di Giovanni responded indignantly, "You don't consider one hundred fifty dollars for an original Jorge Luis Borges piece a gift?" The check and apology went out with our next mail.

The only complaint about payment I received during the years the magazine published was a note from Nelson Algren. An essay by the author of *The Man with the Golden Arm* that appeared in *The Critic* had been recommended by Simone de Beauvoir, when I contacted her to check quotes included in a commentary by Herbert Lottman that we reprinted.

Algren's "The Six Best Novels of World War II, and Why Five Died" generated strong reader response, not all of it favorable. Algren's list—*From Here to Eternity, The Gallery, The Naked and the Dead, All Thy Conquests, The Girl on the Via Flaminia,* and *Catch-22*—seemed "arbitrary and capricious" to apostles of other "classics" including *Slaughterhouse Five, The Young Lions, The Caine Mutiny,* and *Battle Cry.*

Algren anticipated this, and during a phone conversation after his acceptance of our excerpt, he put down his critics. "What the hell do they know? Any writer or critic worth a damn is 'arbitrary and capricious.'"

Catch-22 was the book that made Algren's cut: "The administrations of Johnson and Nixon have brought the lunatic embattlements of Milo Minderbinder into reality. To our own sad cost. The hilarity of *Catch-22* is more terrifying today than it was only a decade past."

I tried to deflect his anger at the criticism by reminding him we reprinted his piece because we thought it daring and in many ways insightful. Soon after our phone conversation I received a note addressed from 1950 Evergreen, Chicago, on a yellow second sheet: "Dear Mr. Offit," Nelson Algren wrote, "Thank you for your presentation of my 'insightful' lines. Are you making any plans to pay for them?"

Although there seemed to be high risk in cutting and editing published lines by William Styron, Barbara Tuchman, John Updike, and, lo and behold, E. B. White, we received unsolicited words of praise from each of them.

In January 1972, Bill Styron wrote, "Dear Sidney, I think the way my interview was excerpted turned out to be most intelligent and graceful and I have no criticism at all. . . ." Bill was a personal friend. His wife, Rose Burgunder Styron, was the poet laureate—local beauty queen of greater Pikesville and points north when I returned home during my college days in Baltimore. Years later, in 1977, when Avi's *The Sexual Self* was greeted with exultant reviews by *The New York Times Book Review, The New Republic,* and other publications both here and abroad, in addition to being a main selection of the Literary Guild, Bill Styron's expression of admiration in a note to me touched Avi most deeply: "I am learning a great deal from her excellent (and excellently written) book."

Martin Goldman had trepidation about touching a line of Barbara Tuchman's. He understood the author of the bestselling *The Guns of August* and *Zimmerman Telegram* was finicky about having so much as a word changed. "Many thanks for the proof . . . ," Barbara, whom I knew from the Authors Guild Council, wrote when I sent her a copy of the version of her essay we were hoping to reprint. "The excerpting is so well done I didn't miss a word."

Although the compliments were directed to me because I was the point man, I was not responsible for all the cutting and editing. During the years of *ID* Marty Gross and then Lucy Burchard, Martha

White, Harriet Shapiro, Anne Atwater, and often Martin Goldman would be responsible for clips and snips. I was impressed, however, that so often two thousand words could do justice to a four-hundred-page book, or 50 percent of a major magazine piece could wind up in the wastebasket without the author's complaint.

George Plimpton was delighted to approve our reprint agreement if E. B. White would accept our excerpt of the interview he and Frank Crowther had written for *The Paris Review*. Among the gems that survived our cut was the author of *Charlotte's Web* and *Stuart Little* reflecting on the writing of books for young readers: "Anyone who shifts gears when he writes for children is likely to wind up stripping his gears. . . . Anyone who writes down to children is simply wasting his time. You have to write up, not down. Children are demanding."

We considered not cutting a word, but we had to chisel and scrape so as not to allow too few pieces to run away with our issue. White's response to the Plimpton-Crowther question about the "present state of letters" tempted us to feature it as a continuation of the Bellow-Rhav-Phillips exchange. "Much writing today strikes me as deprecating, destructive and angry. There are good reasons for anger, and I have nothing against anger," White wrote. "But I think some writers have lost their sense of proportion, their sense of humor, and their sense of appreciation."

Before we sent the proofs I spoke to White at his home in North Brooklin, Maine. His voice suggested the quiet calm of a man just in from the fields who understood perfectly the relationship of earth and sky and a nursing cow, even to *Intellectual Digest*.

I asked him what he had been reading lately and he told me he didn't read much. I was surprised, too, by E. B. White's answer to my question as to what books he would recommend to writing students (Strunk and White's *Elements of Style* was the rage). The grand master said quietly, "I'm not so sure any book or books are necessarily a help to a writer trying to find his way. Reading a good book may be intimidating."

White returned the proofs of our excerpt, correcting several typos and concluding with a note: "I think you've done a good job of excerpting, and it is acceptable to me as it stands, with corrections as indicated." The White endorsement circulated around the office, generating the pride of winning a Pulitzer Prize for excerpting.

Less than a year later I received from White a souvenir of my years with *ID*. It was a clip of a paragraph from the editor's column that Martin Goldman had written: "If *ID* often speaks with seriousness, and it does and will, that seriousness should not be confused with the verbal tonnage that serves as a mock-up of thought. We may ask in glum accents, *'Quo Vadimus?'* But if we have a saving grace, we'll not forget the rest of Robert Benchley's old title, 'Or the Case for the Bicycle.' "

White had pasted the clip to a blank sheet of paper. Under it he typed, "Better to speak with accuracy than seriousness." He identified the title, author, publisher, and year of publication (1939) and then scribbled a note to me: "I love Benchley, but he didn't write *Quo Vadimus*. I did—for better or for worse."

John Updike appeared in so many issues of *ID* that I became familiar with his family routine in Ipswich, Massachusetts. When Updike generously contributed an essay, "Laughter in the Shell of Safety," to *The American PEN,* I read it with admiration for his erudition—Cervantes, Shakespeare, Rabelais, Twain, Waugh—and his bold and ingenious effort to analyze what makes us laugh. PEN waived the reprint rights and we welcomed the opportunity to work it out with the author.

We were doubly rewarded for the "find." Updike accepted our excerpt, writing: "I think you've done a terrific job condensing this. I guess because you do it all the time. I enjoyed seeing myself in the old *ID,* and read Saul Bellow with fascination in the new one." He went on to answer my question as to why six o'clock was always the best hour to call him. "We generally eat around six-thirty; we feel we should eat with the children until they finally reject us. Also, my wife only cooks one meal that way."

I was so impressed, Avi and I wanted to take a shot at the early-dinner routine with Ken and Mike. But Avi cooked for the week on

Sundays and I made hamburgers and steaks between her stews and roast chickens. We had widely divergent schedules. We didn't all live quite as together as the Updike family at 50 Labor-in-Vain Road.

Seeking her approval for the reprinting of her poetry, I couldn't get off the phone with Anne Sexton. She spoke with the intensity of a poet on a break expecting to live a novel. She had already won the Pulitzer Prize when we reprinted selections from *Transformations*. Kurt Vonnegut had written in the introduction: "Anne Sexton domesticates my terror, examines it and describes it, teaches it some tricks which will amuse me, then lets it gallop wild in my forest once more. . . ."

I appreciated her transformation of *Grimm's Fairy-Tales* into myths that we celebrated as "round with wonder," but during our phone talk I admitted I was not consumed with terror and tried to explain why I so often found life "a breeze." Anne Sexton said that didn't sound at all like a person who would be editing a magazine called *Intellectual Digest.* She wanted to know where I thought my good spirits came from.

We went on like that until I'd told her about my parents, my wife, my children. There was not much action from the other end of the line except for Sexton's urging me to tell her more. I tried some lines from her poems to change the subject, "I must not sleep / for while asleep I'm ninety / and think I'm dying." I asked her why she thought she felt so glum. It was the only sound resembling a laugh I heard from her. She suggested we meet and she would tell me all about it.

I didn't meet Anne Sexton, but when I read a year or so after we spoke about her death by suicide I regretted that I hadn't followed up on her invitation. Not that I consider myself a tonic for despair, but it may be a great flaw in my optimism that conceals from me the powerful hopelessness that leads to the suicides of so many talented people I've known.

ID didn't publish W. H. Auden but he held our record for near misses. I spoke to him to unravel a complex attribution to him and his companion Chester Kallman of thoughts expressed in an article we hoped to reprint. After our conversation, Auden sent me a note confirming why he couldn't grant permission. "I'm afraid M Kallman and I cannot give permission to quote from M Nabokov's article. It so happens that every single quotation he makes from the text as attributed to me were written by M Kallman."

During our conversation I told Auden about my encounter with Robert Frost so many years ago. Auden admired Frost and enjoyed the tale of Frost as matchmaker. He mentioned a poem of his that was soon to be published in *The Times Literary Supplement.* Without saying so directly, this tip seemed to be my reward for the Frost story. I followed through with hopes of first American reprint rights to a poem by the bard considered the greatest of twentieth-century British masters.

In March 1973, I wrote to Auden at Christ Church College, England, where he was then in residence. We offered twenty-five dollars for "Unpredictable but Providential." It turned out our offer was neither. "Sorry, you can't," Auden wrote back. "It's appearing in *The New Yorker.*"

Dr. Harry Edwards's contributions to *ID* were so frequent that he and I engaged in a long correspondence. The inspiration for the black athletes' demonstration at the 1968 Olympics, Harry Edwards had written a smoldering essay, "The Myth of the Racially Superior Athlete," for *The Black Scholar.* He argued that "Praise for the black athlete's natural speed or power is the white way of implying he is not there from the neck up. Blacks are channeled into the one or two endeavors that are open to them—sports or entertainment."

It was Edwards, too, who identified sport as an American religion. He supported his thesis by citing the rituals—Sunday games religiously attended, stadiums as temples of worship, and devotion to sports heroes as "saints."

Ernest Hemingway didn't appear in *Intellectual Digest,* but I did receive a warm note from his widow, Mary, when I met her at a party honoring another *ID* contributor whom we both considered one of the greats of

American letters, Albert Murray. "You renew my faith in man's word, as well as coatroom promises," Mary Hemingway wrote. "The trouble with your magazine is I feel it compels one to read it, with all those fascinating concepts lying there ready to bite you on the nose."

Bill Ziff abruptly closed our shop after the June 1974 issue, citing increased paper costs, rising mail rates, and sluggish renewals. A number of contributors, writers, and editors wrote touching condolence notes or called. I never got past remembering Saul Bellow's grim prophecy that the venture was doomed during our walk to the Wailing Wall in Jerusalem.

25

Writing Workshops, Greenwich Village, with a Pulitzer Laureate, a Tenured Brown Professor, the Coauthor of *Animal House,* and Anatole Broyard

1965–2007

When I walked into the classroom to conduct my first writing workshop at the New School in the fall of 1965, I suspected the robust gent sitting in the back of the room was Ernest Hemingway, the fellow stroking his gray mustache was William Faulkner, and the pale, intense lady by the window was Virginia Woolf. What could I teach them? Could fiction writing be taught? I'd applied for jobs teaching at a half dozen New York colleges and universities with the hope I could earn a few bucks to help keep our home fires burning. And there I was facing an evening class of such diversity it would satisfy a casting director's fantasy.

Fortunately, I had a lesson plan. From my years at military school and as a sometime instructor in the U.S. Army, I'd learned the recipe for value received in a classroom: "Tell them what you're going to tell them. Tell it to them. Tell them what you've told them."

(At Johns Hopkins University, where our professors—scholars granting gifts to undergraduates—passed along their lessons in erudite and occasionally witty monologues, there was style to which to aspire but rarely coherent design.)

So I told them that before we read and responded to students' work in class, we would be discussing and writing brief exercises in aspects of the craft: style, viewpoint (what is the story about?), dramatization, point of view (who tells the story), characterization.

The early weeks were relatively easygoing, with references to E. M. Forster's *Aspects of the Novel,* Hermann Hesse's autobiography, Arthur Quiller-Couch's lectures, and readings from Jane Austen, Gertrude Stein, Jonathan Swift, F. Scott Fitzgerald, and John O'Hara. As an introduction to the craft of the humor story, I've shared with the class the delights and lessons of Calvin Trillin's "Roland Magruder, Freelance Writer," an addiction since I read it in *The New Yorker,* August 14, 1965:

> "What kind of freelance writer?" asked Marlene.
>
> "A sign writer."
>
> "A sign painter?"
>
> "No," said Magruder. "I write signs. Cities retain me to write signs on a freelance basis. I specialize in traffic work. 'Yield Right of Way' is a good example."

Then came the challenge of commenting on students' papers. Early on I hadn't understood that it was necessary to let the class know right out of the box that comments would be related to the work submitted—only! There would be no career guidance, no evaluations from me in response to "Do you think I have talent . . . Am I wasting my time?" But before I knew better, I got off lightly and beat the odds with the first student to whom I offered a career tip.

"If you're willing to take the risk, take it now," I advised Stephen Dunn. "I'm impressed by your gifts for language, your lyrical phrasing . . ." After he'd published eleven collections of poetry and been awarded the Pulitzer Prize for *Different Hours,* Steve Dunn told me my precocious words had been among his considerations when he quit his job and took off for Spain to follow his muse.

Before he became a frequently published poet I was so impressed with Steve Dunn's talent I saved a letter he wrote to me in October 1974 requesting a recommendation for graduate school. "The decision to go to Graduate School to obtain a Creative Writing Masters degree is a late one for me. I'm twenty-eight. Naturally, therefore, it is fairly well thought out and reflects a certain seriousness on my part . . . Recently I've had two poems published by *The Atlantic Monthly*." I was honored to write in support of Steve and scribbled a note at the bottom of the page of his letter to me: "Remember Steve Dunn? Of course. Graceful stylist. . . . No show-off. Perhaps more poet than novelist. . . . This kid could go all the way."

In his poem "Art," where he writes about listening to Callas singing Puccini on his car's boom box as he drives to pick up his wife at the airport, Dunn confesses, "I didn't want to move." He goes on to speculate on the nature of artists' relationships to their art.

> *Was Puccini ever taken from such a moment?*
> *Was Callas? They must have been, of course.*
> *And couldn't bear it. Or ranted anyway*
> *because they were brilliantly selfish,*
> *or what involved them just then*
> *was magical, in a sense their lives,*
> *a virtuosity that shouldn't be disturbed.*

I contributed nothing to Steve Dunn's creation of those lines or any other aspect of his craft. Yet, as is often the case, the only assistance a writing teacher provides for the best of students is encouragement.

When Barry Beckham joined my workshop at New York University, I was already teaching four courses a week as an adjunct, hustling around the Village from East 12th Street (the New School), to Washington Square where under the long shadow of the arch and a

Henry James town house, I met with students in the NYU Continuing Ed program.

Warren Bower, who seemed to walk off the pages of a James novel—good manners, cultivated diction, very well read, read, read—hired me for four hundred fifty dollars. I signed up immediately, thinking it an excellent fee for each two-hour class and very considerate of all the time required for reading students' work. It turned out to be the gross for twelve two-hour sessions, my introduction to the exploitive wages for adjuncts, identified as "honorariums."

Barry Beckham was on the rise at Chase Manhattan Bank when he handed in the first chapter of his novel *My Main Mother*. I knew from the bios students submitted after the first session that Barry was a graduate of Brown University, and I could detect from the breezy manner in which he summarized his childhood in Atlantic City and assignments at Chase that he possessed that rarity—a style of his own.

"So it's almost time," began the first paragraph of *My Main Mother*. "I've been coming here for several days to proof-read my history I started writing almost a month ago, and tonight I should finish it off. Tonight should be my last night in this old, wooden station wagon ensconced in the Maine woodlands," the narration continues, and then in the third paragraph comes the stinger: "Listen this old Ford wagon was presented to me by my late Uncle Melvin, who died before I killed my mother. Good-doing, wine drinking, pipe smoking Uncle Melvin knew that no one else could possibly love the old Ford more than I."

It was the 1960s and in addition to Arthur Fields and John Pope, who published my novels, I was acquainted with a half dozen editors who were members of PEN. Impressed by Barry's first chapter, I told him that after he completed three chapters and an outline, if we thought it was ready, I'd ask an editor friend to take a look. The following week Barry approached me at the end of class. He was holding in his hand an envelope with the Chase logo, stuffed with his chapters and outline.

Ed Burlingame, the editor in chief at Walker and Company, had only two questions for me after he read Barry's chapters: "Is he temperamental? Difficult to work with?" My answer to Ed was: "You're going to like Barry Beckham so much you're going to want to take him home to meet your wife and children." Ed did and so did I.

When *My Main Mother* was published, *The New York Times* raved, "The scenes of Harlem, of how it feels to be an aged black from Maine getting a flat tire in Times Square, of encountering a homosexual in the Village, of street gangs and boarding houses, of the ironies of racism are fantastically vivid and compelling. . . . Barry Beckham may well become one of the best American novelists of the decade."

Barry went on to publish other novels and nonfiction. He quit Chase, accepted an appointment to teach at Brown University's Writing Program, and is the only person I've ever known who gave up tenure. He decided it was time he made a contribution to an African-American university. For several years Barry taught at Hampton and then took off on his own to publish *The Black Students' Guide to American Colleges,* which eventually led to his very own independent publishing company.

Through all these years Barry Beckham has been among my best friends. He was "host" to our son Mike when Mike attended Brown. When I was stuck for a writer to contribute an essay on an African tapestry for *Intellectual Digest,* Barry did the quick study and came through with a prose poem. He and his vivacious wife, Monica, are always in touch, and Barry and I over the past decade have fallen into a routine of weekly telephone performances. Like James Stevenson, he is a friend whom I discovered has such a talent for other voices, he can leave a message on my answering machine that could get me in lots of trouble if I mistake the mimicry and respond to the original. Barry drove me to the telephone directory to contact a Nigerian dissident whom he so masterly created that I was actually convinced a desperate prisoner in a cell in Niamey had tracked my telephone number from PEN and was appealing to me to secure his hidden fortune. Fortunately, by the time my messages were returned the telephone Academy Award performer had been identified.

Ezra John Keats was already a bestselling author-illustrator of books for young readers when he popped up in my fiction-writing class. *A Snowy Day* was a children's classic and Keats's other books all had vibrant sales and were in print. About five-eight, with mustache and eyes

so alert they seemed on the verge of a major discovery or wary of disappointment, he was unabashed in his aspiration to write adult fiction.

"I signed up for your class after I read your Catskill novel and
then a book for juveniles that Paul Galdone illustrated. It seems to
me you've done both, so maybe you can help me."

I was flattered but uneasy. The texts for picture books, when
well done, are much like poetry—spare sentences composed with a
jeweler's patience and precision. Often the illustrations create the
mood, the tone, and even the progression of the narrative. There are
writers who have succeeded in both genres—Jules Feiffer and James
Stevenson—but masters of abbreviated prose composition are usually too self-critical to write a novel. I suspected Ezra John Keats had
that disposition.

He had written in his bio for the class that he was told he had
started to draw at the age of four. He went on to tell me, "In our
household, where I rarely heard a kind word, my presence was acknowledged through my drawings. I drew on everything I could
find—paper bags, the enamel kitchen tabletop, on the sidewalk,
scraps of wood, and I colored-in the pictures in newspapers."

During the semester, he submitted several pages that he was considering as the beginning of his novel. They were so reminiscent of
the bio pages I'd read earlier, I encouraged him to write on. "Get it
down and worry about cutting and editing later."

I was right and I was wrong. Jack Keats invited me to join him
for lunch at the Society of Illustrators where, after a second glass of
wine, he told me the story he hoped to write was about his troubled
childhood and the influence it had on his work as a writer and illustrator. But I was wrong to think he could just "blurt it all down." He
told me, "I can't proceed to the next word, the next line, unless I'm
convinced that what I've written is as good as I can write it."

During lunch I had the suspicion that Jack Keats didn't often
have such intimate conversations. I offered to read anything he wrote
even after the semester was over. I was startled when as soon as I'd
made that offer, Keats, a man as fastidious in dress and manner as he
was on the page, brushed against his wineglass and spilled the liquid
over a new camel hair coat he'd carefully folded and placed on the
chair beside him. Neither of us spoke of it as symbol or prophecy.

Several years later Ezra John Keats died. I was invited to speak at a memorial service conducted at a branch library to share memories with an assembly of young readers and fans.

An attractive young lady who seemed to have a strong, intimate attachment to Keats extended the invitation with the acknowledgment that she knew I'd been a good friend. I was touched by the coincidence of his playing out, through his early death, the name he had selected as his own. (John Keats the poet had died even younger.) I was inspired, too, by the audience of vibrant children gathered to celebrate the works of a man who had told me so vividly of the distresses of his own childhood.

I offered this perception on the English poet's work as a reflection on the achievements of Ezra John Keats as an artist. "From the memories of his own pain he was able to evoke buoyant, vivid images and stories to delight and entertain." I went on to tell the young audience, most of whom seemed fascinated by the contradictions between life and work, how often this is true of the creators of the arts we admire—painting and music as well as literature.

I left the library feeling pleased I had paid thoughtful and true respect. Several days later I received a letter from the hostess, excoriating me for totally misrepresenting Jack. He was a happy, joyful man, always aware of beauty, she wrote. She was offended that I had so blatantly misread him and surprised and disappointed that he, who was so unerring in his evaluations of people, had been wrong about me.

I rarely met off-campus with writing students to discuss their projects. "I tend to be more honest in public," I confessed to my classes early in the semester. "One-to-one, all my instincts are to be reassuring, encouraging. I feel reluctant to predict negative odds when I, myself, have been so willing to live the long shot." Marita Golden wouldn't accept a blush and self-effacement.

In her introductory bio Marita (then Bernette) had written, "Even in elementary school I found the heavy, musty silence and book-lined walls of libraries appealing, and often more than after school games. While I often wondered at the absence of my own image in the books

I read in school, and on my own, I will admit I was a fool for *Winnie-the-Pooh,* and addicted to teenage mysteries."

The pages of a novel she submitted during the workshop impressed me by her engagement with her subject: the troubles of talented, attractive black women in gaining the respect of men for their ambitions and feelings.

Although the characters and situations were vivid and seemed authentic, Marita was struggling with the story line. She kept in touch after the semester concluded and invited me to join her for coffee—"not a drink, coffee!"—to discuss the latest development in her life. The latest development turned out to be her marriage to an African that led to her moving to Nigeria.

Her adventures and realizations while serving as a housewife in a traditional African family eventually led to *Migrations of the Heart,* a personal odyssey. I encouraged Marita to write it, but it was Alice Walker who most succinctly described the achievement: *"Migrations of the Heart* challenges some of the myths (about race, sex, and class) that have kept black women committed to dreams that can never come true—in the world we have today . . . It is a book all women will find useful and compelling and all men who love women will find disturbing, painful and instructive."

With her career launched, Marita went on to complete the novel she had begun in our workshop and later to publish fiction and nonfiction. Her crowning achievement has been the founding of the Hurston-Wright Foundation, an organization devoted to the discovery and encouragement of African-American literary talents.

When I joined the guests at the Poets & Writers awards celebration to acknowledge Marita Golden's unique contribution to writers and writing, I was surprised that she mentioned my name. As always she had it just right. No accolades for what I'd "taught her," just to the point: "Sidney was so encouraging and convincingly confident I had something to say."

I followed Avi from the kitchen to the bedroom, reading aloud from the story Patricia Volk submitted to our New School writing workshop. It made me laugh. It made Avi laugh. Our laughter had "build."

My sister Sukey calls to tell me You don't sound so good.

I tell her I've been carrying around a prescription for Prozac for two weeks.

"I once carried around a prescription for Clomid for a year," she says.

"The stuff they put in pools?"

"That's good," Sukey says. Her laugh has no build. Neither has mine . . .

In all the years I taught, not more than a half dozen times did I pass a story along to Avi and only Patricia Volk's humor dared me to read aloud. Again, the gratitude far exceeded my contribution to the "student's" writing career.

Patricia Volk's collection of short stories *All It Takes* was published by Atheneum. The jewel of her career appeared in the fall of 2001: *Stuffed, Adventures of a Restaurant Family.* When I received bound galleys from Patty's editor at Knopf, I read it in one sitting and was convinced my former student had done for Mattie's chocolate cake what Marcel Proust did for the madeleine. I was impressed, too, by Patty's modesty. How could she have resisted telling everyone she ever met that her great-grandfather Sussman Volk was responsible for introducing pastrami to the United States?

This time I didn't read aloud. I passed the copy along to Avi and made sure everyone from my mother-in-law to distant cousins in Texas shared this recipe for laughter on seeded rye.

Gurcharan Das had graduated from Harvard and the Harvard Business School when he dropped by my writing workshop. A small man of regal bearing with eyes so warm and inquisitive it was not immediately obvious he knew most of the answers. Mr. Das wrote little fiction during our semester together. He did pass along a copy of a play in progress. I recognized that there was no smash hit in the works but the characters were exquisitely realized and the theme an arresting probe of ideas east and west. At the end of the semester Mr. Das called to request a visit. He had already written a glowing report on the class that he sent unsolicited to the dean, who forwarded a copy to me.

"You are welcome to visit, Mr. Das." And so Gurcharan Das arrived with one of the two gifts from a student other than books that I've received in all these many years. And what a gift it was—is! A hand-embroidered, jeweled and dressed, two-foot-high elephant. It has grazed by our fireplace, certainly not looking for a place to die, entertaining children and grandchildren ever since.

Gurcharan visited to tell me of his plans to return to India and combine a career as businessman with his part-time writing. He succeeded at both. After a run as CEO of Procter & Gamble India, he became a venture capitalist and consultant to business and government leaders in his native land. He also contributed columns to the *Times of India* and wrote two more plays and a novel.

We met again in New York many years after the gift of the elephant. I was invited to attend a book party to launch Knopf's publication of *India Unbound: A Personal Account of a Social and Economic Revolution from Independence to the Global Information Age.* Gurcharan presented a copy to me with an inscription: "For my guru Sidney with fond regards—you got me started."

I didn't read chapters aloud to Avi, but she was intrigued by the suggestion that I knew anything at all about Procter & Gamble or advising the business community of India.

It was the early 1970s, a period of flamboyant costumes, iconoclastic prose, and no-taking-teachers-wisdom-for-granted. Hayes Jacobs, the Grand Sachem of the New School writing program, had pulled out the stops on attendance. There were fifty students in my Wednesday evening fiction class, and thirty-five composing memoirs, biographies, histories, and essays for the Tuesday morning nonfiction session.

By the time Chris Miller arrived, I thought I'd read and seen them all: gents in Nehru jackets and bell-bottom pants, tattoos and nose rings. Ladies bouncing and sashaying. Gray, blond, brown, red, orange, purple, and green hair. Chris Miller looked like a kid who dropped by while making a pit stop. A helmet was flung over his arm and he moved with the confidence of a fellow accustomed to flashing around town on a motorcycle with a voluptuous belle hugging fast to his waist.

I was aware of him but didn't identify Chris Miller with the story he wrote until I returned it to him after class. It was a piece of satiric pornography—obscene, but textured with humor that occasionally erupted into scenes of Rabelaisian farce. His attitude when he approached the desk was expressed in a half-cocky, half-defiant smile. "Okay, so I'm not Jonathan Swift or Oscar Wilde. Wanna make something of it?"

Miller seemed surprised when I told him how impressed I was. But I had a suggestion. "Consider stronger characterization and a developing narrative. Don't squander your talent on a limited genre." I didn't have to go into details. Miller seemed to know instantly what I meant and how to do it. At the time he was writing for the *National Lampoon*. Several years after we met I was invited to the screening and reception of their film *Animal House*. I brought my son Mike along so he would have some evidence that his old man wasn't a complete square. Chris Miller greeted us with warmth and gratitude. There I was, thanks to my New School experience, standing not with Ernest Hemingway, William Faulkner, or Virginia Woolf, but with Chris Miller, coauthor of what was to become one of the most influential movies of the decade and, what's more, he introduced us to John Belushi.

St. Martin's Press held a party at Sardi's in 1969 on the publication day of Edward G. Williams's young adult novel *Not Like Niggers*. A moving tale of a Negro family living in a small southern town during the Depression, the novel explored the complexity of satisfying the mother's aspirations to achieve middle-class status. The driving premise of her ambition was based on her acceptance of white society's attitude toward Negroes, particularly the ultimate insult "nigger."

Ed Williams, a brown-skinned, charming, understated, and good-looking young author, satisfied his fictional mother's aspirations. His novel so impressed Norma Jean Sawicki, the editor, that she had hopes it would be a prizewinner and perhaps, eventually, a classic.

It was not coincidence that in less than a decade four of the published novels by students in my writing classes were written by African-Americans, including Ed. During that period a dozen blacks attended my oversubscribed workshops. Each and every one had something to say. Unlike the other students who so often were playing with their gifts for language or flirting with a fantasy, Beckham, Golden, Williams, and Blyden Jackson had a story, a passion driving their prose. Publishers were responding to their talents because a great new market was opening up—and they (the publishers) were trying to make up for lost time.

The reviews of Ed's novel were positive until the Sunday before the Sardi's blast. A prominent African-American critic wrote a searing indictment in *The New York Times Book Review* declaring *Not Like Niggers* represented the most self-conscious, self-hating, and least productive responses to racism.

Ed had mentioned me in his dedication, and soon after publication I shared the comeuppance. At a party at John A. Williams's house I was introduced by the host, the author of *The Man Who Cried I Am,* to John Oliver Killens, a novelist and founder of the Harlem Writers Workshop. I recognized Killens from PEN receptions, but I had obviously made a negative impression. "So you are Sidney Offit," he said in a voice so musical yet ripe with controlled anger I thought he was going to launch a Shakespearean soliloquy.

"I think you should know, Sidney Offit, I do not approve nor applaud what you are doing. The gratitude expressed to you by my brothers is disservice to our independence and dignity. 'The good-doing . . . the encouraging Sidney Offit.' No thank you, Massa. We do not need your solicitations—at all!"

John Williams put his arm around my shoulder and led me to other guests with the gentle disclaimer: "Never mind John, he has his ways."

Other reviews were more generous to Ed Williams, but the library sales crucial to the success of a young adult novel were severely reduced by the *Times* review. The publisher's return was so disappointing, Ed received little support for a second novel. He went on to write plays and eventually moved to Norfolk, Virginia, to found the ZWG Repertory Theater, dedicated to defining excellence in black theater.

Although I considered him a master of narrative fiction who integrated important social issues, John A. Williams continued to be underrated and underpraised. I never read a novel by John Oliver Killens, but I did manage to stay out of his way.

My colleagues at the New School and NYU's Continuing Ed writing programs were as diverse and talented as the students.

The year I started at NYU, Sloan Wilson, the bestselling author of *The Man in the Gray Flannel Suit,* told me, "I'm wrapping it up. Teaching takes too much psychic time and provides an excuse for not working on my own novel."

Walter Miller, the poet, critic, veteran of the Lincoln Brigade, was close to rhapsodic about the experience. He expressed his pleasure by not only enlightening and entertaining thousands of students but eventually marrying more than one of them.

At the New School during my early years, I met LeRoi Jones, who was booked in the catalogue under "Introduction to Writing, Tuesdays 3:00–4:40 P.M." We met once briefly and his advice was, "Don't take it too seriously. There's as much fantasy going on here as writing." Years later, after he'd changed his name to Imamu Amiri Baraka and become famous as poet, playwright, and political activist, when I reminded him of this early meeting he remembered me only as the liberal who debated Martin Abend on Channel 5, but concluded pleasantly, "Could be."

Seymour Epstein, Richard Brickner, Ismith Kahn, Bernice Kavinoky, Alice Morris, Kenneth Koch, Robert Phelps, David Ignatow, and José Garcia Villa were all featured on the Hayes Jacobs productions bill, but it was Marguerite Young with whom I experienced a party

time. *Miss MacIntosh, My Darling,* Marguerite's novel, was identified in
the faculty directory as "epic" and clues to her approach to teaching
could be found there, too. When I encountered students whose indifference to plot didn't seem to be compensated for by lyrical prose, I
suggested they transfer to Marguerite's class. With nary an exception,
each and every one returned to express gratitude for the introduction to
this "brilliant woman." My relationship with Marguerite was right out
of *Tristram Shandy.* I don't think in all the years we met, always cordially and sometimes with affection, she or I ever understood what the
other was talking about.

Bill Packard looked like Orson Welles with a beard, and his voice
had just as much resonance. A poet and founder of *New York Quar-
terly,* Bill and I both played the boards at NYU and the New School.
I sat in on one of Bill's classes. It was an impressive hour—filled with
appreciative responses to students' poems that didn't compromise his
criticisms.

Another of the writing workshop's superstars, Anatole Broyard,
picked me up the Wednesday evening I checked in for a cancelled
class. He told me the course descriptions we wrote were advertising
copy. "You have to hook the Kathleen Winsors right along with the
Mary McCarthys and Edith Whartons." We sat on a bench in the
courtyard between 12th and 13th Streets, and he helped me compose
the paragraph that filled the house for more than thirty years.

Anatole was the Village version of the Renaissance man. His
good looks qualified for the profile of the emperor on an ancient Roman coin and his voice was ripe for a lead role with the Actors Studio.
Anatole's dance steps—later immortalized in his daughter Bliss's
short story—were variations of Fred Astaire by Bojangles.

Kafka, Joyce, Sartre, Wittgenstein, Delmore Schwartz, and Dylan Thomas punctuated Anatole's sentences along with parenthetical
references to Freud, Jung, Eric Fromm, Karen Horney, and always
Broyard's favorite jazz impresarios. He carried a gym bag and often
seemed on his way to Stillman's Gym if not Madison Square Garden
for a welterweight title defense. I was impressed, too, by Anatole's

confidence that his occasional short stories were credential enough to conduct a fiction workshop.

When we discussed New School faculty as "working writers" Anatole told me, "Once you're published, that's 'working.' From there on in you're accepted as banging away at the next novel." My conversations with him were always student (me) to Aristotle (Anatole). I appreciated our encounters as among the joys of teaching at the New School during the '60s and '70s.

Our roles were momentarily reversed when I joined Martin Gross to visit the Wunderman advertising agency we were considering for the *Intellectual Digest* account. Anatole was less surprised to see me than I was to realize that this literary raconteur, bard of the postwar Village, earned his baguettes and café noir by copywriting. I reassured Marty we could do no better unless Thomas Carlyle or Mark Twain were moonlighting as advertising flacks.

Anatole made no secret of his New Orleans origins, and I suspected he was a Creole. I never thought about it until Henry Louis Gates Jr. wrote a vivid profile of Anatole Broyard for *The New Yorker.* That was after Anatole's run as book critic for the *Times* and his becoming a recognized name in the New York literary world. (Recently, Bliss wrote a probing and moving account of Broyard family history, *One Drop,* and I realized I had been unaware of the complexity of Anatole's racial identity.)

My association with *Intellectual Digest* may have impressed him, but he made no mention. However, when he ran into me once on Fifth Avenue with Albert Murray, Anatole called me at home that evening. He was intrigued by my obvious friendship with Al who, among other talents, possessed those of a jazz critic and historian.

Anatole wanted to know what Al and I talked about. There was no misreading the message: He thought it unlikely I was in a class with Albert Murray as a jazz commentator. He was right—Al and I were members of a midtown club where we met, often twice a week, for lunch. Our conversations were about books and politics, friends and gossip. As close as I ever came to discussing jazz with Al Murray was our talk about our mutual friend John Hammond, of whom Al said, "John thinks he discovered jazz." I didn't tell Anatole any of this. I managed to squeak through the interrogation, leaving the impression that there was a side of me—the downbeat Sidney—that only Al Murray tapped.

By the twenty-first century, I had departed NYU. My best friend at the New School then was Peter Sourian, novelist (*Miri, The Best and Worst of Times, The Gate*), critic, essayist (*At the French Embassy in Sofia*), teacher, and also my neighbor on East 70th Street.

Peter, his wife, Ev, and their son and daughter, Mark and Delphine, were pals from East 70th to West 12th Street. I rarely missed classes at the New School, but when I did in the '80s and '90s, Peter was a star pinch hitter. One session with Peter Sourian and my fiction-writing students were considering joining his classes at Bard College or petitioning for acceptance to his workshop at the New School for the next semester.

Robert Polito succeeded Hayes Jacobs as head of the Writing Department at the New School in 1996. A poet and prizewinning biographer of Jim Thompson, the noir novelist, Bob Polito launched a thriving Graduate Writing Program on West 12th Street and restructured the workshops so classes rarely exceeded fifteen students and the honorariums could actually be considered part-time "salaries."

With an unerring eye for talent and an administrator's "art," Polito extended the New School writing programs beyond classrooms to a theater for sharing ideas and developments in the literary craft. For that growing constituency of writers young but mostly old who are tempted if not obsessed with writing a memoir, the maestro frequently signed up William Zinsser, the saint of the genre, who moved on from his classic *On Writing Well* to compose the scriptures for *Inventing the Truth* and *Writing About Your Life, A Journey Into the Past.*

Conflicting schedules and my increasing engagements with other activities persuaded me to retire from participation in the NYU General

Studies Program. Once I departed NYU—with silence, no tears—Lewis Frumkes invited me to conduct seminars and teach at Marymount Manhattan, around the corner from our digs on East 69th Street. Lewis, whose writing credentials include several bestselling humor books, is the Fred Allen of that highly competitive genre—the invitation to leave a self-composed message on the telephone answering machine. Example: "After the tone please leave your name, phone number, and the meaning of life as you understand it."

The Marymount all-day writers' conferences that Lewis founded and administers plays to full houses and attracts a billboard of novelists, essayists, critics, biographers, and poets that I frequently regard as a family reunion. Among the old friends with whom I've shared tips and chats at various seminars have been Gay Talese, Patricia Volk, Christopher Lehmann-Haupt, Katherine Mosby, and Daphne Merkin. I was introduced to Susan Orlean the year *The Orchid Thief* was published and recall her saying she didn't rely much on research before satisfying her curiosity in pursuit of a story. On the other side of that "insider's advice" was Debby Applegate, as charming and enlightening a biographer as ever won a Pulitzer Prize (2007 for *The Most Famous Man in America*). At our recent seminar on memoir and biography, she informed the standing-room-only crowd that a writer could never do too much research. The contrast of those approaches may be a guide as to the distinctions between feature writer–reporter and definitive biographer.

As my years pass, I'm reminded often of other former students who went on to publication. They call and write and sometimes acknowledge me with the classic "I betcha don't remember who I am?" Among the published writers I recall, like Mr. Chips as they pass in my fantasy alumni day, are Paul Guernsey and Joe Barbato, Katherine Weber and Sandra Rosenberg, Blyden Jackson and Howard Russell, Ann Jones and Leslie Li, Richard Basini and Tim McClaughlin, Roger Donoghue, Haley Hach and Charles Brush, Astasios Aslanis and Eliot Schrefer, Judith Peck, Peter Siris and Reba Williams, and Esther Benson, David Schiff and Lou Myers, Becket Roset and Charlene Choi!

Perhaps the most challenging and in many ways meaningful reaction to my class was expressed by a gentleman, vaguely familiar,
who approached me at the El Greco exhibition at the Met. Gray-haired,
with sharply defined features and posture so upright my first suspicion was I'd met him at military school, he introduced himself as a
former student. "I'll always be indebted to you, Mr. Offit," he said. "I
took your course years and years ago when I was obsessed with writing a novel. I gave up weekends, holidays, was on the verge of wreck-
ing my marriage, even leaving my job. You cured me."

He never wrote again, but I hope my class made him a more
appreciative reader.

Another chance "reunion" with a former writing student was a Hampton scene—a benefit under a tent on a grand estate to raise money for
Hampton Shorts, the magazine founded by Barbara Stone, who had
participated in one of my New School writing classes. A constellation
of local literary stars, including Kurt Vonnegut, Robert Caro, Molly
Haskell, Andrew Sarris, Marshall Brickman, James Salter, Bruce Jay
Friedman, Daniel Stern, Robert Phillips, Toby Talbot, and Judith
Rossner, contributed to the pages of the journal and rallied for its
continuing publication.

Edward Albee, an early settler in Montauk and the most distinguished of contemporary American playwrights, was there, too, to
lend generous support to this long-shot literary venture.

I had met Ed sixty years ago during his one unhappy year at the
Valley Forge Military Academy. At our occasional encounters over the
decades I'd been impressed by Edward's early insights into the motivation and sexual taste of several of our faculty heroes. We'd given up
that grim nostalgia years ago when Ed told me he'd had enough of
the discussion and didn't want to think anymore about his Valley
Forge year.

Although I didn't regard Edward Albee as intimate family, I did
think of him as a second cousin, related by our mutual adolescent
responses and by affinities for PEN, the Authors and Dramatists
Guilds, and other literary ventures for good deeds.

At the benefit, I was engaged in an "I bet you don't remember who I am?" quiz with what turned out to be another former writing student, a man about my age who had sat in on an NYU workshop. I spotted Ed and he graciously wandered across the tent to greet me. His manner suggested more familiarity than warmth, but when my former student asked if we would allow a photograph, Ed flung an arm over my shoulder and smiled. Then, with a surprising and flattering volley, Ed Albee asked what I recall as, "When am I going to read your next book? Hasn't it been more than five years since that very good memoir?"

My anonymous former student seemed more pleased by overhearing Edward Albee's accolade and admonition than he was by the photograph. "Well, you always said writing habits and disciplines varied, Professor Offit. . . ." A long pause and then: "I suspect that you, like me, would be a more productive writer if you didn't go to so many parties."

26

The George Polk Awards: Izzy Stone,
Murray Kempton, and Other Champions of
the Twentieth- Through Twenty-first-
century Press

1977–2007

"Are you satisfied with your room, Mr. Stone?"

A flick of the wing from the intense gentleman whose resemblance
to a bird was so convincing my suspicion was he would fly off in the
next moment or turn on me for a critical nip. It was 1981. I'd been
curator of the George Polk Journalism Awards for four years, and I. F.
Stone was attending the annual awards luncheon at our invitation.

Among our winners for the year was George Seldes, publisher of
In Fact, a personal newsletter reminiscent of *I. F. Stone's Bi-Weekly.*
Although the Seldes publication predated Stone's launch in 1952,
Izzy Stone was the liberal icon and inspiration for a generation of
young reporters. When Stone won a Special Polk Award in 1970 he
accepted with gratitude so ebullient he not only became identified
with the awards but rallied support for the honors originating from

Long Island University's Brooklyn campus as competitive with the more renowned Pulitzer Prizes, based at Columbia University.

It seemed an inspired idea to invite Izzy Stone to present the award to George Seldes. We knew they were acquainted. Stone had responded positively to the invitation, with the caveat that we pay transportation from Washington to New York and the tariff for two nights' hotel accommodations for his wife and him. We were aware that Stone's wife, Esther, had been his partner and collaborator. The double billing seemed fair enough.

What we didn't know was our guest of honor George Seldes's feelings about Izzy Stone. The award presentation by Stone to Seldes was supposed to be a surprise, a bonus for audience and recipient that would contribute to the tradition as well as provide a warm personal reunion.

For me it was a special treat to discover George Seldes was the uncle of Tim Seldes, the editor at Doubleday who published John Barth's early novels, and also the uncle of Tim's sister, Marian Seldes, my good friend at the Authors League Fund who I considered among the most brilliant stage actresses of our time.

I was on my way through the gallery of the Roosevelt Hotel, decorated with posters representing a dozen prizewinning stories, when Tim Seldes approached me. "What's Izzy Stone doing here?" Tim wanted to know. "Uncle George is very upset by his presence. I hope he isn't going to be *presenting* the award."

It required little time for Tim and me to recognize the dilemma and decide on a compromise solution. We would not ask Izzy Stone to present Seldes's award as we had intended. The plaque and citation would come from a member of our committee. At the conclusion of the program we'd ask Isidor Feinstein, aka Izzy Stone, our former laureate, to say a few words: "No more than three minutes."

Managing Izzy Stone in a room full of his admirers was a job for Leon Trotsky with a script by Sholem Aleichem. I recast the program—which included remarks by award recipients John Darnton, Seymour Hersh, William Greider, Pierre Salinger, Ted Koppel, and Bill Moyers, among others. "Let's save the best for last," I suggested to Mr. Stone. "It would be insensitive to have a speaker after you undoubtedly wow the house."

"You don't have to worry," he replied with a reluctant shrug. "Seldes always has a lot to say."

Izzy Stone seemed to have only the vaguest idea that George Seldes was not flattered by his company. They met briefly for a photograph, shook hands, and retired to their assigned tables with a nod and a grunt to celebrate their reunion.

Seldes received his Career Award with a brief and modest acknowledgment of his good fortune. He cited Bruce Minton and Robert Terrall as editorial associates who had helped him live up to the standards announced in his first issue, May 20, 1940: "*In Fact* is not a commercial undertaking and is published for those who want facts with which to counteract the poison in the commercial press." He mentioned some reports of which he was most proud, including revelations about the dangers to health caused by smoking and how the tobacco industry's advertising power had muted that story in the mainstream press for close to fifty years.

Izzy Stone was more expansive. He elaborated on the sins of newspaper and magazine reporters who rely upon secondary sources rather than read the thousands of pages of official documents to catch the government in contradictions, hypocrisies, and lies. He expressed pride in his circulation, which had reached 66,000 by 1971. But he didn't mention that Seldes's *In Fact,* with its similar muckraking passion, had signed up more than a hundred thousand subscribers before it began its gradual decline several decades earlier.

After the program, when we were providing for the settlement of his transportation and hotel bills, Izzy Stone told me that he was studying classical Greek. Seven years later, the Talmudic scholar of American journalism published *The Trial of Socrates.* George Seldes sent us a thank-you note expressing appreciation for the award that "made people aware of me again." He concluded with the comment, "I don't know what you said to Izzy, but he didn't go on and on about himself as usual."

I became aware of the Polk Awards in 1957 when my friend Mike Levitas, who was a reporter for the *New York Post* at that time, won the award for Metropolitan Reporting. Twenty years later, 1976, I was introduced to the Polk Awards Committee and the proprietary culture of the alumni of LIU's Brooklyn campus by Al Landa, an alumnus of the castle at DeKalb and Flatbush, who had moved on to become vice president of the New School. During his run at the former "University in Exile" at West 12th Street, Landa was responsible for expanding the school's mandate to include the Parsons School of Design and the Actors Studio. Along with his colleague Dean Allen Austill, Landa brought theatrical flair to the programming for adult education. It seems Landa had been tapped by his classmates to do the same for the Polks.

The awards were suspended in 1975 and 1976 after more than two decades. Landa recommended me for the team assigned to bring 'em back alive. I was to work along with Robert Spector, Smollett scholar and authority on eighteenth-century periodicals. After a hitch in the navy in World War II, he returned to the classrooms of the Brooklyn campus for more than fifty years. Landa's and Spector's classmate, a dour wordsmith named Len Karlin, in collaboration with Ted Kruglak, a former reporter for the *World-Telegram*, had been one of the founders of the awards.

It was never made entirely clear to me why the awards had been suspended. The closest I could come to a reason was resentment of the former curator's style. Until 1974, the presentations had been considered a one-man act, dominated by the curator. Karlin had been in on the selections, but there seemed to be an awards committee of two.

Landa proposed that I suggest the names of writers, scholars, and newspaper and television professionals who would provide a panel of advisors for the awards. It seemed to me that inviting recommendations by former winners of the award could do the trick without cribbing from my address book.

Among the distinctions of the Polks was the diversity of its honorees, including television legends Edward R. Murrow (1951 and 1952), Walter Cronkite (1970), Eric Sevareid (1954), Richard Heffner (1957); critics Alfred Kazin (1966), Susan Sontag (1965), John Simon (1968), and Pauline Kael (1970); artists David Levine (1965) and Jules Feiffer

(1961); and defender of the First Amendment Justice William O. Douglas (1959).

In addition, awards were routinely presented to the outstanding reporters of the era: Carl Bernstein and Robert Woodward (1972), Sydney Schanberg (1971 and 1974), Seymour Hersh (1969, 1973, and 1974), Gloria Emerson (1970), David Halberstam (1963), Malcolm Browne (1964), Homer Bigart (1948 and 1950), and jointly to Donald Bartlett and James Steele (1971 and 1973). The awards to these recipients often predated honors by the Pulitzer committee and a number of the pre-1977-revival winners went on to win other Polk citations in the later decades of the century.

My suggestion to contact former winners passed reluctantly. Karlin thought it seemed like asking for a payoff. Spector was not convinced we had archives for their names and addresses. Landa insisted I could do just as well on my own.

So I accepted the assignment as curator and agreed to sit in on the selection process, preside at the awards presentations, and provide an academy of distinguished men and women to illuminate our program and augment our advisory board.

The meetings at Bob Spector's office in Brooklyn to select the winners during the late '70s were attended by Karlin, Landa, Spector, Martin Tucker, an erudite literary scholar, and Ed Hershey, a feisty young reporter for *Newsday,* who seemed to revere the selection process as passing on saints with a College of Cardinals.

I soon recognized that the distinction of the Polks originated from the source of nomination. Unlike the Pulitzers, we were not reliant upon the recommendations of newspaper editors and were also immune to the politics of the newsroom. Nominees for Polk Awards came from multiple sources, including members of the committee, former laureates, our recently appointed board of advisors, and even self-nominations.

The discussions were focused and enlightened if not always cordial. Karlin possessed a connoisseur's taste for composing a varied and deserving list of winners. It was he who suggested the *New England Journal of Medicine* and supported Martin Tucker's recommendation of an award to *The Angolite,* published by the Louisiana State

Penitentiary. Although he continued to regard me as an intrusive outsider, he agreed with my suggestion of an award to Peter Prescott, the literary critic for *Newsweek,* and we shared enthusiasm for Daniel Lang's reports in *The New Yorker.*

When we met at the Roosevelt for the presentation of the awards in 1978, Karlin thrust a script at me. "The less we hear from you, the better," he informed me. "Just follow this script—fast and easy." I was standing with Albert Bush-Brown, the chancellor of LIU, the major-domo of the three campuses, who had made the decision to suspend the awards and, as I now learned, was reassured that I was aboard.

Bush, as he was called, a puckish, broad-shouldered, gray-haired gentleman with a manner and voice that would have been right at home in the House of Lords, overheard Karlin's advice. Before I could respond, he took the unsolicited script from my hands and tore it into bits. "There, there, little man," he said to Karlin. "I'm sure Mr. Offit and I can compose a sentence or two without you."

There was no further prepping or prompting from veteran members of the committee after David Steinberg succeeded Bush-Brown as chancellor (president) of LIU. Steinberg made it clear he would not interfere with the awards process, not even offer a recommendation. Bob Spector, the poet, scholar, and beloved teacher of the Brooklyn campus, and I were in charge of the selection, procedures, and ceremonies. It was easy for me to understand the expressions of affection and admiration expressed by the administrative staff, board, and neighbors of the C. W. Post campus for David Steinberg and his wife, Joan, at a party in his honor in summer 2006.

Perhaps my most rewarding pleasure during the more than a quarter century I've served as curator of the George Polk Awards has been the assignment to break the news to winners. Along the way I've experienced the skepticism often inherent in the best of the working press: "Is this another of your jokes, Harry? Leave me your number and I'll call you back." Or, "You think I'm going to fall for this one? Spell your name slowly and let's have your office address and phone number." I've also been reminded several times about the risks of careless diction.

Carey McWilliams had already retired as editor of *The Nation* when we honored him. Although we had never met, I'd spoken to McWilliams on the phone when we were negotiating for *Intellectual Digest* reprints of *The Nation*'s pieces. Our conversations were so frequent that I had his home phone number, and when I called, I immediately recognized his wife's voice. She told me Carey was out, but she'd pass along my message.

"This is not a call related to *Intellectual Digest*," I thought it important to inform her. "I'm calling as curator of the George Polk Awards—" (I thought I said George Polk Awards.) "We're honored to share our choice of Carey McWilliams as this year's recipient of our Career Award."

"How nice," came the courtly response. "And what award should I tell Carey he's receiving?"

I repeated distinctly as I could without shouting, "George Polk!"

"My, my, my!" was the shocked reply. "I don't believe Carey knows there ever was a *Jewish* pope."

Several years later, when the committee was considering a special award to William Shawn, there was reservation expressed by a member of the committee who was doubtful if the enigmatic *New Yorker* editor would accept any award. I was so determined that we be committed to this overdue recognition, I offered to see what I could find out about Mr. Shawn's attitude toward awards.

We had already honored two *New Yorker* writers—Daniel Lang for his report on anti-Semitism in postwar Germany, and Roger Angell for baseball commentary—as well as the staff writers for "Notes and Comment" and "Talk of the Town" columns. Hoyt Spellman, a congenial member of the business staff and close associate of Mr. Shawn, was pretty sure he'd accept. "Mr. Shawn has grown less reluctant to respond to honors lately."

With this encouragement it seemed easy enough to check with Roger Straus, whom I knew was a friend of Shawn and a good enough pal of mine not to violate the confidence. I tried it out on Roger on my way off the Midtown Tennis Courts where we met just about every Sunday morning. "Do you think William Shawn would accept a George Polk Award?"

Looking down majestically from beneath the tip of his visored tennis cap, Roger said, "I suppose so, but I can't be sure. Bill *is* Jewish, but he doesn't practice or identify much with the religion."

William Shawn did accept the award and wrote one of the most memorable thank-you notes I received. After I finally got it straight with Roger Straus, he recommended I pay less attention to my backhand and brush up on my diction.

When I arrived in New York in 1950, it wasn't the *Times* or *Herald Tribune* but the *New York Post* that featured the writers who shook up the deck. Jimmy Cannon's "Nobody Asked Me But" and "You're Beau Jack," and Murray Kempton's stylish flashbacks to Gibbons, Macaulay, and his seventeenth-century hero, the Earl of Clarendon, were the Menckens of Big Town. Kempton's syndicated editorial columns also provided a daily dose of moral judgment. The Polk Awards Committee never got around to Cannon, but in 1966 Murray Kempton was honored for "Interpretive Reporting."

I met Kempton at the Riverdale apartment of Robert and Ina Caro, and immediately made the Johns Hopkins connection. Yes, he had been editor of the *News-Letter* and remembered the campus radicals—Blumberg and Broadus Mitchell. He also told me he had briefly been a member of the Young Communist League. Joining was necessary: "A password for my first job, which would have inspired neither Conrad nor Melville, but I worked as a seaman."

That exchange was one of many brief but frequently exhilarating conversations with him during several decades. Most often I'd encounter Kempton on his bike, pulling on his pipe and pedaling leisurely, without the slightest suggestion of being a reporter on his way to viewing an historical moment or meeting a deadline.

While holding fast to the handlebars, Kempton would stop and dismount. He would present his judgment or report without preliminary greetings or introduction, as if it were a continuation of an ongoing dialogue.

When listening to Murray or reading his commentaries I was often reminded of Edmund Wilson's observation about Wallace Stevens:

"Even when you do not know what he is saying, you know that he is saying it well."

I learned about Murray's fascinated admiration for Mafia dons and his editorial crusade for what he perceived as justice for the indicted Black Panthers: "The Panthers being the currently fashionable revolutionaries seem to have suffered from jealousy from formerly fashionable and now unnoticed ones."

I was only vaguely aware of "The People of the State of New York v. Lumumba Shakur et al.," the subtitle of Kempton's examination of the trial of the group of young men and women who came to be called the Panther 21. When *The Briar Patch,* a title he acknowledged was suggested by Albert Murray, was published, *Intellectual Digest* reprinted a major excerpt and featured a portrait of Murray Kempton by Herman Itchkawich on the cover.

Kempton seemed to consider that honor enough from me, and when I called in the winter of 1987 to tell him he'd been selected for the Polk's crowning Career Award, he sounded flustered, even defensive. Certainly he respected the Polk Awards but, just as certainly, there were other deserving recipients.

I didn't respond directly but told him about the year's other honorees—Nora Boustany, a *Washington Post* reporter who, in the tradition of George Polk, had risked her life covering the foreign beat; reporters for the *Arizona Republic,* the *Charlotte Observer,* WSMV Nashville, the *Atlanta Journal,* and Pacifica Radio, all of whom would be flattered to receive an award in Murray Kempton's company.

When that didn't seem to quite do it, I told him Gordon Manning was receiving a special award for his contributions to television reporting and Roger Rosenblatt was on deck for an encore. "Rosenblatt won his first Polk several years earlier for 'Children at War,' a feature story in *Time* magazine," I said. "Jacobo Timmerman suggested we honor Rosenblatt for what he considers Rosenblatt's unique and remarkable coverage of the deteriorating situation in the USSR."

With vintage Kempton Shandian dialogue, Murray picked up on the mention of Timmerman and commented on his *Prisoner Without a Name, Cell Without a Number.* He went on a riff discussing the political situation in Argentina. He was deep into a critique of America's

proclivity to back sympathetic dictators, when he was distracted by
another phone call. He asked for the date, what was expected of him
as a Polk laureate, and concluded gratefully as if he'd never considered declining. I hadn't exaggerated what the flattery of his company
meant to the other recipients as well as the Awards Committee. To a
man, to a woman, every reporter on the program considered Murray
Kempton the soul of the working press.

I'd been introduced to Fred Friendly by John (Jack) Chancellor during the years I was debating Martin Abend on Channel 5. Jack was a
close friend and somewhat embarrassed when, as soon as he heard my
name, Fred Friendly turned on me and said, "I don't approve of what
you're doing. Lending legitimacy to that reactionary idiot."

Chancellor was a national star on NBC, whose televised coverage
of the 1968 Democratic National Convention had so enraged Mayor
Daley's monitors, they'd forcefully escorted him off the floor before a
live television audience. Confronting Martin Abend was small potatoes compared to that, but ever the loyal pal, Jack answered for me,
"Better a debate than Abend's solo commentary."

The next time I met Fred Friendly, I was with Charles Collingwood. Charlie, a Rhodes scholar whom Murrow had enlisted as one of
the original Murrow boys on CBS radio, and I had connected instantly when we met at a club bar. Charlie, sipping a midday martini
and enjoying a well-tapped Gaulois, told me he passed his retirement
mornings reading the *Daily Racing Form.* I volunteered that my dad
was a bookie. Charlie and I were off to the races.

A veteran horse player who confessed to scrapping his valuable
collection of modern art, assembled during his years in Europe during and after World War II, Collingwood was as intrigued by my
reflections on my dad as I was by his tales of long shots and parlays.

Fred Friendly knew none of this when he encountered me with
Collingwood. He did recall the previous meeting when Jack Chancellor adopted the role of my impromptu defense attorney and started in
again. "You seem to collect real reporters, Offit. There must be some
hidden charm that never comes through on those awful debates."

Without a blink, Charlie Collingwood pinch-hit for Chancellor and said for me, "Your taste seems to be deteriorating apace with your manners, Fred."

When I finally passed muster with his associates and had the honor of notifying Friendly that he was receiving the award, I called him and was careful to enunciate my name, as well as the name of the award, slowly. The pitch and tone of his voice were so different from those in our previous encounters, I couldn't recall ever having experienced such a change of attitude. Unlike any of the laureates I'd spoken to before or after, Fred Friendly seemed less interested in the award he was winning than in learning about me.

With gentle questions, he drew it all out—the titles of my books, classes that I taught, organizations and boards I served. There was an audible sound of surprise when I mentioned *Intellectual Digest.* When he asked my experience with radio or television, I told him about producing a series of five-minute monologues by PEN members for WNYC radio before confessing to my television "commentaries." There was a pause. I wondered if Friendly was setting me up for another slam. He wasn't. "Of course, Mr. Offit, now that you mention it I remember those debates"—did he say—"very well"?

Fred Friendly was ill the day we presented the awards. He sent a cordial note to the committee. When I called to find out who would be receiving the award for him, he told me his son Andy would be there. Before signing off he mentioned his regret that he would not be able to see me—again.

Friendly died in 1998. A member of the Awards Committee and cochair of the Brooklyn Center's Journalism Department, Ralph Engelman was so inspired by his life and work that he determined to write a biography. Friendly's elegant and devoted widow agreed to full access to his papers, and all but one of the survivors among Friendly's associates agreed to be interviewed. Engelman passed along to me several chapters of the work-in-progress that Columbia University Press has scheduled for publication in 2008.

A companion to Friendly's mother told Engelman that Friendly came back from World War II a changed man. "He returned to civilian life more self-confident, more focused, prepared to conquer new worlds." But Andy Rooney met Friendly during the war. He was later a colleague at CBS. What effect did World War II have on Fred Friendly? Engelman reports Rooney's terse but, I suspect, insightful perception: "None. Zero. Fred Friendly would have been exactly who he was and what he was if he hadn't seen World War II. Fred had more impact on the war than it had on him."

Martha Gellhorn was living in Catscradle, Newchurch West, Chepstow, Gwent, Wales, when she wrote in January 1982:

> *Dear Mr. Offitt,*
>
> *I wish to nominate the article "Lebanon Eyewitness," by Martin Peretz in* The New Republic *for the George Polk Award. I am writing to you as a former war correspondent, seven wars over a period of thirty years. I was scandalized by the reporting of the Israeli invasion of Lebanon, simply as a reporter.*

The letter went on to condemn the Western press for its many false reports. Gellhorn documented the errors with personal "retracing" and "checking" and wrapped up her two-page editorial with a declaration of her feelings about the importance of reporting and a tribute to Peretz's piece:

> *I believe in journalism; I believe the world would be totally dark if it were not possible to receive reports, however sketchy, from all over the world. But I believe even more passionately in the need for careful, exact reporting; and the strange sight of the world's press turning the PLO into heroes and martyrs, and the Israeli army into the hordes of Genghis Khan, was alarming. I believe that "Lebanon Eyewitness" is an essential part of getting the record straight.*

Thomas Friedman and David Shipler won the award that year for foreign reporting. They were honored for their reports from the Middle East. Stanley Kauffmann of *The New Republic* was our honoree for criticism. Martin Peretz was considered but the *Times* team's reports over the span of the year were regarded as more comprehensive and consistent with the tradition of celebrating the best of the beat reporters.

I was so impressed with the Gellhorn letter, I proposed her for a career award. I cited her foreign reporting and mention in Robert Caro's *The Power Broker.* Caro quoted Gellhorn's description of Depression families circa 1933. "No one could see a state of mind; all one could do was try to describe it, as Martha Gellhorn did: 'Everywhere there seemed a spreading listlessness, a whipped feeling . . . I find them all in the same shape—fear, fear . . . an overpowering terror of the future.' "

Members of the committee were only vaguely aware of Gellhorn's work. She was identified as a former wife of Ernest Hemingway who had "some distinction" as a foreign correspondent for the AP. Ralph Engelman suggested Gellhorn a decade later and was no more successful than I. Unfortunately, we let Martha Gellhorn pass without honoring ourselves by honoring one of the most committed and frequently heroic reporters of her generation.

If ever there was a book that represented what the George Polk Awards were all about, it was Horst Faas and Tim Page's *Requiem,* a collection of photographs and brief bio notes of the one hundred thirty-five photographers killed while covering the battlefields of Southeast Asia. David Halberstam (Polk Award, Foreign Reporting, 1963) offered the nomination and wrote the introduction.

I received my introduction to the politics of *The New York Times* from Clifton Daniel, who was among the first of my acquaintances to respond enthusiastically to the invitation to join our panel of advisors. Daniel had retired from the *Times,* where he served as managing editor, and was working on *Chronicle of the Twentieth Century,* a mammoth anthology of press clips that provided snippets of the history of our times.

A gentleman from the South who had artfully adopted the

manners and dress of the English, Clifton Daniel seemed more an ambassador than the crack reporter and editor he had been for all of his professional life. Daniel was reserved and not inclined to gossip, but the fireworks evoked by his successor, Abe Rosenthal, were so incendiary that some time after Abe, too, had retired, Clifton shared with me reflections on the hierarchy.

He respected Rosenthal as a reporter. (A. M. Rosenthal was the recipient of a Polk Award in 1959 for Foreign Reporting, and again in 1964 for Metropolitan Reporting.) "Many good reporters are ambitious," Daniel acknowledged. "You are unlikely to progress up the editorial ladder unless you have a touch of fire in your belly, but Abe Rosenthal was an inferno." Daniel went on to describe to me Rosenthal's progression from honored correspondent to boss. As I understood it, Daniel had been the one to call Rosenthal home from a foreign assignment in Poland and assigned him to cover the United Nations, which Rosenthal did for seven years. "He was deserving," Daniel said. "No doubt about that."

When I asked what accounted for Rosenthal's rise to his former job, Clifton Daniel chuckled softly and said, "When he thought his time was right, Abe read the Sulzbergers correctly and eased me out." He expressed no bitterness, and when I wanted to know what the "reading" was, Daniel said, "The Sulzbergers are careful not to tell their editors what to do, but on those rare occasions when they have a strong opinion, they subtly let you know. Abe was attuned to that. I think, for example, the Sulzbergers, who had for a long time been so sensitive about their Jewish identity that they shied from any suggestion of support for the state of Israel, began to feel differently after the Six-Day War. Abe picked up on that. It certainly wasn't the only reason Punch Sulzberger made room for him at the top, but Abe selected his moments and played to the powers that be."

Clifton Daniel also told me that Abe Rosenthal could be charming and accommodating to the people he courted; not unlike many men who rise to the top in severely competitive situations, Rosenthal was often insulting and mean to his subordinates. In summary, Daniel acknowledged quite generously that there were few reporters he met in his long career at the *Times* who were more devoted to it. "Abe Rosenthal lived and breathed *The New York Times*."

The Rosenthal passion and identification with his job was expressed to me every time I called him to share the names of *Times* reporters we were honoring for the year.

I felt no hint that he was dissatisfied because the list of *Times* winners wasn't longer. When he appeared at the presentations, Rosenthal beamed like a proud parent with no suggestion of displeasure that there were so many other leads in the show.

During his years as executive editor, Rosenthal had introduced the special sections that many accountants of the press considered the crucial money cows that enabled daily papers to survive the reduction in advertising revenue caused by competition from television and later the Internet. Abe Rosenthal was considered for a Career Award, but the suggestion was summarily shot down. Evidently it wasn't necessary to be a friend of Clifton Daniel to have the inside story on Abe Rosenthal's manners in the newsroom.

My experience with Rosenthal's successor, Max Frankel, was bland and uneventful. I recall him as regarding my congratulatory calls as relatively routine. When I mentioned this contrast to Len Karlin he said it was to be expected. He did not recall Frankel ever winning a Polk Award.

Joe Lelyveld, who was appointed executive editor after Frankel's retirement to the Sunday *New York Times Magazine*, spoke in a voice that seemed to reflect a trace of anticipation. A two-time winner of the Polk (Education Reporting, 1971, and Foreign Affairs, 1983), Lelyveld managed to suggest a modest disappointment with the number of awards to the *Times*. He would express this by inquiring politely about other stories submitted by the *Times* or asking if our list was complete.

It's unlikely Joe Lelyveld and I would have discussed this subject in greater depth if we had not coincidentally met at a party a year later, on the evening of the very day the Polk committee had just wrapped up its choices for the season past. During our conversation, after I'd mentioned—without naming names—what I'd been up to that day, Lelyveld said with a slight smile that it seemed the *Times* was "rationed to two Polk Awards a year."

I said recklessly, "You're not altogether wrong. There's definitely resistance to giving too many awards to the *Times*. We try to spread it around."

(Years later, after I'd become a casual friend and ardent admirer of his memoir *Omaha Blues: A Memory Loop,* Lelyveld told me he recalled me saying, "There are people—judges—who hate the *Times.*")

Less than a week later, when I called Joe Lelyveld to tell him the *Times* had won two awards, he graciously didn't rub it in. That same afternoon I received a call from Arthur Sulzberger Jr. I had met him the year he graduated from the Browning School, the East Side prep that our sons attended at the same time. It was difficult for me not to feel like a retired don talking to one of the privileged students whose current station was beyond my expectation when he was being scolded by Headmaster Cook or as a rebellious senior responding to the allure of the librarian who set all the preppies' hearts into overdrive.

"Is it true as Joe suggested at lunch that you told him Polk Awards to the *Times* were rationed?"

I recalled "rationed" as Joe Lelyveld's word not mine, but I said straight out that as publisher Sulzberger must know it gave a newspaper award's committee a greater sense of discovery to find a story in the *Sacramento Bee* or *Norfolk Virginian-Pilot* or *Fairbanks Daily News-Miner* worthy of an award than to celebrate a piece that appeared in the newspaper conceded throughout the world to be not only the best but the one with the deepest resources. Then, I reassured Sulzberger, whom I couldn't think of as anyone but the Kid from Browning, that we were aware of how much an award meant to the individual reporter, and that value remained our standard.

Two years later I was on the phone with Lelyveld's successor Howell Raines, whom Sulzberger appointed to the top editorial perch after what appeared to be a photo finish beating out Bill Keller. Much like Rosenthal, Raines accepted the news of two laureates with enthusiasm. Raines had never won a Polk, but he was a mutual friend of Nick Taylor, president of the Authors Guild, and that was recommendation enough for me. I had no suspicion of the hostility to Raines's management style felt by his staff. My guess is it wouldn't have surfaced had it not been for the Jayson Blair disaster and the pages the *Times* devoted to evidence of the frauds and mea culpas.

I shouldn't have been surprised by the revelation that Blair had been getting away with plagiarism and fiction. In the early 1980s, when *The Washington Post* entered a story by Janet Cooke, Bob Spector and I disqualified it because we thought the dramatizations—dialogues—smacked of fictional invention. We preferred a *Post* report by Jonathan Neuman and Ted Gup that had been nominated by one of our panel.

Ben Bradlee, executive editor of the *Post* and Pulitzer Prize director, responded to our call announcing the choice of Neuman and Gup with an accolade. "I don't know how you do it," he said. "You get it right." Later, when Janet Cooke acknowledged her fiction and returned the Pulitzer she'd won, I wondered if Ben Bradlee, as well as Howell Raines, suspected the inventions all along.

Clifton Daniel died in 2000, so I didn't get to talk to him about the "early retirement" (firing?) of Hal Raines due to the Blair frauds and lack of staff support for their wounded leader. There was a tragic Shakespearean overtone to Raines's run as executive editor of the *Times* that reminded me of Daniel's comment about the "inferno" that was Rosenthal's "fire in the belly." It fueled Howell Raines's achievements (seven Pulitzer Prizes for the *Times*) and perhaps burned him up.

Bill Keller was appointed executive editor after a brief transitional encore by the classic pro Joe Lelyveld. On the phone Keller sounded like the effervescent younger brother of his predecessors. He expressed delight that the committee had selected Somini Sengupta to receive the 2003 Foreign Reporting award for her West African reports. When I also passed along news of the selection of the *Times's* stories on dangers in the workplace as recipient of our labor reporting honors for the year, Keller said, "Two awards! That's swell. I thought we usually won just one."

Arthur Sulzberger, too, expressed such gratitude. I moved on to another subject and asked if he was supporting his fellow Browning alumnus, Dr. Howard Dean, for the presidency. "Oh, I can't make political endorsements," he said cheerfully, "but my son is for him."

We agreed that the sudden outburst of rage Dean expressed after he lost the New Hampshire primary was reminiscent of the outburst of Charles Cook, the headmaster of the Browning School, during the days Dean, Sulzberger, and our sons Ken and Mike were students there. "That sounds right to me," said the alumnus, circa '71. "Howard Dean may have learned his temper at Browning." It was a contagion of rage that didn't seem to infect our sons, or the publisher of *The New York Times.*

During the years of my association with the Polk Awards, Bob Spector invited a growing number of LIU faculty to join the committee: David Medina, a working reporter who had graduated from the Brooklyn campus; Donald Bird and Ralph Engelman, Ph.D.s and cochairs of the journalism department; Abby Kenigsberg, adjunct professor, Media Ethics, C. W. Post; adjuncts JoAnn Allen, Mike Bush, Jennifer Rauch, Melvin McCray, and Michael Jordan; representatives of the Southampton College radio station Wally Smith and Judith Cramer. Perhaps the most tempered and informed contributors to our dialogues have been Len Hollie, our authority on the business beat, and the late Kalman Seigel, who for forty-one years wrote, rewrote, and edited for the *Times* before joining the LIU faculty.

Even with such a large, eccentric, and racially diverse group, the quality of the selections measured by responses of both the press and other awards committees was consistently distinguished. Spector's posse, although younger than our original four, was often just as capable of reaching into the past to honor historic careers. Among the triumphs of the decade was the award to the *Pittsburgh Courier,* a weekly nationally acknowledged as a vibrant and influential resource for the African-American community, and to Morley Safer for his ingenious and daring reports from Vietnam and later as a signature investigator-commentator for *60 Minutes.*

There was unanimous agreement, too, that Philip Hamburger, who contributed "Mayor Watching" columns and reports from the battlefield during World War II, in addition to profiles and talk pieces for more than fifty years to *The New Yorker,* was past due for recognition. (The Hamburger award reminded us that we had overlooked A. J. Liebling.)

Hamburger, along with Herbert Mitgang, whose bold column on the *Times*'s editorial page was honored for being one of the earliest and lone voices to challenge American engagement in the Vietnam War, joined the Izzy Stone chorus praising their Polks as crowning moments in their careers.

Both Philip Hamburger and Herbert Mitgang agreed to join our advisory committee. Supported by Russell Baker, who was selected as the outstanding reporter/columnist of the award's fifty years, they recommended honoring John Oakes. Oakes, a relative of the Sulzbergers, was credited with founding the op-ed page, opening up columns opposite the editorial page for a variety of opinions. A daring advocate, Oakes was among the first to recognize the exploitation of the environment and to write about it, naming names and advocating reforms.

It required the experience of an "insider" to be aware that Oakes's major contributions to American journalism had overcome the reluctance of the committee to agree to one more Career Award for a contributor to *The New York Times*. Fortunately, the jury in Brooklyn, impressed by the sources of recommendation, agreed just in time.

It was my privilege to deliver the good news to John Oakes. In his ninth decade, Oakes was in the hospital when we spoke. I was touched by the gentle, almost inaudible voice, expressing elation. "Thank you. Thank you. I'm honored and will certainly do my best to be with you." John Oakes died less than a month after our conversation. His son wrote a warm and grateful note to the committee, expressing the great satisfaction winning a Career Award had given to John Oakes at the end of his life.

On the eve of the awards presentation in 1990, soon after the publication of Kati Marton's *The Polk Conspiracy: Murder and Cover-up in the Case of CBS Correspondent George Polk,* the LIU journalism department organized a seminar open to the public to discuss who was responsible for the death of George Polk.

With an early movie sale, rumored to be in six figures, and endorsements by Morley Safer ("A sweeping international thriller, meticulous dissection of duplicity and paranoia in high places"), Ellen Goodman ("A compelling book about journalists and government"), and Ted Koppel ("A fascinating and profoundly disturbing book"), the Marton report was the trigger for the panel discussion.

Marton argued that Polk had been murdered by a right-wing assassin, but Edmund Keeley, Princeton University professor, translator, and critic of modern Greek poetry, wrote that there was no conclusive evidence identifying Polk's murderer. In his study *The Salonika Bay Murder, Cold War Politics and the Polk Affair,* Keeley, like Marton, questioned the conclusions of the American committee headed by Walter Lippmann and General William "Wild Bill" Donovan that led to the Greek government's prosecution and conviction of Reuters correspondent Gregory Staktopoulos. Keeley, however, found insufficient evidence to accept Marton's scenario.

Since its inception, the Polk Awards program has commemorated the correspondent's death with the following lines: "Polk was murdered during the Greek Civil War while trying to reach the guerrilla leader Markos Vafiades for an interview. The circumstances of his death and the conduct of the investigation following the discovery of his body in Salonika Bay are matters of continuing speculation and controversy."

At the conclusion of the panel discussion that evening, a young lady stood during the question period and identified herself as a niece of Markos Vafiades. Her uncle, recently arrived from Greece, was with us that evening. She was his translator and wished to share his comments with the audience. Vafiades, frail but erect, spoke in impassioned tones. He alone understood the true circumstances and perpetrator of Polk's murder, he insisted. The world would know when *he* published *his* book.

Neither Marton nor Keeley was convinced, and there was no later word about a Vafiades exclusive. To the Polk Awards Committee, and I suspect the Polk family, George Polk's death remains "a matter of continuing speculation and controversy."

John Chancellor never won a Polk Award, but he should have. His defiance of the floor managers who forcibly escorted him from the

Democratic Convention in Chicago, 1968, as well as his reports of the desegregation of Central High School in Little Rock, Arkansas, 1957, were major achievements of his long career as an NBC News correspondent.

Ira Lipman, to whom I was introduced by my son Dr. Kenneth Offit (recipient of the Association of American Publishers Award for Best Book in Medical Science, 1998), was so impressed by Chancellor's "grace, civility and sly wit, as well as the depth of his reporting," he founded and funded the annual John Chancellor Award for Excellence in Journalism.

In 2005, the Chancellor Award was presented to Jerry Mitchell, a reporter for the Jackson, Mississippi, *Clarion-Ledger.* Mitchell was presented with the twenty-five thousand dollar honorarium by Nicholas Lemann, the talented reporter, essayist, and historian who presides as chairman of the Columbia Graduate School of Journalism. Mitchell's citation commemorated his relentless investigation of the unsolved murders of civil rights activists in 1963, a series of stories that led directly to the arrests and conviction of four Ku Klux Klan members. Later that same year, Jerry Mitchell was the recipient of a Polk Award, but his footnote to history didn't make the final cut for a Pulitzer Prize. Awards are like that—always subjective, at times repetitious, frequently arbitrary, but never, in my experience, capricious.

During the years I've contributed to the deliberations of the Polk Awards Committee, our failures to honor John Chancellor and Martha Gellhorn weren't my only disappointments. David Schiff's *Insurance Observer,* recommended several times by a former Polk laureate, Joseph Belt, was routinely dismissed by Ed Hershey, a formidable articulator of vetoes. Hershey insisted that Schiff's lifetime contribution to monitoring the integrity of insurance companies with a publication he financed and wrote was "too self-promotional." Besides, didn't Sidney Offit say David Schiff was a school friend of his son Mike?

When celebrating its seventieth anniversary, *Esquire* magazine elected to reprint the greatest story it ever published, "Frank Sinatra

Has a Cold," Gay Talese's 1966 pioneering adventure in what came to be called New Journalism. I had no luck with Gay Talese as my candidate for a Career Award. Too few members of the committee were familiar with Talese's contributions to American journalism's craft and style.

I would also have been honored to celebrate James C. Goodale's championing of the First Amendment and his indispensable role as a board member of the Committee to Protect Journalism. But the year he was considered, the committee was determined to restrict our selections to working reporters and producers of a documentary film.

My links to Johns Hopkins and Baltimore were gratified by Polk Awards to Murray Kempton, Phil Hamburger, and Russ Baker, but we overlooked another JHU-Baltimore gift to New York. Robert Kotlowitz helped introduce *NewsHour* to WNET TV and was later cited by our 2005 Career Award winner Frederick Wiseman for his early and indispensable support of Wiseman's career as a documentary film innovator.

Wiseman's tribute, a spontaneous acknowledgment expressed as the salutation to his brief acceptance remarks, delighted me almost as much as that moment in 1984 when the committee agreed to present our National TV Reporting Award to Alexander Kotlowitz, reporter, writer, news producer, author of *There Are No Children Here,* and—the son of Carol (Billy) and Robert Kotlowitz!

As I consider my adventures as curator of the Polk Awards, I'm reminded of a question asked years ago by our then eight-year-old granddaughter Anna. I escorted Anna and her younger sister, Caroline, to visit the Roosevelt Hotel, April 1991, the day before the presentations, so they could see the posters celebrating the achievements of our laureates. After a careful review, Anna asked, "Tell me, Grandpa, is it better to receive or give awards?"

I wonder what our panel of advisors would have answered to that ironic query. Kevin Buckley, Lionel Garcia, Matt Clark, Phyllis Malamud Clark, Paula Giddings, Barry Beckham, Patricia Bosworth, Robert A. Caro, Thomas Fleming, Jill Krementz, Gail Lumet Buckley,

Lionel Tiger, Nancy Larson Shapiro, John A. Pope Jr., Adam Van Doren, Kurt Vonnegut, Harriet Zuckerman—all are or were as worthy of receiving as of giving awards. I never asked.

One of these days, perhaps, we'll branch out and spread the glory—a prize for Best Letters to the Editor to Joel Conarroe; and for Press Coverage to Ken Auletta; and for Local Weekly Culture Commentary to the *Southampton Press*'s Fred Volkmer and Andrew Botsford; and a Book Award to Nancy Sorel for *The Women Who Wrote the War*; and for Weekly Editorials to Helen Rattray, *East Hampton Star*; and for Maintaining the Family Publishing Legacy to Elinor Tatum, *Amsterdam News*; and, for *Propositi Tenax* (firm of purpose) and *Proprio Vigore* (by its own force), independently, to Robert Silvers, *The New York Review of Books*, David Remnick, *The New Yorker*, and Katrina vanden Heuvel, *The Nation* (second woman president of the U.S.A.?).

So you see, Anna, I do feel better giving awards than receiving them, maybe because I've given and wanted to give more than I've received. It's a wonderfully selfish way to be generous.

IV

Games and Play: From the Beginning of Time Through the Twenty-first Century

27

Sundays at Ten, Double-Faulting with Artists and Writers, and Playing Rorschachs at the Court

1964–2005

At the memorial service celebrating the life of the artist Joe Hirsch, Art Students League, 1981, Kurt Vonnegut said about our former tennis pal, "It's a real privilege to have known a first-rate artist as a second-rate tennis player." Kurt went on to acknowledge that the quality of tennis played by our Sunday gang was at best second-rate and most likely third-rate.

Earlier, Jimmie Flexner, who, in addition to his Pulitzer Prize–winning biography of George Washington, had written about American art, commented privately that it was baffling that Joe, who had so mastered brush and canvas that his works appeared in museums throughout the world, never caught on to the design of the Midtown Tennis Club. "Joe's shots were right down the middle. He ignored the deep lobs that benefited from the limited backcourt or the cross-court volleys that could exploit our compromised flanks."

Kurt, Joe, and Jimmie were the nucleus of a group of six who had first call on our weekly doubles matches. If more than four of us showed up—rarely—we'd roll Sid Simon's dice when that distinguished artist was in our company, or flip fingers, odd man out, to negotiate the lineup.

Jimmie and I shared rides to and from the courts at Eighth Avenue and 27th Street with Harry Geyelin, a six-foot-two gray-haired baritone who had the demeanor and style of a local champion right off the courts at Roland Garros. And he traveled in style. Harry had inherited from David Rockefeller one of the first Mercedes-Benz imports after the war. It had originally been driven by Peggy Rockefeller, whom I assumed grew weary of its reluctant stick shift for which the ceiling panel that rolled back, letting in the sky, did not entirely compensate. Harry presided at the Council of the Americas, a goodwill business agency founded by David, his summer neighbor and friend, and from time to time he entertained us with tales of sailing with the Rockefellers at Northeast Harbor, Maine, or tuning up the markets in Buenos Aires, Rio de Janeiro, and Caracas.

Jimmie's remarks reflected his fascination with our tennis games as a kind of Rorschach test of ego and character. "Your friend Kurt's service is modest, and he seems less interested in winning the game than just having fun and not embarrassing himself." After his daughter Nellie informed her father that Kurt was the sage novelist of her generation, Jimmie's reflections became a mite more myopic. "Your friend"—I was always credited by Jimmie with Kurt as my friend, with connotations of responsibility—"Your friend Kurt seems to have a unique and rather fatalistic humor. If you recall his response to my winning lob, by the bye . . ."

When Morley Safer joined our game, Jimmie identified the champion of TV news reporters as "a better athlete than any of us," but qualified by observing that Morley "seemed unwilling to accept the effectiveness of the light touch." Jimmie viewed Gus Peterson, a native-born German businessman who had defied Hitler and immigrated to the United States, as *his* friend. Peter had a summer house near Jimmie's in Washington, Connecticut, and although I never heard them refer to games in the summer, Jimmie regarded Pete's play as "elusively daring." He told me, "My friend Pete is too willing to take a chance on the winning placement. He is thinking strategy all the time."

Jimmie never mentioned directly what he thought of my game, but as he continued to play into his early eighties he insisted I be his partner. With a gentle ballet of his fingers he would instruct me to "cover the court."

I was not alone in my enthusiasm for the matches. Although frequently two or more of our original six would call in with an excused absence, there was always a bench of reserves available to supply the balls as a ticket to join our games.

On the court adjacent to ours for close to a quarter of a century, we were aware of a passionate singles match accompanied by a musical score of grunts, groans, and rhapsodies of delight. Roger Straus, the premier American publisher, sliced and cut with the fierceness of a master as he engaged his younger but talented opponent Roger Hirson, the author of, among other scripts, *Pippin,* the Broadway hit that starred Ben Vereen.

The rabid Rogers played only with each other and, even though engaged in visiting international book fairs (Straus) and Hollywood script conferences (Hirson), they seemed perennials, far more regular than any member of our group. We often chatted while waiting for our courts. Roger Straus was the liveliest of Sunday raconteurs. He spoke as he played, without inhibition, slashing down the line. One Sunday afternoon, when neither Harry nor Jimmie was about, Roger offered to drive me home. When we tried to check out at the street parking lot, his car wasn't there. "I dunno wha' 'appen to it. It missing," the shifty-eyed attendant said.

"You know damn well where my car is," Roger responded. Standing tall, barelegged in tennis shorts but still a majestic presence looming beneath his beaked cap, the publisher of more Nobel Prize laureates than any publisher in the whole wide world demanded, "No nonsense. I want my car right away."

Sure enough, it was delivered pronto—not so mysteriously produced from a shed around the corner.

I only played singles twice at Midtown, once with my son Mike, who wiped me out in two sets, and once as a sub for Morley, who couldn't keep his date with his *60 Minutes* buddy Mike Wallace. I had seen Mike Wallace hold his own with Palmer Williams, who was to our bush league tennis what Archie Moore was to boxing, a contender at every level, but Wallace had just recuperated from an illness that had restricted him from the courts for several weeks. It was my intention to keep the ball in play and not try to run him back to bed rest and Advil. Although my strokes were poor—no racket back, no follow-through for me—I was a veteran hacker since the age of seven, when I broke in wearing white ducks, white cap, white Keds, and waving a wooden Wilson for lessons at the Druid Hill courts in Baltimore.

From my observations of Mike playing with Palmer, I concluded he was as intense about the racket sport as he was about nailing rackets off the court. By my standards, Mike Wallace played a classic game—good strokes, lots of ball movement, and going for the lines. I was convinced after several games that to keep the match competitive I'd better forget who was recuperating from what and go for the points. Mike later told Morley, who reported it to me, that I was a better player than he'd concluded I was after observing me play with our Sunday "Arts Academy."

Over that long run of years Joe Hirsch's wasn't the only teammate's memorial service I attended. At the commemoration celebrating Sidney Simon's life, I was asked to talk about my memories of this most versatile of artists. I mentioned that when he was in his late seventies though uncomplaining, Sid was so deaf he couldn't hear the score. Playing with him as my doubles partner slowly broke my lifelong habit of daydreaming between points. Not only did I have to know the score, but I was frequently roused by a chorus emanating from my invisible partner to the rear. "Oh, Sidney! Sidney! Sidney! Sidney! What's happening to you, Sidney Simon?"

During the summers I rarely played tennis with anyone but my family. My delights in the game as sport and exercise were so powerful that when we traveled with Ken and Mike for two weeks, touring the West Coast, and later on a ten-day car tour from London to Edinburgh, I insisted we bring tennis rackets. Avi and I had compatible games. She, too, covered the court and rarely went for winners. Although her strokes were fluid and her movements considerably more graceful than mine, Avi was no more concerned with winning than I was. But my wife did recognize my growing frustration with chasing our youngsters' balls as they learned the game. It was her suggestion that the boys attend a tennis camp.

So it came to pass that Mike and Ken took their turns with me as their partner playing against Don Budge and his lucky mate at Don Budge's Tennis Camp, Mcdonogh School, Baltimore.

At the age of eleven Ken was the art director of the two-week session, designing the award's program and tournament ladder, but Mike was rookie of the year. When he and I played against Don Budge and his partner, Mary Tydings, the granddaughter and daughter of U.S. senators, it was obvious that Mike was more consistent than the young lady, who seemed to be grooming for Forest Hills. Budge controlled the match with such artful manipulation of points that Mike and I won one game of the best of three. Coming off the court I congratulated Mike. "You can remember that all your life. You and your dad took a game from one of the greatest tennis players in the history of the game." The pragmatic New York kid's rejoinder was, "Are you kidding, Dad? If this wasn't Don Budge's business we wouldn't have won a point."

The timing of the tennis camp experience was on the mark. The next summer our Water Mill landlord, a farmer who had inherited a potato field overlooking the Atlantic along with other properties in the neighborhood, died. His son, who had been laboring as the last

of the village blacksmiths, returned to manage the estate and immediately uncovered a buried tennis court not twenty yards from
the cottage we rented. The court, along with the potato field, so enraptured me I insisted we continue to rent while our friends were
securing their summer retreats, buying houses, barns, estates, everything under the big Hampton sky.

We didn't have a pool, but who needed chlorinated water to
splash in when we had free potatoes and a tennis court. We shared
the court with the tenants of three other rentals on the premises: the
"big house" of the deceased "baron," an apartment over the garage,
and a two-bedroom guesthouse adjacent to the court.

Ken, Mike, Avi, and I enjoyed our family matches but no more so
than batting it around with the best of our neighbors. The jewel of our
campus was Connie Jewett (later Ellis) who, with the exception of the
two weeks each summer when she ran off to Martha's Vineyard to join
our mutual friend Rose Styron's tennis party, was ours, all ours. Connie routinely provided one partner and I was responsible for the other.

When Avi, Ken, and Mike were fulfilling other promises, I enlisted Kurt Vonnegut, who contributed the same enthusiasm and
entertaining commentary familiar to our Sunday game at Midtown.
Sometimes Kurt would bring along a houseguest to fill in as a
fourth. Morley Safer showed up for a weekend's diversion. He was
not only a workout on the court, but Morley's presence so impressed
the reclusive young Hearst headliner who secretively rented the
guesthouse near the court that she risked talking to us for the rest of
the summer.

Soon after their debut as summer residents in East Hampton,
Bob and Ina Caro dropped by, rackets in hand. Avi was deep into
writing the book that would pay our sons' tuition through college
and graduate school, and didn't join us until after the games for
drinks by the potato field.

No guests could have been more gracious and supportive than
Bob and Ina. Not only were they reassuring about our reluctance to
give up our little patch of Elysium to own a house in the Hamptons,
but they respected and encouraged Avi's dedication.

Connie agreed to fill in as my partner. Ina, who in addition to her research for Bob's classic biographies also managed to write *The Road From the Past: Traveling Through History in France,* celebrated by Arthur Schlesinger Jr. as "thoroughly delightful . . . the essential traveling companion," was in a league with Connie, *Chevalier de l'Ordre National du Mérite,* as a Francophile and top seed on our home court. It was obvious that Bob Caro had once been a top-notch player but had laid off, perhaps because of the back injury that inspired the dedication of the first of his Pulitzer Prize biographies to, along with Ina, Dr. Janet G. Travell, the physiatrist renowned also for her services to John F. Kennedy. We played an inconclusive set, but I had the impression that banging the ball around that afternoon in Water Mill was among the last of Bob's adventures on the court.

Other memorable matches of our summers included the afternoon Kurt and I played Richard Spooner, the principal of Southampton High School, and Bud Burnett, our landlord himself, who agreed to fill in when the principal's partner didn't show up.

Bud came in from the field, his wide-brimmed straw hat shading his shirt and overalls, as he pitched his boots aside and went to work blasting holes in the net and riveting the court.

A week or so later, Kurt and I were treated to a match with Bud's son Eddie, a blond giant who made his partner's blood pressure rise even as the ladies' hearts went pitter-patter. With even more vim than his pa, Eddie attacked the ball as if determined to kill it in time for supper. Kurt christened him the "Butcher Boy of Flying Point," a prophetic tag for the young man who was later to expand his family kingdom by selling off the property and developing a resort town of his own near Wilmington, North Carolina.

As the Burnetts began to sell their land, among the first lots to go was their grandfather's, including the tennis court alongside his big old house. My distress at losing the home field was soon soothed by an invitation to play with a member of the Meadow Club, an elite sports haven with grass courts, and to knock the ball around at the North Sea Racket Club, where matches were arranged. It was at the North Sea that I discovered poetry in motion, playing sets at twilight with Kenneth Koch.

Although the Meadow Club was "selective and exclusive" and

the North Sea available to all who could pay the season's fee, my matches at the Meadow Club were relatively noncompetitive—doubles with old friends Chris and Juliet Moore, singles with a congenial gentleman to whom our neighbors Bob and Heidi Jenkins introduced me.

The arranged engagement with Kenneth Koch began with a not-so-subtle audition. A handsome, wavy-haired six-footer, with a modest bow to his legs, the poet suggested we volley before committing to the first of our evening matches. His understated invitation for the games to begin was "I suppose it will be all right."

I admired Kenneth Koch as poet and teacher, but the spiritual fatalism suggested by his line "Biographies are written to cover up the speed with which we go . . ." didn't prepare me for the poet's intense concern for the score.

Our matches were long, frequently into the night. Koch kept the ball in play with deft strokes and a deceptive speed that seemed frequently on the verge of giving up the point before connecting at the last moment for a drop shot or crosscourt volley. I enjoyed the workouts and was so inspired by his competitiveness that I played my best game. It seemed to me obvious that Koch and I were evenly matched and, as I recall, the scores indicated that. Although we played by mutual agreement, the late starting hour—around six P.M.—was not my preference, and we concluded only when he thought it too dark.

Koch seemed so dissatisfied with himself at not beating me that he set the date for the next match as if it were mandated by a Fate, decreeing that after one convincing, lopsided victory, he could be done with me. Eventually he was. After we had played a half dozen times, splitting sets like familiar logs, Koch sighed with resignation, acknowledging the cursedly slow-floating eccentricity of my game that made it impossible for him to win, win, win as the superiority of his strokes so clearly indicated he should.

When I met him at literary events that included our mutual friend Arnold Cooper's annual August lawn party, he seemed reluctant to greet me, responding to mention of our matches with perfunctory nods of dismissal as though embarrassed to be included in an anthology of doggerel when he knew very well he was a master of prosody.

Peter Maas, with whom I played summer weekend matches for more than a decade, didn't invite me to his court. Peter summoned me. The author of bestsellers that included *Serpico* and *Underboss,* Peter and I met when we were both breaking into hardcovers edited by Arthur Fields at Crown. Arthur introduced me to Peter with the notice, "Maas is one tough baby. He's going to make the Mafia his beat and it's going to pay off." It did.

Peter had no memory of our meeting. Although relentless in research and getting the story, he expressed no particular interest in people with whom he had no specific relationship—either professional or functional. He would get to know the gardener, the antique-shop proprietor, the real estate agent—with whom he did business (and invite them to join his tennis games!) as determinedly as he became acquainted with the underworld characters, law enforcement officials, writers, agents, and publishers who served his career.

I'd been recommended to Peter by Stanley Cohen, an international lawyer-historian whose homes in Paris, the south of France, and the Hamptons near Mecox Bay, provided hospitality to a sufficient number of literary stars—Joe Heller, Ed Doctorow, Marshal Brickman, Patricia Bosworth—for Stanley to qualify as a Maas referral source. First, there was the certifying exam: singles with Peter on his court located in a clearing surrounded by lush trees and flowers near a pond off Scuttle Hole Road. In tennis whites, standing on spindly legs and puffing a slim cigar, Peter faced the sun, the net, and me with neither sunglasses nor peaked cap. When he misplayed a point he chastised himself, as if to impress us with the anomaly of an off day. But for all his lanky determination, he moved slowly. Had it not been for the disappointment he projected when losing a point, I would have assumed that Peter was a beginner just learning the game.

I made the cut, and Peter invited me to join his weekend matches, to begin promptly at ten A.M., Decoration Day through Labor Day. No excuses. During my early years as a Maas apparatchik, Bill Holtzman was eventually assigned as my partner. Bill, who later worked in the Giuliani administration, has a talent for getting on with people whose politics may differ from his own without ever compromising his candor or integrity. When a shot was out and he thought so, Bill Holtzman laid it on our host. As a grateful guest, I had become accustomed to a more accommodating game, not only deferring to my opponents' judgments, but giving them the benefit of *all* the close calls.

I suspected that Peter's "contractual" arrangements with Bill and me were motivated more by his determination to have a lineup that didn't require phone calls to set up a match than by the compatibility of our games. Holtzman and I were disciples of the same school: lots of hustle, keep the ball in play, with no nuances of movement that would inspire Balanchine or Jerome Robbins. We understood that Peter preferred to play his game at net, and so we concentrated on lobs and backcourt volleys. Over many summers, a series of celebrities joined Peter as partners to deal with our hackers' game.

The Greek aristocrat-columnist Taki was so impressed by the level of our grace, he reported with considerable irritation that he and Maas had sunk so low they had been beaten by "a couple of sluggish old Jews."

Peter Stone, a frequent fourth who like Taki seemed to have been trained in classic strokes, joined us throughout the years only as a concession to Maas's insistence. An award-winning author—an Emmy and an Oscar—Stone had a compulsive wit that entertained us so extravagantly we didn't suffer much from his critical condescension toward our game. "Why don't you just bring a sledgehammer and be done with it. . . . Your serve was so out they're chasing it in Quogue. . . . Now that was a shot that was undoubtedly the best sneak attack since Pearl Harbor. . . . Would you mind very much if we tried to play tennis rather than snatch the bacon. . . ."

Another Peter, Peter Jennings, arrived for the Sunday-morning game dressed in whites, with a can of balls, impatient for the games to begin. I had met him several times at Polk Award events, but I made no effort to remind the TV news anchor of our acquaintance. He made it clear during the pregame volley that he was on a tight schedule—a plane waiting somewhere to fly him to an exotic destination that would no doubt be featured on the evening news report from Mount Olympus.

Jennings attacked the ball with a ferocity reminiscent of Kurt's discovery of the "Butcher Boy of Flying Point." I suppose his percentage was .300—Hall of Fame for a baseball player, but not much fun on a tennis court. Maas was restrained but critical. "Slow it up, Peter. The plane isn't going anywhere without you." I remember my unsuccessful effort to adjust to Peter Jennings's fast-paced, aggressive game. Fortunately, Bill Holtzman was less empathetic and carried us to an easy but joyless win.

My favorites among the Maas cameo stars were Kevin Wade and Griffin Dunne, Hollywood transfers who played with no histrionics but rather the good manners associated with older generations on the courts. Kevin's game had the grace of a British colonial trained at Sandhurst but reared on the classics. He had just come off a triumph as the author of the film *Working Girl.* Griffin was on his way from a successful career as an actor to producing films.

Although unsure of their ages, I judged Kevin and Griffin were about as old as my sons. Unlike Peter, who was my partner for the match, I thought it a triumph just to hold our own. Maas postmortemed all matches that he lost, but through the years I played on his court, frequently as his partner, he never said a harsh word about my play. It was a gentleness that I saw him extend to his sons John Michael and Terrance, both of whom he nurtured with patience and pride.

During the summers of our play, the August majordomo was Sam Cohn, another of Peter's Hollywood imports, all of whom lived in New York but worked at beating the long odds on the West Coast. Sam's weight, height, gait didn't suggest his passion for any game played away from a negotiating table. I didn't know until several years after I met him that the portly gent to whom Peter related like Laurel to Hardy (or was it Hardy to Laurel?), skeptical but accommodating, was the agent who had sold the screen rights to so many of Peter's books.

Sam Cohn was also, I heard, "a sought-after agent . . . king of the hill" who represented Susan Sarandon and Woody Allen, among others. He was a negotiator who seemed accustomed to getting his way. Sam's first serve, preceded by a corkscrew motion, usually plopped to a corner of the court. He played with the pragmatist's strategy "hit 'em where they ain't." I considered Sam a better player than his physique and movements suggested, but from the other side of the net, I was aware, too, that Sam seemed to be conducting a tutorial for his partner. "Come up. Up to the net. Now. Now . . . Not behind me! Cover your side of the court. . . . Hit the ball harder. Don't be a wimp!"

These messages were delivered with growing irritation when Holtzman and I were on a run. Maas shrugged them off and frequently fired back with a criticism of his own: "Where were you, Sam? We're never going to win from the backcourt."

I found these running commentaries distracting, but Bill Holtzman was amused and entertained. "That's Sam. Always the Boss."

There was no suggestion during the summer that I would be hearing from Sam in the fall. I was surprised when his secretary called to invite me to join Sam for doubles at his club Tennis Port across the East River. I was picked up and chauffeured by Sam Cohn himself. During our rides across the bridge, restricted as we were but with no distractions, I suspected we were on our way to an intimacy reminiscent of that I'd experienced over the long stretch of years driving back and forth from the Midtown courts with Jimmie Flexner.

I learned that Sam Cohn, who had gone on to Harvard and a law degree, was, like me, a graduate of a military school. But unlike my warm regard for Valley Forge, Sam looked back with revulsion on his experience at Culver. "When they persist upon calling me for a contribution, I say, 'Yes, of course, I'd be delighted to make a considerable gift if you can assure me each and every cent is spent to tear down the place.'"

Sam asked questions about my wife, children, grandchildren. He had the art of poking at confidences without expressing any commitment to friendship, a caution he must have developed to protect himself from a call the next day probing for "Any chance to sell my book to the movies?"

At his club we played with two pros—Marian, a young lady with a demon backhand, who was often assigned to me, and a lithe Puerto Rican gent who seemed to have picked up his racket at the same spot King Arthur located Excalibur. The sessions always ended at the bell with the scores so close only a game or two separated the winners—most often Sam's team.

Invitations to the winter sessions—perhaps a dozen over the stretch of several years—ended after the August that Bill Holtzman was away and Peter assigned me to team up with the player-coach. Peter's partner was Alan Siegel, a former Ivy League basketball player from Cornell who, with a helmet and spear, could pass as a visitation from a Roman centurion.

Alan was new to the game, but he caught on fast. Before long he was smashing serves to deep corners and poaching effectively at net. With a script not much different from the one I'd heard him divine for Peter, Sam expressed irritation along with instructions for my game.

It must have been a miscalculation of my speed or flexibility that led to my tearing the meniscus of my left knee. I resisted an operation and rather than do nothing to cure it I followed Avi's advice and worked with a therapist to restore strength. It worked and in less than a year I was back on the courts.

My postinjury debut was at Central Park, where during the spring I played with Bob Silberstein, my roommate at Valley Forge in 1945 and perhaps the best amateur tennis player with whom I'd ever mixed it up. Bob had slowed up considerably over the years, but he could still rally for the big points.

Although he humored me when playing one-on-one, I don't recall ever losing a match with Bob Silberstein as my partner. At Central Park we were sometimes invited to play with the proprietary teachers and retirees who had taken possession of the center courts. It was there that I encountered my PEN pal Gay Talese, teamed with a radio talk-show host whom everyone but me seemed to recognize. Bob and I so impressed Gay he suggested I join him for winter play at the indoor courts at the Armory at Park and 67th.

Gracious, princely, and with hand-eye coordination capable of swatting tennis balls as if they were nuisance flies, Gay kept me hustling for the erratic bounces from the wooden surface. He didn't say so, but I'm sure my singles play was a disappointment.

To brush up and take advantage of my membership (joining the Armory Club required not only recommendation but an interview with their admissions committee), I played pickup games three times a week. I was aware that my ability to cover the court was declining and attributed the growing aches in my knees to aging. After drubbing me in one set, my son the doctor suggested we call it a day. As we were drying off in the locker room, Ken spoke to me as "son to father," strongly advising me not to play ever again on a wooden surface. "There's no cushion, no give—you'd best quit now before you destroy what's left of your knees."

I laid off indoor tennis until tapped by Peter Schwed for occasional appearances with a group of eight that Peter assembled to join him for two hours at a court deep in the heart of Queens. Peter had run Simon & Schuster and brought to his tennis enterprise the same dedication and curiosity that characterized his years as an editorial administrator.

Players were auditioned, evaluated, and assigned to teams that Peter determined would provide the most vigorous competition. At the end of the first hour, we were rotated. By the time I joined this group of journalists and publishing savants, Peter was already close to eighty. Even at that advanced age he had competitive company. Charles (Cy) Rembar, the attorney who argued and won the case that allowed *Lady Chatterley's Lover* to be published in the United States, was a fierce athlete. The guy on your team you would want to be at the plate when the winning run was on base, Cy's cousin Norman Mailer wrote in the introduction to Cy's landmark, *The End of Obscenity.*

Among the younger athletes, the undisputed star was Richard Craven, a gentlemen so modest, even though he had played world-class competition during his Harvard days, he insisted he had so slowed up he was right at home with Schwed's league.

New York Times editorial writer, Pulitzer Prize winner Bob Semple, was the life of the Schwed party. Bob's good humor and wit made veterans and rookies feel welcome and secure during the treks through side streets to the dead end that provided the two flights of steps where Schwed's King Solomon's Mine of tennis courts magically appeared.

I was often assigned to team up with Cy Rembar against Peter and his protégé of the morning. Peter and Cy were both tough competitors, familiar as well as comfortable with winning. At the time I engaged with them they were both long past their prime and I, along with them, was limping into decline.

The defining moment was a line call. With the game score even and the tie-breaker knotted at six, Peter sent a sharp serve deep into Cy's court. Cy called it out. Peter protested, "Come on, Cy. I could see that ball hit the line from here."

Cy answered with a quietly rhetorical, "Do you think I would cheat you, Peter?" And then the verdict, "The serve was out."

It was an awkward moment, flirting with the embarrassment of witnessing an eminent professional of the law challenged by a retired apostle of books and both seemingly determined to win.

"I can show you. There may even be a mark just where it landed," Schwed threatened as he came across the court, waving his racket as a weapon? Pointer? "There. There's the spot." He stopped at the deep corner of the receiver's court, his grizzled face and narrow eyes focused on what I perceived as most likely a smudge, a footprint.

Although I was the closest witness, neither Cy nor Peter called upon me.

At the moment I felt great trepidation about being involved, Cy said, "You really think that's a mark on this court resulting from your serve, Peter?" Again, the tone was quiet but the rhetorical scorn undeniable.

"Yes. Yes, I do," Peter insisted. "That serve was clearly in."

Cy may very well have surrendered what he knew to be a truth for the first time in his life. "Then it's your point, Peter. If it means that much to you, be my guest."

As Peter turned and headed back to his court, Cy said to me, "I guess winning means so much to him it distorts his vision as well as his manners." He shook his head from side to side. "And at our age."

In my seventies I attended two more memorial services for former tennis partners. Peter Maas had been in and out of the hospital during the summer of 2001 for a mysterious infection. The last time we played he suggested we have another go at singles. It was midweek, a warm afternoon, and it was obvious that his recuperation was slow and painful. I encouraged Peter to rally rather than play a set, but Maas had made up his mind. Even weakened, the voice of command was still there. I was thinking as we played, "We're the same age but right before my eyes Peter is growing older and older."

After we left the court he talked about the match, searching for a reason, a problem that could be remedied to improve his game. He ran through the litany "eye on the ball . . . racket back . . . follow through," and then after a long pause said, "I think your style of play intimidates me. I don't know why. It's not that way with Holtzman or Cohn, Stone or Siegel."

Of course he was wrong but I didn't correct him.

Less than three weeks later my old tennis maestro was dead. At the memorial service in New York, Hugh Carey, the former governor of New York, spoke about Peter as an indispensable advisor, a political wise man. His son John Michael mentioned his uncompromising devotion and their pleasures fishing together. A half dozen speakers reflected on Peter Maas's career as a bestselling author and crack reporter. No one mentioned his pleasures on the court.

My Allen Room friend Jimmie Flexner died at the age of ninety-five. His daughter Nellie flew in from England for a memorial service at Jimmie's social club. Our nation's great man of letters Louis Auchincloss celebrated Jimmie as satisfying Dr. Johnson's standards for being perfectly "clubbable." Robert Caro, the leading biographer-historian of our time, rejoiced in his twenty-four books still in print. The venerable Arthur Schlesinger Jr. surveyed Jimmie's versatile literary career as historian, biographer, and art critic. Even there among so many of James Thomas Flexner's colleagues and friends, only his daughter Nellie and I seemed to remember him as a tennis player renowned at Midtown for "the Flexner Lob" and to me as the friend who introduced me to the pleasures of playing Rorschachs at the courts.

28

Locker Rooms, Treadmills, and Hot Air with Buster Crabbe, Rod Gilbert, Bruce Springsteen, Tom Wolfe, Bruce Jay Friedman, Joe Heller, a Contender, and a "Champion"

1971–2007

An entry in my journal for Sunday, 24 January 1971:

> When you are discussing boxing in the sauna it is a help to know the big man with the broken nose is a professional boxer who has exchanged punches with Cassius Clay. Alex Miteff comes from Argentina. "No, no," says Alex, moving his hands as big paws jabbing for an opening. "Clay is best. He can beat them all."
>
> The little bald-headed man with an aggressive paunch and no behind says, "You're crazy. Clay can't take a punch. Frazier will kill him."
>
> By the coals two musclemen sit blinking. If they have a thought relative to the dialogue it must be "I couldn't care less."
>
> I've been going to the Shelton Hotel Health Club four or five

times a week for the past three years. It is at Lexington and 48th. I'm usually in and out in less than an hour. I read the paper in the sauna, spend five minutes in the steam room, shave and rinse, and then twenty to thirty minutes in the pool. After I shower and dry off I drop into the sunroom for a minute or two and then douse myself with palms full of lotion and oil before I dress and take off. This Sunday someone in the sauna is talking about the two and a half million Clay and Frazier have been guaranteed for the championship fight.

I'd seen Alex before, but never spoken to him. He is big and broad-shouldered and resembles Anthony Quinn. He genially concedes points with the grace of a man who is accustomed to giving in to other people's greater need to be right.

It isn't until the bald-headed man leaves the sauna that I ask Alex if he ever fought Clay. He shrugs as if to say "Yes, I tried."

Then, he starts slowly evaluating the arguments of the man who has insisted Frazier will win. "The Bonavenna fight is nothing," says Miteff. "He fights a style makes everybody look bad. Bonavenna throws off—rhy-thm, the rhythm."

The paunch is back again, moving to the heat of the coals. "Hey, they tell me you were the heavyweight champion of Argentina."

"Not Argentina," says Alex. "South America. Is not the same thing."

There is a change in the bald-headed man's attitude, but he is unable to renew the conversation. "What you do?" Alex asks me suddenly.

I tell him I've written some books and I'm working on a new magazine.

"You writer." His thin eyes narrow and he nods. "Lemme ask you—how come everybody write and write about boxing, but nobody say what is really like?"

I'm prepared for a discussion of the abuses of the fighter by the manager and promoters. That's what I get.

The bald-headed man agrees with Alex. "It's a rotten business. The boxing game is run by racketeers."

"Not so." Alex lifts a finger like an impresario. "Not all racketeers. Some good men. Many men mean good in the boxing business. But still, the fighter——" He shrugs helplessly.

I ask him if he's read *The Harder They Fall.* He tells me he has and liked it. "Schulberg know his business." He mentions Rod Serling's *Requiem for a Heavyweight.* "But not exactly the same thing. Is not so simple. I wish I write book—my story."

Later, after I finish my laps and shower, I sit near the sunroom where Alex is reading the *Times.* Because I want to get in and out of the Shelton quickly, I rarely talk to people. It is one of the places in the world I have no desire to make new friends.

"But I could tell you story——" Alex looks up from his paper as if we have been talking straight along. "When I boy I leave home, live in room in Buenos Aires. I shine shoes until I meet Perón." He tells me then about his friendship with the Argentine dictator. Perón had given him a car and a house and money. "He good man. Good for Argentina," says Alex. Spelling out the changes in the Argentine economy during and after Perón, Alex establishes his case. "There. Again. What you know about Perón? What they write about him. Always Perón he is dictator. Evil man. Cruel to the people. Not true. But why nobody write that?"

I suggest that his view of Perón is a very personal one. Although I don't know too much about Argentine history I can understand why a reporter might not be impressed with the indulgence of the Perón administration, the expenditures of public funds to preserve private power. That doesn't elude Alex. He shakes his head. "Is not that simple. What my people have now? Was better then or now?"

I say I don't know, and then I tell Alex that if he feels so strongly he should try to write it down. "No, I no artist," says Alex. He explains that his wife is the artist in the family. She is a ballet dancer. "They say it cannot be a boxer and ballet dancer. But it is." Alex laughs and moves his large shoulders. "It is. We are." He tells me he has three children—Alex Jr., Fernando, and Kareem. I promise him a book for his children and he waves as I leave him sitting with the *Times.*

———————

It was a familiar face and a familiar body I saw reflected in the wall-length mirror of the Shelton's locker room in 1971. He was undressing by a bench about twenty feet from me where I was changing to my bathing suit. Could he possibly be Buster Crabbe—Flash Gordon! Buck Rogers! Tarzan!

During the late thirties, my brother, Benson, and I had been addicted to double-feature Saturday afternoons at the Rialto Theatre, North Avenue, Baltimore. It wasn't the feature-length movies, the short subjects, "The March of Time," or previews of coming attractions that enraptured us. A weekly serial, *Flash Gordon,* was such a hit not only with us but the other kids in our neighborhood, it was repeated week after week, year after year, until Buster Crabbe, the blond hero with cropped hair, perfect features, broad shoulders and Olympian body, was recast for a serial version of Buck Rogers and cast for a brief run in *Tarzan the Fearless.* But Buster Crabbe was always Flash Gordon to us.

I was too awed to approach him directly, but continued to stare with visions of spaceships, Dale Arden, and Princess Aura flashing through the locker room. Later that same day, I was swimming my thirty laps when Flash Gordon plunged into the other lane. He swam with perfectly measured strokes reminiscent of Johnny Weissmuller, the legendary Tarzan and another Olympic swimming champion, holding his head out of the water. I couldn't resist the temptation to try to keep pace. Even when Buster Crabbe switched to the breast stroke I continued to fall laps behind him.

It may have been the longest session I ever indulged in an indoor pool, probably close to an hour. I didn't dry off until Our Hero called it a day and was on his way to the shower. I shadowed Buster Crabbe discreetly and when he was fully dressed and exchanging greetings along with offering a tip for the locker attendant, I introduced myself and told him how my brother and I skipped a weekend in Atlantic City because we were such devoted fans of his Flash Gordon adventures.

"I'm always surprised at how many people still remember that," he said disarmingly. When I asked what he was up to now he invited me to visit him at the Concord Hotel where he sometimes gave swimming lessons.

Buster Crabbe was not a weary celebrity. He seemed even a mite grateful to be recognized. Fernando, the pipe-smoking former Spanish aristocrat who had been making do distributing towels and toilet articles for several decades while he quietly attempted to convert the exercise factory into a social club, told Buster Crabbe that I was a writer, as if to certify my compliment.

"And what do you write?" asked Buster Crabbe.

"Nothing in a class with Flash Gordon or Tarzan," I said. "But I've recently published a collection of stories for young readers, *Not All Girls Have Million Dollar Smiles*."

"That's not entirely true in Hollywood," Buster Crabbe replied. "If the smile isn't worth a million, they find a way to do something about it."

Then, Buster Crabbe smiled his Flash Gordon smile and was on his way by bus, subway, taxi, or rocket ship to further adventures in Big Town.

Bruce Jay Friedman's first novel *Stern* was published in 1962, just about the time I met the critic David Boroff, who thought I should be acquainted with two young novelists whom he considered bound for the literary pantheon—Bruce Jay Friedman and Philip Roth. I had brief chats with Roth and Friedman at a party at Boroff's West Side apartment, read their fiction, and confirmed David Boroff as my literary handicapper.

I became such a fan of Philip Roth that later I brought his novels along as a prescription for a perfect holiday. During the years that Avi and I joined British walking groups for rambles through Provence, Tuscany, Malta, Majorca, and Delphi as well as the highlands of Scotland and Wales, I was such an enthusiastic reader of Roth's novels Avi suggested it might be more fun for both of us if we invited Philip Roth to join us and read aloud.

I encountered Bruce at the locker room of the Shelton. Tall, with the gait and bearing of a running back, he certainly did not qualify for casting as the somewhat nerdy leads in either his novel *Stern* or *A Mother's Kisses*.

A year before Roth's *Portnoy's Complaint*, a triumphant monologue of the Jewish experience in America as a psychiatric tragicomedy, Friedman told the story of assimilation as a bewildering, frequently humiliating laugh fest. Reading his novels—and even after meeting him—I had difficulty identifying the Maccabee warrior he appeared to be with the befuddled victim of his novels. I had never consciously experienced anti-Semitism—my defenses against insult have always been strenuous—and so to me reading Friedman was education as well as fun.

Bruce had worked at Magazine Management in the 1950s at the time I was employed by Mercury Publications. He spoke of talented friends such as Mario Puzo, who, like him, was putting in time for the weekly paycheck while "banging away at the old novel." We talked in the steam room and sauna and after several encounters we compared notes about our voluntary and irrational presence in rooms filled with sufficient heat to invite the entry of the mythical demon with his pitchfork.

With a wry smile that I couldn't read, Bruce mentioned that he was writing his second play and calling it *Steam Bath.* He was. It wasn't quite the literary triumph of his novels, and had nothing that I could recognize as inspired by his experience at the Shelton. But *Steam Bath,* along with his later scripts for films, short stories, and novels, confirmed for me David Boroff's prediction that Bruce Jay Friedman was among the most talented and versatile satirists of his generation.

When the Shelton Hotel closed shop, I moved on to the Jack La Lanne Clubs with branches all over town. I settled at the unit located in the East Fifties off Madison and close enough to the offices of *Intellectual Digest* for me to drop in at lunch breaks or after work in the evening.

Unlike the Shelton, which was more a spa than a gym, La Lanne's focus like that of its founder was on body building. The pool provided a dunk rather than a lap. I learned to make do by devising exercises, stretches, stationary kicks, and jogs to satisfy my daily quota for water sport. This seemed a waste of time to several of the members conspicuously committed to "definition" (jargon for what in my younger days we suspected was being "muscle-bound").

The most garrulous and popular member, an aging gent mysteriously addressed as "the Baron," was my advocate. With flaring gray hair and a trimmed gray mustache, the Baron's pale, pudgy body suggested he was not—and would never be—the least interested in swimming or exercise. Soon after introducing himself to me, he solicited copies of *Intellectual Digest* and asked to see my novels. The Baron told me he was a former columnist for the now defunct *New York World-Telegram & Sun*. He still solicited insiders' dope as well as scandal with a genuine curiosity that was as seductively friendly as it was flattering.

When he learned that my novel *He Had It Made* was set in the borscht belt, I became the audience for his total recall of routines, gags, and stories. In addition, the Baron insisted upon introducing me to other members. "Do you know Sid? You have to know Sid. He's a famous writer and a certifiable intellectual. You should subscribe to his magazine, buy his book. He'll autograph your copy for you."

I don't recall the Baron selling a single subscription or copy of my novel, but among the members he introduced me to was a young actor-screenwriter to whom he recommended, "Collaborate with Sid." A jab of the thumb to identify me. "He's already published. Famous. He could help you out." The gentleman to whom this pitch was addressed wasn't much taller than I, but there was no mistaking the body movements and self-assured demeanor as that of a serious workout apostle.

The square-jawed, muscular young actor-writer seemed as dismayed by the attention as I was. Evidently the Baron had elicited from him that he was writing a film script about a boxer. He seemed unwilling to discuss it, and registered visible relief, a relaxing of the cramped brows, when I mentioned several boxing movies of the past—Kirk Douglas in the film version of Ring Lardner's short story

"Champion," Robert Ryan in—"What was the name of that film? *The Set-Up?*"

The literary muscleman was as much a film buff as he was an impressive presence. I left with the sympathetic feeling that it was too bad such an intelligent, obviously dedicated young man was addicted to an illusion—a produced film script about a boxer?

As my old man might say, "The odds were off the chart" that the actor-writer the Baron introduced me to in the locker room was Sylvester Stallone, who would go on to write *Rocky,* winner of the Academy Award in 1976 for best film, and then enjoy a thriving career on the screen as Rambo, man of muscle—courtesy of Jack La Lanne?

It was Avi's idea that I allow my membership in Jack La Lanne's to lapse in order to join her as a charter member of the Atrium, a deluxe facility opening on 57th Street between Park and Lexington that one of her patients had touted as a bargain. "You can swim real laps in the pool, the locker rooms are carpeted, free towels, and we can rendezvous in the coed sauna and steam rooms."

Soon after we signed up I was invited by the manager to be a member of their board. Misled about my prominence by my debut as a political commentator on Channel 5, one of the more generous administrators suggested I join Joe Namath, Richard Todd, Bess Myerson, and Sal Marciano with complimentary membership and "no real responsibilities to speak of."

We'd already paid our relatively modest dues and I declined the invitation, convinced it was bad manners to exploit what I was certain was the well-meaning agent's misreading of me as some kind of celebrity. Several weeks into my daily visits, sure enough, there were Joe Namath and Richard Todd sitting side by side, draped with towels over their laps, in the sauna.

Todd, blond, had a perfectly toned body that made him look like he had modeled for Rodin. But Namath, dark complected with earnest eyes, seemed too engaged by personal and emotional dilemmas to be concerned with the achievements of his flexible body.

As the Jets' quarterback, Namath had been more villain than hero in the mythology of Baltimore Colt fans. His 16–7 devastation of our home team in the 1967 Super Bowl had been a shock as well as a tragedy to twelve-year-old Ken and ten-year-old Mike, our sons who passed up the New York Jets and Giants for allegiance to the "family farm." In the steam room and locker rooms of East 57th Street, the Jets' star and bad boy was mannerly and friendly with all and, rumor had it, seductive with one.

Among the staff of the aspiring city/country club was a pinup candidate referred to by male members and locker room attendants as "Barbie." From time to time Barbie, whose assignments included signing up new recruits, appeared in the steam or sauna rooms in a bikini. It was reported that when Mr. Namath was visiting for a late workout, the centerfold would appear wrapped only in a towel. This cast of characters—two—and costumes inspired scandalous speculation among male members of the locker room, along with occasional complaints from women who wandered into the precinct.

Joe Namath signed a few autographs and soon moved on. Barbie eventually hooked up with a Wall Street tycoon and visited only to show off the late stages of a pregnancy. Those of us who inherited the Richard Todd legacy rooted for the Jets with the satisfaction of loyalty but never much hope for their victory.

If Fernando was the reigning prince of the Shelton Hotel's men's locker room, Victor Noel Sepuleuda is the psychiatrist-in-residence at the successor to the Atrium, the New York Health and Racquet Club's branch at East 57th Street. Dispensing good cheer and therapy along with the towels, lotions, and locks, Victor, or Papé, as he is sometimes addressed, is the most overqualified, yet satisfied, person I encounter in my daily routines.

It is not uncommon, when arriving for steam and workout in the pool, to see Victor, squat, broad-shouldered, with a graying mustache and speckled locks, in T-shirt and khakis, nodding sympathetically as one of the members shares with him a tale of woe—abandoned by wife, out of work, being driven nuts by a maiden aunt. Although he never met the distinguished *New Yorker* editor, the late Gardner Botsford, Victor like Gardner responds to all inquiries as to his health, no matter what the current diagnosis, with "Never felt better." His sympathetic rejoinder to unsolicited complaints is frequently a nod, a pat on the back, and the conviction, "You feel that way now, but it will get better."

Because I bunk my clothes in the locker adjacent to Victor's station, we share greetings and chitchat five days a week. With an exquisite sense of respect for privacy, he nevertheless sees to it that members he considers to be of congenial interests are made aware of each other. As our locker room host and ambassador, Victor introduced me to Steve Horn and Robert Layton, matinee idol attorneys and world travelers as committed to good cheer as they are to beautiful ladies.

Years ago, when my friend John Hammond, identified as the impresario who "discovered jazz," was in the hospital, Victor made sure I had a passing conversation with one of John's "discoveries," the rock musician Bruce Springsteen, who was wandering through the locker room on one of his rare visits. It was a brief exchange but the poet of "Born to Run" and "Born in the U.S.A." responded to my mention of John's name with immediate recognition and an affection that suggested gratitude. I assured him I would relay the message to John, but Bruce Springsteen seems to have done better than that. He contacted John Hammond in his hospital room. I later learned from other friends that the Springsteen connection was grace from heaven. Nurses, doctors, orderlies, and other patients expressed increased courtesy, even reverence, for modest John Hammond, who had suggested to no one his association with Springsteen—or Bessie Smith, Benny Goodman, Duke Ellington, and other deities of American song and dance.

Rod Gilbert, the Hall of Fame New York Rangers hockey celestial, was a regular in the workout rooms for several years, and visited the pool frequently for a quick dip. I suppose I saw Gilbert more often and spoke to him more intimately than I did with any great athlete, including those I met during my three years visiting the locker rooms, of the Yankees, Dodgers, and Giants for *Baseball Magazine.*

Gilbert was approachable and friendly. When I asked him how he adjusted to the bullying and violence that was so integral to professional hockey, he told me he established right away that he wouldn't tolerate intimidation. He described how he hauled off on the first player who deliberately fouled him, explaining that it's better to have a reputation as a hothead than an easy mark.

We also talked about our impressions of Mickey Mantle and Billy Martin, whom Rod knew as friends. He described their self-destructive drinking, and while he cherished Mantle as a friend, he recognized a sense of doom in the great Yankee's feelings about himself. It may have had a lot to do with Mantle's father's early death, but Rod Gilbert wouldn't play analyst—a locker-room exercise in our neighborhood. Gilbert did, however, venture into medical advice, a "prescription" for me that may well have saved me the loss of my voice.

The symptom—clue—was increasing hoarseness that I was quietly treating with ever longer sessions in the steam room. Defying Avi's wise and generous counsel, I refused to track the cause. During one of our ritual conversations among the steam clouds, the Rangers' ace spontaneously diagnosed my hoarseness as a problem with my vocal cords. When I insisted it wasn't anything an extra dose of steam wouldn't cure, he suggested I was wrong. Then Gilbert went on to tell me he had the same problem himself, and it required a laryngologist, and perhaps an operation. "You may have to rest your voice for a day or two afterward. See Dr. Blaugrund, he'll tell you all about it."

Dr. Stanley Blaugrund, a member of the staff of Lenox Hill Hospital, was an old friend of my wife's and an acquaintance of our son Ken, too. Avi had served her internship at Lenox Hill after graduation from the NYU School of Medicine. Ken elected to return to our neighborhood after five years in Cambridge where he received both his M.D. and M.P.H. from Harvard.

But it was Rod Gilbert's name I invoked as my reference, and sure enough the consultation in the steam room "cleared the air." Two weeks later Dr. Blaugrund removed a polyp from a vocal cord, and after two days of the silent treatment, I was back in action, sounding off in classes, meetings, and the steam room.

Andy Warhol had "immortalized" Rod Gilbert in 1977 with an acrylic and silkscreen on canvas. The scholar and recipient of the George Polk Award for Criticism, Arthur Danto, whom I revered for recognizing and writing the introduction to the artist Russell Connor's "civilized comedy" *Masters in Pieces,* identified Warhol as the "Philosopher of Contemporary American Art." When I told Rod about this he expressed only incredulity at the cosmic value of the posters. Overhearing fragments of this exchange in the locker room, another of the fresh-towel subscribers, Peter Palazzo, a designer who is credited with revolutionizing newspaper graphics, waited two days before acknowledging he'd overheard mention of Warhol during my conversation with Rod.

Peter had that quiet tough-guy manner that seemed more appropriate for a street-smart negotiator than the artist who created the typographic format that distinguished the 1963 *New York Herald Tribune* and became a model for newspaper design ever after. Peter asked if I knew Warhol, with an inflection that suggested *he* did.

I mentioned meeting Warhol briefly. A student in one of my New School writing classes was so certain her god Andy and I would strike up the band together, she insisted upon introducing me to him. "You and Andy have so much in common," I recalled her saying. "You're both so interested in people."

I told Peter my visit to Andy Warhol's factory had been as amusing as a social disaster could be. I remembered Warhol as devoid of affect other than that of an obsessed voyeur. He didn't respond to his acolyte's effort to create a conversational bridge between us. Warhol just nodded, unimpressed. He was absorbed in observing people across the room. I recalled faint oriental music, several overly made-up, anorexic young ladies enacting a harem dance scene, and two young men playing "rock, paper, scissors." That was it. Not a word from Warhol stored in my memory bank.

Warhol was "Andy" to Peter. He told me, "I gave Andy one of

his first commissions. Hired him when I was creating newspaper ads for I. Miller. Warhol did these line drawings—kinda shaky—of legs and shoes. He couldn't have been more grateful for the job, easier to get along with." Peter seemed surprised, even disbelieving of Warhol's great success. "Beats me," he said. "The only thing unusual was the way he sent out all these personal drawings for Christmas cards. I figured he was a self-promoter, nothing particularly wrong with that. I kinda liked the guy, rooted for him. I've hung on to a couple of his old drawings." Later, Peter Palazzo told me he sold the original Warhols for so much money, "I'm embarrassed to tell you."

It may be the therapeutic wonders of the steam or just the ole Roman appeal of guys hanging out at the baths, but another songbird Victor made sure I met was Jerry Leiber, who, among his other top-of-the-chart compositions, was responsible for Elvis Presley's "Hound Dog."

With a towel draped around his midsection, thinning gray hair, and a complexion that suggested he'd just come out of a long session in the steam room, Jerry was nonetheless an imposing presence. It was his smile. He always seemed one up on you.

When I learned Jerry Leiber was raised in Baltimore, I passed along, through Victor (no postage), a copy of my memoir. Less than a week later, much to my surprise, the composer of rock and roll greeted me with a grin and the one-upper, "So your old man was a bookie in Baltimore. He must have known my uncle, who was the biggest of the big shots in the same line."

Georges Borchardt isn't quite in the swim with Buster Crabbe and Rod Gilbert as a legendary athlete, but among literary agents he's an international favorite as the person a writer covets to create the first splash for the marketing relay team. When I recognized Georges in the pool at the NYHRC 57th Street, it was early on a Saturday afternoon. There he was, the agent responsible for the publication of more than two thousand translations from the French, swimming with his head above water. Right by his side was his very own mermaid–wife, Anne, a conventional freestyler just like me, with goggles.

What a bonus it has been these many years to encounter Georges in the locker room for literary chat and gossip. He who helped introduce the works of Roland Barthes, Samuel Beckett, Marguerite Duras, Elie Wiesel, Jean-Paul Sartre, and Alain Robbe-Grillet to readers in the U.S.A. awarded me an uncorrected bound manuscript of Pierre Bayard's *How to Talk About Books You Haven't Read.*

About ten years after our first summer rental in Water Mill, Long Island, the Omni Health Club in Southampton opened. The spa has little to recommend it to summer residents of mansions and beach houses, but it is a club and church to the locals who are as addicted as I to daily steam, sauna, Jacuzzi, and swimming pool. The health club, located in the building that houses the offices for the Hampton Jitney, was founded by the generous entrepreneur who got the jitneys rolling from Manhattan to the Hamptons. It is one of the few spa facilities—if not the only one—on the East End west of Montauk.

During the twenty years I've subscribed to daily visits, summer months and weekends, I've run into less than a half dozen members who were not locals. Gene McHam, a former member of the Lindsay team that ran City Hall in the late 1960s, has worked out on the machines from time to time. For reasons I have never quite understood, Jacques Leviant, an international trader who owns the mansion next door to George Soros's at the Southampton beach, has routinely walked for twenty minutes in the pool and sat for another ten in the hottest of the two hot tubs.

Perhaps Joe Heller qualified as a "local." He and his wife, Valerie, lived in East Hampton. The first time we ran into each other at the Omni, Joe told me fiercely, "This is the only club I'd join." Joe's mischievous eyes seemed to question whether I would be as happy with my "medication" as he was with his.

We shared notes on our routines and I learned the spa had no attraction for him at all. "Is it sanitary? I don't even shower here." Seems Joe Heller worked out on the treadmill, or was it the stationary bike? "None of that Charles Atlas stuff for me. A muscleman kicks sand in my eye, I go to the ophthalmologist."

Other members seemed unaware of Joe's presence or literary reputation. That, too, pleased Joe. "I prefer to sweat unobserved." When Joe's memoir *Now and Then* was published in 1998, I reviewed it for the East Hampton *Star.* "We were children from poor families, but didn't know it," Joe wrote about his childhood in Brooklyn. There is not a complaint or a line of self-pity or an indictment of any friend or family. I praised the memoir as a "celebration of life." Soon after the review appeared, Joe caught me by the check-in desk as I was leaving off my membership card and he was picking up his.

"You are a gentleman and a scholar," Joe Heller proclaimed, "A wonderful writer and a superb literary critic. I love your book reviews! What's more, I just dropped you a note telling you just that."

True to his word I did receive Joe's note, but his Omni legacy was a mite complex. Picking up on Joe's enthusiasm, the knockout number who attended the desk said, "I didn't know you are a writer. How exciting. What do you write?" Not a word from her or anyone else at the Omni ever suggested they were aware of Joe Heller or *Catch-22.*

The other literary great who qualified for an attendance medal at the Omni was spotted and acknowledged by Frank Zyckowski, Southampton born and bred, veteran of the Korean War, and the object of my bird-watch at parades down Main Street on Memorial Day and the Fourth of July. Frank whispered to me in the locker room that Tom Wolfe had signed a copy of *A Man in Full* for him and, "You know, he actually complimented me for that letter to the editor I wrote for the *Press.*" Tom is like that, gracious and responsive, an egalitarian in the gym and at the desk.

I had met Tom and his wife, Sheila, when she designed the Buckley-Little catalogue sponsored by the Authors Guild for writers to sell copies of books considered by conventional markets as "out of print." I was immediately impressed by the manners, taste, and off-the-cuff brilliance of the Bard in White. Walking up Third Avenue on my way home from my midtown health club, I'd sometimes see Tom with friends, dining near the window at the Isle of Capri on the corner of 61st Street.

I was a devotee of Gino restaurant at the time. The prancing zebra wallpaper evoked memories of Ed Sullivan introducing me to Chicken Gino (a broiled half chicken saturated with fresh garlic). It was a ritual at lunchtime for the deadpan host of the country's top-rated Sunday-evening variety show to feast on the house specialty and enthusiastically—even with a smile—recommend it to other guests. It was also at Gino on a late-evening visit with son Ken in the early '70s that Frank Sinatra, himself, told us he did not, "definitely did not," like garlic.

It wasn't until decades later that Avi and I decided that if the Isle of Capri was good enough for Tom Wolfe, we should test the Isle's garlic for ourselves. Vincenzo and Maria Lamanna's legacy, preserved by their daughter Jane and granddaughter Donna, soon became my company "cafeteria." Even when Gino wasn't overcrowded, I dined at the Isle with family, friends, or solo.

Standing by the check-in desk at the Omni with Tom, a thin, graying gent with a warm boyish smile, we often exchanged commentary and family notes as well as restaurant reviews. Tom's Omni outfit was always the same: a modest navy blue gym shirt and pants outfit, with comfortable sneakers for his warm-up stretches and ballet on the Precor Elliptical Fitness Trainer.

When I mentioned his coincidental endorsement of the Isle and our pleasures at the discovery, Tom shared a history of the restaurant as formerly offering a buffet that attracted a following of writers and editors. He also informed me of the wisdom of the Lamannas, who had bought the property as well as neighboring tracts.

My family's admiration for Tom Wolfe includes three generations. *The Painted Word* was passed down to several of our grandchildren. Anna, the eldest, was impressed sufficiently to find Tom's negative perceptions of some contemporary art an inspiration for a critical piece she wrote in her junior year for the school paper at Dalton. A sculpture by Sol LeWitt that dominated the front court and blocked the view to the garden at the Whitney had ticked Anna off. Apparently the staff and advisor to the school paper were not pleased by Anna's iconoclastic spirit. She wasn't invited to serve on the editorial staff in her senior year, and took a number of hits from the children of families who collected the fashionable "masters."

In the midst of this brouhaha, Anna and I encountered Tom Wolfe, suited up in his white urban uniform, strolling down Madison Avenue. I introduced Anna to my Omni pal, and told him the tale. Tom expressed empathy, support, and most flattering of all, requested to read Anna's piece. Two days after mailing it, she received all the endorsement she would ever need. "Your piece is wonderful (and makes me feel very special)," Tom wrote. "I'd say you won the duel. . . . How can anyone get excited over a work in a visual medium that's about 'ideas pure and simple'?"

V

*Doers of Good Deeds, PEN and
Authors Guild: 1960s Through the
Twenty-first Century*

29

PEN American Center: Langston Hughes, Arthur Miller, John Steinbeck, Pablo Neruda, and Pearl Buck, Championing the Legacy of Franz Schoenberner

1963–1971

"I recognize you. You're the Spanish poet." With this miscasting, John Farrar endorsed my nomination to be a member of PEN American Center soon after the publication of my second novel, *The Other Side of the Street,* 1962. The international writers' association was founded in 1921 by C. A. Dawson Scott, a Cornish novelist, and John Galsworthy to "dispel race, class, and national hatreds" and to encourage the principle of "unhampered transmission of thought within each nation and between all nations." I was introduced to John Farrar, the publisher and president of the American Center, at a cocktail party at the Pierre Hotel.

Offit has been taken for other national identities and associated with various contractions. Was the original name Ofsowakowski? Ofsowitz? O'ffit? But Offisata? I never did find out with whom John Farrar confused me, but I did discover it was my complexion and something "about the eyes" that he later told me persuaded him I was

Spanish. "Did anyone ever mention you resemble the portrait of the young Picasso?"

The bimonthly cocktail parties (the Pierre called them "PEN receptions"), celebrating three or four recently published authors, started at five and concluded at seven, just enough time for me to visit the Elysian Fields and be home in time to check Ken and Mike's homework and short-order a late supper for our home team's medical student, who had to spend nights at Bellevue Hospital, covering for striking nurses, or doing her stint monitoring pregnant women in labor all night when she was on ob-gyn service.

The presiding deities of the American Center were Marchette and Joy Chute, midwestern versions of the Brontës who settled in New York and adopted PEN as their church. Marchette in a broad-brimmed hat, long skirt, and no-nonsense shoes was distinguished for her biography *Shakespeare of London.* She looked Elizabethan. Joy's books for young readers, many of them sports stories, were published with the initials "B.J." preceding her family name. "It was assumed a woman wasn't able to write a good sports story," she told me. "I even hid from some of my publishers." Both Marchette and Joy served as presidents of PEN and they were constantly scouting young writers to whom to entrust the legacy.

I wasn't aware of this until after I'd written a piece about an international congress in Piran, Yugoslavia, and the Chutes insisted I meet Franz Schoenberner.

The former editor of *Simplicissimus,* Schoenberner had survived three concentration camps and attributed his escape from Nazi Germany to PEN. This I learned from the Chutes as we sipped sherry at their East River apartment, seated by a bay window and flanked by a table that held (did they say?) an original Shakespeare folio. I was as uncertain about the folio as I was about the reason Franz Schoenberner was sitting in a wheelchair when I arrived at his Gramercy Park apartment.

My perhaps mistaken impression that *Simplicissimus* was a satirical magazine led me to respond to his questions about the PEN congress with brief dramatized sketches of the delegates playing Talmudic scholars over various administrative issues. I tested my French, Slavic, and English mimicries with no sign from Mr. Schoenberner that he was amused. After my brief sketch, he asked me questions like a relentless interviewer in pursuit of evidence or a self-incriminating statement.

Attempting to change the subject, I interrupted and asked if he had ever seen Adolf Hitler. "Of course. Of course." Franz Schoenberner's neck tensed, his head jutted forward. "We saw Adolf Hitler all the time—at the cafés, in the street, always strutting, always lecturing."

The eagle face nodded agreement with himself and repeated, "Of course I always saw him." I realized I had evoked a painful image, but it was too late to retreat. I asked, "What did you think of Hitler back then?"

"What did I think? I thought—what else was there to think—Hitler was a madman. Why would anyone pay attention to a madman?"

Mr. Schoenberner went on from there to tell me how the Nazis had threatened and then destroyed his magazine. I was surprised to learn he was not Jewish. His father was a minister. The narrative of his experiences in the concentration camps was brief—a recitation of the names and an affirmation of his stubborn refusal to accommodate their demands for renunciation of his satiric indictments of Hitler and the Nazis, culminating in their destroying his legs. "Were it not for PEN I would not be alive today." He paused and reached across the wheelchair to take my hand. "You must remember, young man, that PEN is not a party, not a club. It is a trust, a trust upon which writers' lives often depend." He let go of my hand and added with a faint smile, "Your English and French characters are quite convincing, but I am not sure you will get by with your Slav."

Although attendance varied from week to week, perhaps a dozen members showed up routinely at the Pierre. I soon became acquainted with Langston Hughes, who seemed to find the gatherings as entertaining as I did. A stout man with a receding hairline, friendly flushed face, and a gentle manner that neither imposed nor suggested he considered himself a major contributor to American literature, Langston Hughes often relaxed on one of the few couches in the room with me by his side. He was much more aware than I of who was who in the crowd, and frequently offered brief evaluations of careers to guide me. One evening he spotted John Cheever among the guests. I was vaguely aware of Cheever as a short-story writer, but Hughes was considerably more impressed. "Cheever writes a good tale of the world he knows, an upper-class society, but he brings them alive. I suspect his stories will be read for quite a while."

He also observed that Cheever was having "a bit too much of the party." Another writer, aristocratic, handsome, athletic (could he have been Glenway Wescott?), seemed to have reached the same conclusion and we assisted as he graciously escorted John Cheever from the party and to a taxi.

Conversations with Langston Hughes over the course of several years rambled from his observations on writers and the writer's life to discussions of childhood and our feelings about our families. He told me he disliked his father. I confessed I could imagine no more supportive father than my dad. That sounded so privileged and sentimental that I shared our family secret. I told him my dad was a bookie. Langston smiled and nodded approval. "Well, what do you know about that!" It seemed to justify his passing friendship with me and confirm the reason for our mutual trust.

He told me that Vachel Lindsay was most responsible for "discovering" him. He was working in a restaurant at the time and plunked several of his poems in front of the famous poet. "I wasn't so happy about all Lindsay's poems, his so-called study of the Negro race, but the man could sing. He could sing." Lindsay praised Langston Hughes's poetry, and that led to publicity and eventually a scholarship to Lincoln University in Pennsylvania.

As he spoke I felt tremors of his reluctant gratitude and, without much thought, responded with several lines of a Langston Hughes poem: "Why should it be *my* lonelinesss / Why should it be *my* song / Why should it be *my* dream / Deferred overlong?"

After a moment Langston came right back with a recitation from Lindsay's "General William Booth Enters Into Heaven": "He saw King Jesus. They were face to face. / And he knelt a-weeping in that holy place. / Are you washed in the blood of the Lamb?"

I concluded, "I am. I am, Brother." We both laughed, and Langston said we better cut it out before they kick us both out for turning a reception into a poetry jamboree.

Langston Hughes and I eventually realized we shared an editor, Arthur Fields, who had published my novels and was responsible for Crown signing Langston's *An African Treasury*. He expressed admiration for Arthur, a vibrant editor who refused to be slowed up by the World War II injury that required him to conduct his life from a wheelchair. "Fields was candid, a straight shooter," Langston said. "He encouraged my book but promised little more than publication. No big promotion budget, no book tours, but lots of review copies and an effort to keep my book in print."

Then he confided that he was the greatest single purchaser of his own books. "I buy them without apology. You write a book, you make sure the people you'd like to read it have a copy. Family, friends, most folks believe you get the books for free, so I just send them copies. Been doing it for years." He smiled wistfully. "Now that *African Treasury* our friend Arthur Fields published—Arthur saw to the author's forty percent discount. I just about broke even."

It had not occurred to me that an author of such stature would buy and distribute his own books, but if Langston Hughes could do it, so could I. The next day I sent him a copy of *The Adventures of Homer Fink* and received a postcard response and later a copy of his *African Treasury*.

"None of us comes here as a representative of his country. None of us is obliged to speak here as an apologist for his culture or his political system," Arthur Miller, the president of International PEN, kicked off the weeklong congress that met at New York University in 1966.

Lewis Galantière, a translator who had knocked around Paris with Ernest Hemingway, and Julius Isaacs, a sidekick of Mayor LaGuardia who had written a well-received memoir of that experience, were responsible for raising the money and getting the show on the road, but once again it was Marchette and Joy Chute who dotted the *i*'s and crossed the *t*'s for the congress of world scribblers.

Along with Charles Bracelen Flood and Franklin D. Reeve, I was frequently commissioned by the Chutes to fulfill various "hospitality" assignments that week.

I had been conducting a fiction workshop and a nonfiction workshop at NYU since 1963, when Warren Bower invited me to Washington Square to participate in the university's continuing education program. The courses were listed in the widely distributed catalogue and mentioned in an ad that appeared in *The New York Times,* but I was surprised that the Chutes knew about my part-time "employment."

"You teach at NYU, don't you, Sidney? Perhaps Mr. Neruda would enjoy a brief tour of Washington Square." It wasn't easy shaking off the crowd, but we managed to escape through a side door and stroll under the arch. Pablo Neruda seemed less surprised to be at the congress than he might be, considering all the fuss related to a communist poet receiving permission from the U.S. State Department to join us. He told me about the congress in Bled, Yugoslavia, he had attended in 1965. It was his first and it had convinced him of the importance of writers organizing and "expressing ourselves politically as we do through PEN."

I had read Neruda's *A New Decade,* but knew little about his early *Love Poems and a Song of Despair.* I don't know how he came to mention it, but I recall the haunting resonance of his voice when he told me the title in Spanish and then translated it into English. Although a diplomat and obviously a man with dramatic as well as literary gifts, he talked to me as a teacher to a student defining the importance of Arthur Miller's plays and his delight that Miller, an American, was deeply concerned and committed to political-social justice in the world. He went on, but I lost track of the conversation after we encountered a former student who passed us with a startled glance and who I realized was not informed by her recognition of the famous Chilean poet-diplomat but rather perhaps by his appearance, so immaculate and well-appointed in a double-breasted pinstripe suit—just like a home-team capitalist. There was nothing about his dress or demeanor to suggest that her teacher was strolling the local precincts with the poet who wrote:

> *America, from a grain*
> *of maize you grew*
> *to crown*
> *with spacious lands*
> *the ocean foam.*
> *A grain of maize was your geography.*

Pablo Neruda wasn't the only guest whom the Chutes assigned me to serve during the week. When John Steinbeck arrived from Sag Harbor to attend a talk by Saul Bellow, Joy instructed me to stick with him. "Mr. Steinbeck doesn't particularly seek attention."

I was still reflecting on my encounter with the dapper Mr. Neruda when I shook hands with the rugged, bearded bard of the disinherited. John Steinbeck looked more like a retired fullback than a recent recipient of the Nobel Prize. He called me "son" and made it clear I was his blocking back as we made our way to the lecture hall where Saul Bellow was scheduled to speak. I was surprised by Steinbeck's intense interest in Bellow.

I sat by his side and was entertained by the various sounds he made responding to Bellow's commentaries. With magisterial flourishes Saul Bellow attacked academics and critics whom he perceived as defining the literary culture. Steinbeck sniffed and snorted, shook his head, and occasionally glanced at me and winked. I tried to remember lines from his novels as a kind of background music for his company, but all I could conjure was a vision of Henry Fonda, forlorn but valiant, in the film version of *The Grapes of Wrath* and the memory of a jacket photo of the novelist sitting with a dog for *Travels with Charley.*

While we were listening to Saul Bellow, the photographer Stefan

Congrat-Butlar snapped a picture of us. John Steinbeck whispered, "He's wasting his time. There's not enough light." When Saul Bellow concluded his address, Big John stood, winked again, and said to me, "Talk about biting the hand that feeds you."

The congress concluded with a banquet at the Plaza Hotel. Marchette and Joy asked me to arrive an hour before the guests were due. We had learned early on, at the boat ride around the tip of Manhattan launching the week's events, that making reservations was not a priority for members of the American Center. At dockside Frank Reeve, a handsome and chivalrous poet, together with Charlie Flood, a master statesman, and I were granted battlefield commissions to turn away all those without reservations. Several dozen poets, essayists, and novelists anticipating an evening of wine and music on the river, with a picnic basket at sunset—*pique-nique sur l'eau*—responded to our apologies with nary a bon voyage among the literate growls of frustration.

That awkward debut was mild compared to the hurt feelings at the Plaza celebration. The Grand Ballroom had been booked for five hundred, but more than eight hundred delegates, PEN members, and guests showed up. My assignment for the evening was to soothe Pearl Buck who, although a recipient of Pulitzer and Nobel Awards, had not been included at the dais—a long stretch of elevated podium that was the one place in the room to be seen.

No one seemed to know if Pearl Buck had been invited as an honored guest or signed on for the event as a paid subscriber. Marchette suggested I "keep her busy" while table rosters were shuffled and seating arranged for acceptable table company. I didn't know Pearl Buck and had no idea what she looked like. It didn't contribute to my confidence that I had never read one of her eighty-odd books. Once again I was stuck with the image of a movie star. This time it was Luise Rainer, whom I remembered as a destitute beauty, the Chinese farmer's wife in the film version of *The Good Earth*.

When at last I met Pearl Buck I was confronted by a gray-haired, straight-backed, well-dressed missionary's daughter who seemed quite aware of her stature but totally unaware she had been overlooked. I'd been informed that the best we could do was seat Ms. Buck and her escort at a front-row table with perhaps Leon Edel and John Hersey. I was to walk through it, keeping the chatter going with no apology. Pearl Buck seemed satisfied, but her escort signaled for a whispered instruction before being seated. With a voice as commanding as Paul Muni, costar of *The Good Earth* but also the convincing lead in *Scarface,* he made it clear Ms. Buck's appropriate place was at the head table.

Arthur Miller, Pablo Neruda, Lewis Galantière, and the rest of the starting lineup moved over and Pearl Buck sat among the all-stars.

I suspect I had a more enlightening time that evening sitting with Fred Morton, author of *The Rothschilds,* and his lively wife, who made me aware that for all her fame and regal manner, Pearl Buck's remarks about our relationship and responsibilities to China were "condescending."

Soon after he accepted the presidency of PEN in 1969, Charles Bracelen Flood invited me to join him at the University Club for dinner with the chairman of the National Endowment for the Arts. The subject of our discussion was to be funding—money. The success of the International Congress had left the American Center with enough bucks to move our records out of "Betsy Cenedella's kitchen" and James Putnam's basement. Both had served as executive directors during the years when there was no central office, but now we roosted on the second floor of a building at 20th Street and Fifth Avenue. The program had expanded, the staff increased, and there was rent to pay.

The National Endowment could consider continued funding to PEN, the chairman made clear to us, only if we were a "service organization." Congress was not inclined to authorize taxpayers' money to be spent on an international writers' group.

Charlie and I, as most writers, were uncomfortable with the hustle involved in asking for money. But Charlie caught on fast and by the time we knocked off the last of our after-dinner coffee, we were ready to celebrate with cigars. The chairman was satisfied with Charlie's suggestion that PEN would initiate a series of writing workshops for youngsters in the ghetto. We called it PEN-in-the-City.

Before long I was making rounds at the East Harlem Tutorial Center as well as uptown public schools and Daytop, the narcotics rehab facility.

In addition to contributing pieces by workshop participants to *The American Pen,* PEN's magazine, I soon became acquainted with Kitty Kirby, an energetic programmer for the Police Athletic League who conducted interviews with writers and young readers on WNYC, a local NPR outlet. Kitty enlisted me as a representative of PEN to judge the annual PAL essay contest, Tales My Grandparents Told Me. The entries by New York City public school students, ages ten through fifteen, offered a unique and frequently startling glimpse of our "mosaic" of cultures and ideas.

It was an assignment that enchanted me and kept me busy for four decades, but only once, when I was writing a weekly column during the first year of publication of *The New York Observer,* did I have an opportunity to share this experience. It always seemed to me the names of the participants and titles suggested the story. This last year, among the selections were "The Collapse of a Risky Business," by Dongho Shin; "An Inexplicable Turn," by Valentina Izyayeva; "Polish Survivors," by Natalia Uruska; "The Mango Tree," by Martha Duran Ruiz; "Madade Marie Gustave," by Kiaka Shepherd Kiara.

When Charlie invited me to join him as a delegate to the PEN congress in Menton, France, 1969, Arthur Miller spoke to me warmly about the workshops. I sat with him and his wife, Inge Morath, at the Hotel Napoleon overlooking the Mediterranean and felt over-rewarded by the interest and admiration for what I'd considered an experience that was a gift to me.

I don't suppose there was any writer in the world more respected for his commitment to the ideals of PEN, but if Arthur Miller was the least bit impressed with his reputation I didn't experience it. He and Inge were concerned about the severity of the division between haves and have-nots in America and finding ways to heal the breach.

We discussed the possibilities of PEN organizing nationwide writing programs for young people. I recall Inge Morath as the first person to mention that there should be some foundation or benefactor to contribute funds for a modest honorarium. Arthur was genuinely concerned that I keep at it. He presciently perceived the workshop's program in New York would grow because it was so "right."

Inspired by Arthur Miller's enthusiasm, I enlisted two other writer friends whom I'd met at my New School and NYU workshops. Barry Beckham had scored a major hit with *My Main Mother,* a novel listed among the best books of the year by *The New York Times. Not Like Niggers,* a young adult triumph by Ed Williams, qualified Ed as a pro, and he, too, bailed me out by sharing the workshops at Daytop.

In 1966, Budd Schulberg launched a Watts Writers Workshop and a year later, Galen Williams rustled up funds to create Poets & Writers, an organization that paid writers to visit schools. The poet Elliot Figman and bestselling writer Susan Isaacs inspire and monitor the programs that currently serve thousands of readers and writers.

Samuel Johnson writes in *The Lives of the Poets*: "Cowley, Milton and Pope are distinguished among the English poets by the early exertion of their powers; but the works of Cowley alone were published in his childhood."

Don Kurth Jr., Joe Agnelli, and Schuyler Miller were past their childhoods when their workshop prose appeared in the 1971 edition of *The American Pen.* I never read a word by any of them in print after that debut, but some years later I did receive a letter from Kurth. He wrote that after moving on from Daytop, "I decided to take some evening courses at Fairleigh Dickinson in English to try to improve my style. I found that I enjoyed school and realized that I did very well if I applied myself . . . After a year of straight A's I transferred to Columbia College. Somewhere along the line my interests shifted from

English to medicine. I just graduated Phi Beta Kappa from the College and I will be starting medical school at Columbia in the fall."

By the mid-1970s, when Nancy Larson Shapiro recharged the programs of the Teachers and Writers Collaborative, and diverse groups were also sponsoring writers' visits to schools, PEN-in-the-City seemed not only underfunded but a mite redundant. We momentarily closed the shop only to revive it several years later with a similar service identified as PEN's Readers & Writers program, an engagement Francine Prose generously and perceptively defined "as much a gift to the writers who participate as to the readers they serve." To me it seemed another contribution to the public's awareness of PEN to help us with our commitment to freedom of expression throughout the world, Franz Schoenberner's legacy.

30

Continuing Adventures at PEN with Jerzy Kosinski, Norman Mailer, Susan Sontag, Gay Talese, and a Cast of "Thousands"

1971–2005

There is a fading picture taken at a PEN congress, Jerusalem, 1972. As a delegate of the American Center, I am standing before a memorial at Yad Vashem commemorating the victims of Nazi persecution. I am flanked by V. S. Pritchett, the British critic, and Heinrich Böll, the German novelist. Pritchett and I are wearing yarmulkes; Böll's head is covered by a black beret.

That ceremony, along with a walk with Saul Bellow to the Wailing Wall and a private lunch in the Arab quarter with an assembly of angry Palestinians, are my memories of Jerusalem. I recall nothing of our administrative sessions or the business of PEN.

Böll seemed perpetually in mourning during our time in Jerusalem, lamenting the tragedy that had contributed to the creation of the state and the political tensions endured by the valiant survivors surrounded by hostile neighbors. Victor Pritchett and his wife approached Israel with a mix of curiosity and wonder and what seemed to me a disciplined detachment. Saul Bellow later wrote a short book about his visit to Israel. It was much richer in detail and positive feeling than the skepticism and bitterness I felt during my encounter with him.

In 1973, during the last year of his term as PEN's president, Tom Fleming invited me to join him as a delegate to the International Congress in West Berlin. When he addressed the assembly, Böll, who had just been awarded the Nobel Prize, quoted the Russian poet Joseph Brodsky. Brodsky had spoken of the writer as belonging to no nation but belonging to his national language: "The measure of a writer's patriotism is not a loyalty oath . . . but the way in which he writes the language of the people among whom he lives."

A. den Doolaard, a delegate from the Netherlands and an ambassador of PEN's fund for writers in prison, told Tom and me, "Heinrich Böll is a brave man, a fearless man." He went on to say that Böll had given a share of his Nobel Prize money to help the families of writers in prison. "But more than that he has used the prize to challenge governments to let the jailers of the world know he will use his notoriety to call attention to their repression of writers."

Tom and I passed up the guided tour of East Berlin to visit the novelist Stefan Heym at his home on Tagore Street. Heym had left Germany before World War II. He served in the U.S. Army and his war novel *The Crusader* was widely praised and read. Heym returned to the communist-controlled sector of Berlin because "I am a communist, and wish to live in a country founded on Marxism. But, I am persona non grata now. So my work is not published here." He didn't explain the reason he was censored nor did he complain of being persecuted. Heym insisted he remained a committed revolutionary.

He entertained us with tea and Johnnie Walker Red and was pleased when I told him I would be writing a report on our visit for *The American Pen*. "Our PEN center is enormously important to writers of East Berlin," Heym said. "And any mention and support we receive from other centers gives us some leverage at home."

Heym drove us back to the Berlin Wall, where we picked up the passports we'd left as security. His last words to us were: "Perhaps we will meet again if you can arrange to invite me as a speaker to a PEN congress."

Neither Tom nor I had much to say about programs for the International Congress. As far as I know, Stefan Heym passed his last days in East Berlin before the Wall came tumbling down.

At the conclusion of his successful tour as president of the American Center, it was Tom Fleming's inspiration to suggest Jerzy Kosinski as his successor. Unlike many of the native-born American writers who were skeptical about the "fees" for the honor, Polish-born Jerzy, whom I and a handful of his early acquaintances addressed as Jurek, responded positively and without hesitation.

Kosinski and I had met several months before the publication of *The Painted Bird,* his internationally acclaimed novel of a Polish boy's ordeals during the years of Nazi persecution. Jurek had expressed fascination, even incredulity, that I taught fiction-writing classes. When I invited him to visit an evening session at the New School, Kosinski suggested we meet for an early dinner.

Thin, with hawklike features and eyes that seemed ever inquiring or on the verge of a definitive revelation, Kosinski radiated a desire to entertain. I felt sufficiently charmed to invite him for dinner at our house, where Avi and our sons and I frequently feasted on roast chicken or hamburgers before I took off for my fiction workshops in the Village.

Jurek arrived promptly at five-thirty—an early hour even for cocktails—but he didn't seem to mind or notice. He was dressed in a dark suit and a starched white shirt with pointed collar and muted blue tie. He accepted a glass of wine, which he fondled but didn't drink. Kosinski seemed genuinely fascinated by teenage Ken's collection of model ships and airplanes—inquiring about the identities and histories of the sailing ships and World War II fighter planes. Our younger son Mike's audio equipment seemed to intrigue him, too. It was as if Kosinski were visiting a foreign land and had determined to absorb as much as he could of its exotic culture.

During dinner, Jurek continued in the role of fascinated observer and interrogator. On our way downtown to the New School, he summarized as if informing me, "The very attractive woman who is your wife is a doctor, a psychiatrist. You can rely upon her. The boys—obviously brilliant—on their way to becoming doctors or shipbuilders." Then, he paused and concluded with a definitive smile, "Still you write and they tolerate you."

His impression of the fiction workshop was less a reflection on the stories read and my observations of the craft than what he perceived as sexual intrigues in progress. "The young lady, smiling all the time with the visible breasts, she is going to have an affair with the bearded man who had something to say about every story. Unless of course you want her. You can have any one of the sixteen ladies but I am not so certain about each of the seven men."

When he returned from Europe after the filming of his novel *Being There,* Jurek invited me to his apartment at East 79th Street, a studio that he would soon be moving from to live with Kiki von Fraunhofer, who was eventually to become his companion, caretaker, wife for the rest of his life. That afternoon he displayed for me his photograph collection, including scenes from foreign places, and studies of street people and transvestites.

"But I am not a camera," he said. "I am writer and—" he paused for melodramatic effect before informing me he was a ski instructor, too, and introducing a series of photographs of him on the slopes in Europe.

For lunch he selected a Third Avenue bar where he had made a reservation. The place was empty when we arrived, and when Jurek announced his name to the bartender who was doubling as waiter-host the response was, "Sit anywhere you like. There's not much action here for lunch."

Jurek insisted upon the table in the far corner with a seat that provided a view of the room and early notice of other customers arriving or departing. "I am always aware of a route of exit or a place to hide as well as other company," he told me, with an expression that combined the flattery of a confidant with the amusement of a prankster.

The Painted Bird had won Kosinski world renown, and his novel *Steps* a National Book Award, but it was Peter Sellers's performance in

Being There that elevated the film to a cult classic and enabled Kosinski to play the full Hollywood hand. He became acquainted with Warren Beatty, who commissioned him for a cameo role in his film *Reds.* Yet he was sufficiently insecure about his presidency of PEN to consult with me about the "diplomatic way" to sever our ties to the Columbia University Translation Center. "They tell me we can no longer afford it," he said with a fatalistic shrug. "How do I know? I am a writer. I avoid numbers, but our treasurer is very wise man, John Macrae the Third. He is publisher and advises me it is not possible." With a pathetic shrug, eyebrows lifted, he concluded, "We do not have the money. Who is Kosinski to make issues with Macrae the Third."

Alas, poor Jurek had neither the time nor energy to make the necessary personal phone calls to consult, petition, and persuade all the people involved in the decision. But he accepted my support as "enough" and shared all of his french fries and half of the hamburger he'd left uneaten. On the way out of the empty bar he tapped my shoulder, embraced me, and said, "I would suggest you be president of PEN, but you are much too busy, married as you are to a sex therapist."

Although he was well received in Europe, where he represented American writers at international conferences, Kosinski's break with the Columbia Translation Center was the scar in the memory of his years as PEN's president. Frank MacShane, a former member of the board and chair of the Graduate Writing Program at Columbia, expressed disappointment and at last betrayal at Kosinski's reneging on what had been considered a commitment. A poet, translator, and author of one of my favorite memoirs, *Army Brat,* William Jay Smith brought the letter Kosinski had written declaring the separation. He read it to the PEN board, noting grammatical errors, misspellings, awkward phrasing. "I cannot believe the president of PEN wrote this letter," Smith said, addressing Kosinski directly. "It must have been ghostwritten."

At the time it seemed a harsh and vengeful dig, but several years later the *Village Voice* featured an indictment of Jerzy Kosinski as a pretender—a Jew who posed as a non-Jew—a literary hoax, who borrowed an obscure Polish story as the narrative for his first novel; a stylistic fraud who hired freelance editors to write and restructure his books.

To me it was a tragic exaggeration of his mischief, poor judgment, and eccentricity. I remembered Jurek telling me that he made a point of avoiding discussion of his Jewish identity after the publication of *The Painted Bird* because the book was a novel and he did not want to temper the charges of Nazi-inspired cruelty as a Jewish boy's invention.

I was aware, too, of the writers upon whom he relied for proofreading and reassurance about his composition in English. The agonies that eventually led to Jurek's suicide were defined in James Parker Sloan's biography *Jerzy Kosinski,* a study Tom Fleming appropriately applauded as a "riveting historical detective story."

Soon after she was elected president of PEN and prior to her attendance at her first International Congress, Muriel Rukeyser invited me to meet with her. "Oh, you teach at the New School mornings as well as evenings. Then we can lunch at the Cedar Tavern and be Abstract Expressionists with words." Since its days as a hangout for the New York School of artists, Jackson Pollock, Mark Rothko, and Willem de Kooning, the University Place wood-paneled bar was a meeting place for New School writing faculty. I had been delighted more by chance encounters with Frank O'Hara, a curator of the Museum of Modern Art, who had written: "I am not a painter, I am a poet / Why? I think I would rather be / a painter but I am not."

I was familiar with the booths that ran along both walls, the dim lighting, the overdone hamburgers and good beer. When she arrived several minutes after me, Muriel was impressed that the waiter knew me by name and anticipated my order. "Everyone seems to know you," she said like a kindly elder sister. Muriel Rukeyser seemed to find it a good thing that a writer be social.

A large woman with an imposing forehead emphasized by the stiff broom of hair that flowed back on her head as if modeled on a porcupine, she was slow getting to the point of our rendezvous. It was an invitation for me to join her as a delegate to the congress scheduled for Vienna. Unfortunately I was committed to family duties in Baltimore that spring so I had to pass. It seemed a great disappointment to the newly elected president of the American Center, who expressed trepidation about meeting strangers on her own. For all her size and imposing presence, Muriel was shy and unsure of herself. When I referred to a stanza from her "The Poem as Mask," she seemed flattered and reassured.

Sitting there at a far-corner booth of the Cedar Tavern, we together recalled the lines of her poem:

> *When I wrote of the women in their dances*
> *and wildness, it was a mask*
> *On their mountain, gold-hunting, singing,*
> *in orgy, it was a mask, when I wrote of*
> *the god, fragmented, exiled from himself,*
> *his life, the love gone down with song*
> *it was myself, split open, unable to speak, in*
> *exile from myself.*

Muriel Rukeyser went on to Vienna and during her term proved to be a forceful advocate for the imprisoned Korean poet Kim Chi Ha.

After the two-year term of Henry Carlisle, a writer who appeared the incarnation of an international diplomat, I participated with the Nominating Committee in convincing the poet, translator, critic Richard Howard to accept the laurel wreath that passed as a crown. I was acquainted with Howard as the author of an essay celebrating the poem "They Flee from Me" by the sixteenth-century poet Sir Thomas Wyatt. The poem's durability had been a mystery to me until I read Howard's celebration of Wyatt's lines as introducing to literature "what we have come to know as the Proustian mechanism: life becomes reality only when we can remember it. . . ."

I took a shot with that esoteric if not pretentious reference when, several months after he conducted his first meeting of the PEN board, I ran into Howard at the railroad station in Baltimore.

Richard Howard's perfectly sculpted balding dome presided above eyes that seemed to be critiquing everything in sight for a verdict of unqualified condemnation or, conversely, observing the beauties of the visible world for a verse in praise of it. His classic but mobile features had the fascinating ability to express either emotion, or both at the same time, at any moment the muse moved him. Before realizing it was a risky intimacy, I settled at his side for the three- to four-hour ride back to New York.

Howard was returning from a lecture at Johns Hopkins. For me it was the conclusion of an overnight visit with my family to celebrate my mom's seventy-fourth birthday with dinner at Marconi's. By the time we reached Wilmington I had exhausted my repertoire of Howard-related scholarship. We had gone on to discuss my former student Tom Victor, a handsome, disarmingly modest young photographer who had obviously passed along some good words about me to Richard Howard. That credential seemed far more impressive to the poet-scholar-translator than my mock recitation of Wyatt's lines: "They fle from me that sometyme did me seke/With naked fote stalking in my chambre."

By the time we reached 30th Street Station, Philadelphia, we'd agreed that Karen Kennerly, our full-time paid executive director, was an appropriately tough administrator with just the right dose of ambition beneath her charming, witty manner. I didn't have to think about an agenda for the final laps to North Philly, Trenton, Newark, and finally Penn Station. With a satisfied sigh Richard Howard said, "Very well," removed a book from his briefcase, and with a summary smile announced, "Time to catch up on some reading."

It was a modestly bonding experience and less than a year later Richard graciously responded to my desperate request for a translation for *Intellectual Digest* of an early-sixteenth-century French poet.

Bernard Malamud, who agreed to succeed Richard Howard in 1979, was considered one of the masters of American fiction. He was right in there with John Cheever, Saul Bellow, Ralph Ellison, Flannery O'Connor, Philip Roth, and Kurt Vonnegut on college reading lists as well as occasional appearances on the bestseller list. With a bald crown and wreathlike hairline, well-trimmed mustache, and slightly hunched shoulders, Malamud presided at board meetings like the patriarch of a legal aid society.

Sometime during his second year I encountered him in the men's room of PEN's office. There he was, the author who had touched me with *The Magic Barrel* and enthralled as well as bewildered me with *The Natural,* meticulously ordering his thinning crown. I nodded in the mirror expecting neither recognition nor response, but Malamud smiled warmly and with a Talmudic nod said, "So, Sidney, I hear you are a writing teacher."

I had no disarming rejoinder so I confessed and then asked, "How would you know that?" Bernard Malamud smiled again, kindly, and told me a friend of his family was in my class, but she preferred he not mention her name until the end of the semester. "She is admiring and very fond of you."

Some semester. Two classes, seventy-five students, and in addition to reading and critiquing papers, I'm searching in vain for the mystery guest.

That riddle was resolved three years later when I encountered Malamud on Madison Avenue. He had passed on the presidency of PEN to the drama critic Richard Gilman, one of my good friends and a walking encyclopedia of baseball, opera, and the dramatic arts.

Malamud seemed genuinely pleased to see me. He hadn't been attending PEN board meetings after his term ran out and was curious about my responses to Dick Gilman. I reported that Dick seemed very comfortable in the role. I also mentioned what I considered a characteristic piece of Gilman esoterica.

I recounted for Bernard Malamud Dick's announcement of PEN's growing role as a dispenser of literary honors. When one of the members had inquired about who was receiving the *kudu* for translation, Gilman cautioned us to be careful not to mistake a "kudo" for a "kudu." "A kudu," he reminded us, "has very little to do with translation. It's a large grayish-brown African antelope." That definition, I mentioned to Malamud, is word-for-word Gilman, right off the top and exactly as it appears in Merriam-Webster.

Malamud accepted it as amusing and then reminded me of his

promise to tell me the name of the student who had spoken to him about me. He mentioned her name. I nodded and attempted a non-committal, "Oh, yes." It didn't pass with Malamud. He commented not unkindly, "Well, with so many protégés and acolytes, we can hardly expect you to remember everyone."

He rewarded me with a hot bit of PEN news. "Norman Mailer has agreed to serve as PEN's next president." Then, with a smile of modest triumph, he added, "I was asked to call Norman and I did."

When I asked Bernard Malamud what was the hook that convinced Norman Mailer to accept the presidency of PEN, he said, "I just told him, 'Norman, you have to accept it. There's a time when we all have to give something back.'"

The Salmagundi Club, at Fifth Avenue and 12th Street, a show-place and social base for artists, served as the temporary office for PEN while we explored for more spacious accommodations. It had a gallery on the first floor where we were allowed access for special events. However, PEN's board meetings were conducted in cramped quarters: a long table that could seat perhaps twelve or fifteen members with bridge chairs also stationed along the sides and back of the room. When Norman Mailer presided, it was standing room only.

Mailer became the president of the American Center in 1984. In the early '60s, when I became a member of PEN, visits by Norman to the authors' receptions were welcomed like a "Second Coming." Usually there was the word, a rumor that the most notorious author of his generation was on his way to tipple with the Chutes' crowd. My first impression of Mailer was of the all-around camper, athlete, student, and hail-fellow, always on the make for a good time. He seemed to be perpetually smiling for the sheer joy of being Norman Mailer. On the other hand, there was no mistaking his grimace when crossed or identifying with what he perceived as injustice.

Mailer's hair, which grayed and became straighter through the years, was cropped and curly, and early on his face had the hearty look of a kid who would refuse to grow old—animated blue eyes, mobile lips, and those Frank Sinatra–Bing Crosby ears that heard all—every consonant, vowel, and rhythm. Yet as he aged his liveliness became more of an illumination of deeper feeling than an invitation to play.

He was early into his run when he announced to the board that it was time we hosted another International Congress. I was the only veteran of the '66 Congress team in the roomful of board members. I expressed a cautionary note to temper our president's enthusiasm. Mailer listened attentively to my reminders about the difficulties of fundraising and my rehash of the tainted money we had received from the Fairfield Foundation, with whom we had severed relations as soon as we were aware the foundation was a conduit for CIA funding. Then he responded, speaking directly to me with a disarming affection. He said he appreciated the eyewitness history but he was certain there were foundations and individuals of "good fortune" who would be willing to underwrite such a major literary event. He added with a twinkle that there were ways, too, for PEN to cash in on our potential box office appeal to pay the way.

I should have known better than to question the fundraising confidence of the author of *Advertisements for Myself.* Although he had run unsuccessfully for mayor of New York and come off as less than an Academy Award contender with his films, there was no more versatile writer-performer-promoter in the history of American letters than Norman Mailer.

True to his prediction, Mailer had the PEN show on the boards two years after he assumed office. In 1986, the International Congress was scheduled to begin with a benefit performance at a Broadway theater, featuring a debate between Mailer and Gore Vidal, and an event at the New York Public Library including remarks by George Shultz. The invitation to Shultz, presented by Mailer in an informal conversation, created a tempest when it was announced to the board.

We were meeting at our new office, on Broadway near Prince Street, a much larger accommodation than the Salmagundi Club. Once again the meeting was well attended, but there were no expressions of gratitude for the president who had put it all together. Members of the board expressed outrage that Ronald Reagan's secretary of state had been invited to exploit our company. Kirkpatrick Sale attacked Mailer, demanding to know by what authority was he empowered to speak for PEN without the board's consent. Two of my good friends, Grace Paley and Ed Doctorow, among the most respected members of the board, were unequivocal in their protest.

Although I was in combat with Martin Abend on Channel 5 television and consistently criticizing the Reagan administration, I was sympathetic to Mailer's position. My experience at International Congresses suggested that there was often an effort to attract representatives of the host's government.

Mailer acknowledged to the meeting that the invitation was offered impulsively and he hadn't expected Shultz to accept. But it didn't satisfy members of the board who insisted Mailer rescind his offer. The clamor was so intense, noble Kurt Vonnegut expressed visible stress. He trembled and in a voice cracking with passion announced that he was leaving the meeting.

Mailer offered a modest apology, and was obviously stunned by the members of the board who refused to accept anything less than a cancellation of the invitation. At last he stood like a punched-out Caesar exhausted by a roomful of Brutuses. He headed to the door, following the route Kurt had pioneered. It was Gay Talese, our master of good manners and diplomacy, who intercepted Mailer and attempted to persuade our president not to walk out. Patricia Bosworth, a writer who was also a colleague of Mailer's at the Actors Studio, and I, joined Gay. For me it was an intuitive response. I was convinced Norman Mailer was a generous and bold leader of PEN and deserving of our grateful respect. The three of us managed to calm Norman sufficiently for him to return to his chair and wrap up the meeting with another apology, although George Shultz remained on the congress marquee.

The people of "good fortune" that Norman Mailer rallied for the PEN congress were Saul and Gayfryd Steinberg. Saul, a pleasant fellow with a talent for exploiting underpriced assets for big bucks, was a Park Avenue millionaire and art collector who enlisted Richard Feigen, a dealer with a Ted Williams eye for the old masters, to help museum the walls of his thirty-four-room penthouse. Among the premiums for his friendship with Feigen, the art dealer introduced Saul Steinberg to Gayfryd, who with Saul's connections became a grande dame in the tickets-for-benefits derby that was the hottest social game in New York at the time.

Saul and Gayfryd Steinberg lived around the corner from us in their mansion-museum at 740 Park Avenue. It was there they entertained a select group of PEN members, the literary table hosts and sponsors of the gala. When we were composing the list of distinguished writers for consideration for our second time around, my suggestions of Louis Auchincloss and Ralph Ellison had been accepted with glee tempered by skepticism. Would Ralph Ellison, author of *Invisible Man,* regarded by many as the outstanding American novel of the twentieth century, show up for a PEN event after so many years of absence? Did I know Louis Auchincloss well enough to offer the invitation in person?

Louis did agree to join us as a literary host, but I have no memory of him at the Steinbergs. When I called Ralph Ellison, his wife, Fanny, recognized my name from talking to her husband about the Thursday-evening dinners at the social club where Ralph and I hung out.

Ralph was friendly but not immediately responsive to the invitation. Since the publication of *Invisible Man,* Ralph Ellison had been overwhelmed with requests to join boards, present speeches, attend benefits, and show up as a signature of support. I knew about his experience as a PEN delegate to the International Congress in London, 1956, because Marchette Chute had written about the enthusiasm he expressed for PEN after that experience. When he seemed reluctant to accept another distraction from his appointment with his muse, I reminded Ralph of the good things he'd said about PEN and how much his presence would mean to the members who had been knocking themselves out so this fundraiser would be a success.

With a sigh and chuckle at my hard sell, Ralph accepted. I said I was looking forward to sharing the experience and would be there to greet him.

But I wasn't there to greet him. I'd miscalculated my role as one of the hosts, and although I'd arrived early I was engaged by other guests, particularly Mortimer Levitt. He of the Custom Shop empire, considered among the best-dressed and most spirited of New York doers of good deeds, connected with me because we were the only gents among the early arrivals sporting bow ties. I had no idea you could talk about bow ties for fifteen uninterrupted minutes without repeating yourself until I met Mortimer Levitt.

Then there was Allen Ginsberg, thin face, full beard, all decked out in a well-cut suit—a chameleon on the culture circuit from Beats to Beater-Uppers. I wasn't aware that Allen even knew my name until he engaged me to help him set up photographs so he could pop away with his camera. "Just ask that pretty lady to stand still a moment and smile—what's her name again?"

"Molly Haskell. Surely you know Molly Haskell, Allen. She and her husband, Andrew Sarris, are the Matthew Arnold and Virginia Woolf of movie criticism."

"Matthew Arnold and Virginia Woolf? I'm not sure I get that."

I tried again. "Robert Silvers and Barbara Epstein. Of film criticism."

"Is Bob Silvers here? I didn't see him."

It was then I spotted Ralph Ellison standing by the receiving line. A chipper gent with well-groomed mustache and a smile awarded for warm feelings or appreciation of wit, Ralph dressed meticulously, carried himself with intuitive grace and a posture more frequently identified with veterans of the service than scribblers who hunch over writing tables.

I joined him immediately and apologized for not waiting for him in the lobby. Ralph expressed no complaint, but he was obviously restless and regretted his presence at what appeared to be a celebration of literary celebrity. Gayfryd didn't recognize him and I promptly identified Ralph Ellison parenthetically as "America's greatest living novelist."

"That's not necessary, Sidney," Ralph said. But Gayfryd came as close as I'd seen her come to a smile and graciously greeted him. "We're honored you could join us—" Pause. Name escaped her? She concluded, "Sir."

From there on it was all Ralph Ellison, with me as the walk-on. The playwright and novelist Wesley Brown approached with awe and acknowledged candidly, "I've always wanted to meet you, Mr. Ellison. I'm a great admirer of your work."

Ralph nodded modestly and said, "Remind me again, Mr. Brown, what it is you've written." Wesley didn't get deep into it before Norman Mailer fell upon Ralph with a hug. "The party is a success," he declared. "The champion has arrived."

During a brief break from his fans, I asked Ralph Ellison if he had ever been in a private house that was so overflowing with masterpieces.

A massive painting by Peter Paul Rubens, *Death of Adonis,* dominated the gallery. Works by Vasari, Cranach, Rembrandt, and Brueghel's *Christ Preaching at the Seaport* were among the collection identified as "a veritable textbook of the high points of seventeenth-century art."

Ralph Ellison hesitated before responding, as if leafing through the visual archives of his memory before telling me he had seen equally impressive collections in a private home. When I asked where, he said, "Europe."

It was only when he returned from the restroom, where it seemed the walls and corridor were decorated with paintings by Eglon Hendrick van der Neer, Jacob Jordaens (*A Boy Singing*), and other Flemish masters, that Ralph changed his mind and acknowledged, "No. I think I have never been in a house so overwhelmed with classic art. Who are these people, anyway?"

Toward the end of his term as PEN's president, Mailer suggested an inspired collaboration to relieve us of our dependence upon fundraisers and the party-circuit tycoons who underwrote them. He proposed that the Actors Studio produce an evening of plays by PEN members. He mentioned that Kurt Vonnegut, Ed Doctorow, Bill Styron, Susan Sontag, and, surely, he himself had plays to offer, on the house, for the good of PEN. As a member of the Studio, he was aware of their money woes and was sure Paul Newman and Company would come through for an evening of performances.

Mailer set up a meeting with representatives of the Studio to draft the plan. He asked Patty Bosworth, who was also a longtime member of the Studio, as well as a current vice president of PEN, to join him. I had no idea until I arrived at the meeting that I'd been selected by Mailer as the only other delegate representing the PEN board. Karen Kennerly, who by this time was concluding her first decade as the organization's executive director, joined us as the "resident pro."

The tentative plan was for there to be an early evening of plays at various Broadway theaters and then on to a reception at a venue that could accommodate the anticipated throng.

Karen wanted to know how we would share the loot. Norman suggested PEN receive the money collected from its patrons and the Studio would be entitled to the balance rallied from their list. I suspected it would be a risky mix of temperaments: Henry James coproducing with Greta Garbo? But Norman had proved his talent for fundraising and he had my support. Patty, too, thought it a daring idea worth trying. The Studio delegates, including their executive director, were contemplative, recognizing that this would be a time-consuming project, but they affirmed their commitment.

It seemed the coproduction was launched. Then Norman, who was informally conducting the meeting, recognized that Karen hadn't said a word in support. An attractive woman with short, straight schoolgirl-styled hair that fell seductively over her forehead, Karen spoke in a richly textured voice that seemed cued for a poetry recitation rather than an administrative message. There was no mistaking her skepticism. "Publishers, agents, our other supporters budget funds for the PEN galas," she reminded us, and then went on to say that while the collaboration might well be an exciting theatrical event, it seemed to her a major risk with little to gain. It would certainly have to be discussed and approved by PEN's board.

Mailer concluded abruptly, "If you don't support it, Karen, let's forget it."

There was a brief exchange about this being a matter for the boards of both the Studio and PEN, but Norman insisted that a presentation to the board would be a waste of time without Karen's endorsement.

Our meeting adjourned on this sour note. Karen expressed no apology or qualification. After she took off, Norman squinted and he bobbed his head with the movement of a boxer who had just taken a shot and is trying to shake it off. "I don't understand why Karen did that," he said to Patty and me. There was no reference to his contribution to PEN or rehash of how he had so dramatically increased public awareness of the organization Karen Kennerly was paid to manage. Then he shrugged and grinned, accepting what he considered a betrayal and, perhaps, offering the compensation of excusing him from the responsibility of providing future inspirations for the critics of PEN.

After Ken Auletta, a *New Yorker* writer who covered the publishing and business beat, was quoted in *New York* magazine rebuking PEN for allowing a "sleazy character" like Saul Steinberg to exploit his association with PEN, his wife Gayfryd "retired" from her roles as benefit chair and patron.

By the time Larry McMurtry galloped in from the west to serve as PEN's president, 1989, and lead our cavalry charge for writers' rights throughout the world, Barbara Goldsmith had signed on as one of the sponsors for the gala.

I'd met Barbara Goldsmith a year or so after she joined Clay Felker to found *New York* magazine. A slim, attractive woman with a disarmingly modest smile and a manner that belied her sophistication and brilliance, Barbara went on to write a novel and several prizewinning biographies, in addition to mounting a successful campaign for book preservation that led to the use of acid-free paper nationwide. Not only did she rally sponsors, but Barbara underwrote an award to be presented annually.

The Barbara Goldsmith/PEN Freedom to Write Award provided cash prizes for the high-risk, frequently persecuted world champions of free expression. Her award, along with the PEN/Newman's Own First Amendment Award introduced by A. E. Hotchner and Paul

Newman, became the messages of the gala. Eventually the PEN benefits attracted the support of Toni Goodale, as elegant and vibrant a hostess as ever rallied dollars for good deeds. It wasn't just party time; the themes of the evenings were what PEN was about.

In the fall of 1998, Michael Roberts, a former secretary to the president of Harvard University, with a law degree and doctorate in comparative literature, was the wise choice of Michael Scammell and the informal search committee to serve as executive director, heir to Karen Kennerly's last hurrah: a reorganization of PEN's structure. There were no longer six vice presidents and seventy-five (75!) members of the executive board. The increasing overdose of board members during the reigns of Larry McMurtry, Edmund Keeley, Louis Begley, and Anne Hollander provided a cast for meetings that frequently compelled our presidents to preside over sessions that seemed less like a literary seminar than group therapy.

I wasn't included among the twenty-three trustees of the new board, but I continued as a member of PEN's Membership Committee. Michael Scammell, during his last year as president, asked me to serve as head of the Nominating Committee to propose his successor. Michael, who was born and raised in England, was a reluctant administrator but had a talent for it. His English charm, always courtly, seemed self-assured and was backed up by his literary achievements as a translator and biographer of Aleksandr Solzhenitsyn.

After brief consultations with other members of the nominating committee, we concluded our first choice would be Frances Fitz-Gerald. I'd invited Frankie to be the Nominating Committee's candidate for president of the Authors Guild twice and been delegated decades earlier to invite her to head the ticket for PEN. With feelings of amusement for what must surely be among my most repeated experience with rejection, and a rush of the oddsmaker's confidence that it was all a matter of timing, I made the call.

The long shot came through and PEN entered the twenty-first century with one of the most respected chroniclers of the history and realities of Vietnam (Pulitzer Prize for *Fire in the Lake,* 1973), as our leader. During the process of selecting the ticket that included Ron Chernow and John Guare as vice presidents, I also became acquainted with the versatile prose artist Francine Prose, whose son provided background music for our telephone conferences (was he practicing the saxophone?), and Roxanna Robinson, a master of the short story who lived right in my neighborhood so we could confer on subway rides home from PEN's SoHo offices.

PEN was on such a roll that at the conclusion of Frankie's two years, I felt it was time I "retired" as the resident custodian of PEN's memory. I faded from the Membership Committee, diplomatically chaired by the novelist Beth Gutcheon, but hung in for what I thought would be my last roundup as a member of the Nominating Committee. Our assignment: Michael Roberts's next collaborator.

The committee met in Michael's small office. All the seats were taken when a hearty young man, long hair dangling to his neck, with a baseball cap on backward, arrived and sat on the floor. Who was this "unacknowledged legislator of mankind"? Rick Moody, the author of *The Ice Storm, The Ring of Brightest Angels,* and *Purple America,* told me he had spotted my bow tie walking up the street. Less than two minutes into our conversation, the kid on the floor had the morning line for the best bet of the day. "How about Joel Conarroe? He's just retired from the Guggenheim. We can't do any better than Joel for president of PEN."

Joel was not only the Winston Churchill of literary orators, his anthologies of American poetry were masterpieces of that often underrated genre. And he had the touch—the muscular hug that expressed friendship, warmth, and compliment. I'd met Joel when we were both backbenchers at board meetings. I introduced him to my family at a serendipitous encounter on a trail through a nature preserve in Long Island where Avi, our son Ken, his wife, Emily, and granddaughters Anna, five, and Caroline, three, were tracking wildflowers and bright birds. All three generations adored Joel Conarroe and here was Rick Moody endorsing our family's hero.

It was considered a coup for PEN to persuade Joel to accept the presidency. Since his retirement as president of the Guggenheim Foundation, it was an open secret that foundations, libraries, editorial offices were attempting to sign him up.

Once again the timing was right, and Joel Conarroe agreed to serve a two-year term. And what a glorious two years it was for PEN! Michael Roberts quietly but ingeniously balanced the books, while at the same time successfully coordinating the expansion of PEN's program for translation. Joel's references to a "poem a day" achieved an eloquent balance between the literary and administrative at meetings, events and, of course, the annual gala.

Although presidents of PEN are not traditionally celebrated for their recommended reading lists, it was Joel who introduced me to a number of writers whose personal charms led me to the satisfactions of buying and reading their books. Among them, Michael Cunningham's *Flesh and Blood* and *The Hours,* Benjamin Taylor's *Tales Out of School,* Amy Hempel's *The Collected Stories,* Jhumpa Lahiri's *Interpreter of Maladies* and *The Namesake,* A. M. Homes's *The End of Alice,* and Honor Moore's *Red Shoes,* a collection of serenades to colors actual and emotional.

I'm sure Langston Hughes would not have considered my investments an extravagance.

Salman Rushdie had been an honorary vice president of the American Center since 1994, soon after the publication of his novel *The Satanic Verses* had provoked a death threat by Ayatollah Khomeni. When writers throughout the world rallied to Rushdie's defense, he became as symbolic as one writer could be of what freedom of expression—the principle of PEN—was all about. Joel and Mike Roberts believed Salman would be the ideal choice as Joel's successor.

Once again as chair of the Nominating Committee I checked in with other members of the committee for their approval. They couldn't have been more congenial. Among them was Betty Fussell, who during her service as chair of the Membership Committee, catered the late-afternoon meetings with her very own homemade treats for high tea. Betty was as wise a handicapper for PEN members and officers as she was an authority on recipes. "Salman Rushdie for president of PEN—a wonderful choice, and my guess is he cares enough to do it." Ed Hirsch, a stand-up impresario of poetry and humor, immediately signaled with a rhapsodically verbal green light. A Gibbons of twentieth-century Cuba, Wendy Gimbel, wrapped it up with more reserve but unqualified support.

Joel and Mike and I conspired to offer Salman Rushdie the nomination as president of the American Center at our midtown social club where we knew we could sit quietly, unobserved, and at the same time lend a touch of ceremonial dignity to the proposition. As soon as the white wine, Perrier, and Diet Cokes were on the table I asked Rushdie if he could hear the drum beat and bugle call or was it an imaginary musical accompaniment of Brahms's Fourth? We would be honored if he would accept the Nominating Committee's recommendation that he serve as our president.

I'm sure it wasn't a surprise, but Rushdie came as close as I'd ever seen him to a blush. Eyebrows arched, eyes intense, face aglow with the fire of his message, he immediately launched a spirited and engaging monologue on how much PEN's support had meant to him, his feelings of debt and desires for reciprocation. He had ideas, too. Perhaps PEN should expand its representation of poets to include the creators of lyrics and musical ballads. He spoke of the younger generation's expression of poetry through song—the Beatles, Bob Dylan, and other names far less familiar to me.

Joel, Mike, and I toasted and "bottoms-upped." We had our candidate.

As we were leaving the club, I asked Salman to sign a copy of *The Satanic Verses* as a gift to Anna, our eldest granddaughter, who was graduating from high school that year and awaiting word as to what college had accepted her for the following fall.

"Is it an anxious experience?" Salman Rushdie asked.

"Absolutely," I responded.

With a mischievous smile and his glasses descending low on the bridge of his nose, the writer who survived the most publicized death threat of our time wrote to my granddaughter: "Be brave!"—a priceless souvenir and two-word salutation to my four decades of association with writers of the world.

31

The Authors League, Guild, Fund, Foundation: Writing as a Livelihood with Rex Stout, Herb Mitgang, Toni Morrison, Robert Caro, Madeleine L'Engle, Robert Massie, Mary Pope Osborne, Roger Angell, and the Poet of Lake Wobegon

1961–2007

The Authors Guild was founded as the Authors League in 1912. It seems ironic that such an assembly of novelists, dramatists, poets, and distinguished historians of their time has no chronicler like Marchette Chute, who wrote a brief history of PEN American Center in 1972. My own recollections, garnered from random files of personal memories, seek to recount important moments of enlightenment—and the fun I had along the way.

In the summer of 1961, soon after the announcement of the publication of my first novel, I received an invitation to join the Authors

Guild. It was like a bugle call sounding salute and call to arms. Less than a year later, I was among the members crowded into the Sky Garden Roof of the St. Moritz Hotel, Central Park South, for the annual meeting.

"What is the Authors Guild about?" Rex Stout, the president, asked, then declared, "Three words—contract, contract, contract." A small man with a beard, who resembled a photograph of George Bernard Shaw, Stout was the bestselling author of a series of erudite mystery stories starring the detective Nero Wolfe. There seemed no conspicuous motive for Stout's profound devotion to the Guild and League, composed of representatives of both the Authors Guild and Dramatists Guild. Although I never saw his contracts, the success of his books suggested he was among the handful of writers who made a living from royalties.

Stout conducted the meeting more like a political rally than a report to stockholders. There was assumed unanimity among the assembled authors—we were at war with publishers for a fair shake and improved contracts. At that time, contracts with my publishers seemed to me a gift from Apollo, if not Zeus himself. Peter Van Doren, G. P. Putnam's Sons, Arthur Fields, Crown, and John A. Pope, Jr., St. Martin's Press, were among the last people in the world to whom I felt the slightest hostility. The ten percent royalty and sharing of reprint and dramatic rights all seemed fair to me. Although not in the warrior class, I did feel in the company of colleagues, mentors, and friends and honored to be a member of the Guild.

During the discussion of new business, Rex Stout called upon a well-groomed, athletically lean gentleman whom he addressed as John. I would not have anticipated the proposal coming from this stately gent: "The Guild should be offering programs to acknowledge the memberships of writers of books for young readers." He didn't say "juveniles" and certainly not "kiddie-lit." Rex Stout nodded agreement in such a cordial, informal manner, it seemed there were only the two of them in conversation.

When John sat, a voice to the rear of me, with awed tones, identified the author by title, *The Kid From Tomkinsville*. The novel Philip Roth later defined as "the boys' Book of Job" was certainly a scripture for my brother and me. We read and suffered Roy Tucker's tormented career as a major-leaguer, not quite sure what to make of it. Was the message to stay away from professional baseball? Or, no virtue without pain? Putting those theological contemplations aside, Benson and I opted for the insider's tips, among them Roy Tucker extending a tar-taped ball from a rope anchored to the roof of the barn so he could practice hitting in winter.

The best we Bawlamer boys could do was a tennis ball extended from a wire wrapped around the base of a ceiling chandelier. For a bat we substituted a broom handle.

When he'd had enough of the random therapies that followed John Tunis's remarks, Rex Stout announced summarily, "Meeting adjourned." I moved against the outgoing tide to speak to the man who turned out to be John R. Tunis in the front of the room.

"No, it isn't absolutely necessary to swat at a ball with a bat," he reassured me. A broom handle may be lighter, but the narrow extension could possibly sharpen hand-eye coordination." He smiled when I asked why Roy Tucker suffered so much. "It's been quite a while—" The Kid was among Tunis's early books. He'd followed with a volley of bestsellers—*Iron Duke, Keystone Kids, Rookie of the Year.* "I suppose he did suffer, but then again, nobody ever said a professional athlete's life is easy. It's a rare bird who plays the game day in, day out without injury."

My very first meeting at the Authors Guild provided me with a report for my Baltimore home team, and a tip from a Hall of Famer of sports stories: There are lessons for young readers experiencing through stories how their heroes deal with setbacks and lost games.

Several years later, when I was writing a series of sports books published by St. Martin's Press, the Tunis model inspired the not always happy endings for *The Boy Who Won the World Series, Soupbone,* and *Cadet Attack,* all now out of print, unlike the John R. Tunis classics.

In March 1966, New York hosted the National Book Awards. Encouraged by a *Look* magazine colleague of Leo Rosten's, I joined the audience for a panel that the author of *Captain Newman, M.D.* and *The Return of H*Y*M*A*N K*A*P*L*A*N* was conducting for the Authors Guild on the vanishing boundaries between fact and fiction. I was feeling moderately flush with the reception of my young adult novel *The Adventures of Homer Fink*: good reviews and a paperback sale to Scholastic. It seemed time to settle down and write another adult novel, a story of role reversal where Dad stays home to mind the kids while Mom goes on to medical school. (Husbands making the best wives was a hot new topic then.)

There was also the possibility of attempting to write my story as memoir, a reflection on the experiences Avi and I shared. Fact or fiction? Exactly what the Rosten panel—Richard Whalen, Leon Edel, John Gunther, Gordon Parks, and Jean Stafford—was all about.

They weren't long into their discussion when it was clear all the panelists agreed facts should be reported without invented dramatization. No entering into the minds of real people or dialogue without documentation—journals, letters, interviews. Tell it straight. With fiction all bets were off. Stafford, who had written a novel with the arresting title *Children Are Bored on Sunday* and a collection of short stories, *Bad Characters,* said it was among the delights of writing fiction to allow for the free play of the imagination without feeling the pressure of violating "facts."

When the panel concluded, Elizabeth "Babs" Janeway, the president of the Guild whom I had met earlier at PEN, suggested that as a younger member of the Guild I should be acquainted with the panelists. Persuasive as a schoolteacher, Babs Janeway led and I followed to meet Jean Stafford. In black turtleneck and checked suit, hair bobbing over her neck, with no makeup visible to me, it was easy to see why this sharply focused lady had bowled over Robert Lowell and A. J. Liebling. Jean Stafford, divorced from Lowell, was Liebling's widow. (The master of the journalistic essay and monitor of *The Wayward Press* died in 1963.)

Babs no sooner introduced us than she was engaged by other members of the Guild. Stafford's expression suggested she was evaluating a potential date and not entirely sure she wanted to see any more of him—me. I told her how I identified with her comments about the liberations of fiction. There was a long silence, and I was prepared to move along when Jean, with a kind of midwestern purr, asked what kind of experience was I thinking about fictionalizing? I briefly described Avi's attending medical school and mentioned the good times

I had at home with Ken and Mike. "Well, you may need a little more time to think over what it all means," she said quietly. "Although it does sound like a situation for lots of comedy."

We were interrupted by a tall, anorexic-looking fellow in tinted glasses who asked if it was true A. J. Liebling had been kicked out of Yale for refusing to attend chapel. "Let's get our facts straight," Jean Stafford replied. "Dartmouth!"

I moved on to a brief exchange with John Gunther about our enthusiasm for the political future of Bill vanden Heuvel (we had both supported our favorite East Side Democrat in the congressional race he lost to John Lindsay). Babs thought it important for me to meet Leo Rosten, who was a member of the Guild Council. As we turned from John Gunther, I heard an admirer of his *Death Be Not Proud* say in a hushed, tearful voice, "Your tribute to your dead son was inspiring, Mr. Gunther. I'm sorry to impose but I'd be so grateful if you could take a look at a book I've written about my twelve-year-old daughter who died of polio in 1953."

Babs Janeway immediately turned back and with a sympathetic "Oh, dear," distracted the petitioner from her focus on John Gunther. "What a tragedy," Babs said softly. "I can very well understand why you want to write about that." Then she said, as if it were an inspiration of the moment, "I'm sure if you call Peter Heggie at our Guild office he'd be more than pleased to suggest the names of agents or a list of agents who may be able to give you far more help placing your book than any of us."

The Gunther fan seemed to appreciate that. John Gunther certainly did. "I'm going to be traveling for a while," he confessed. "I really wouldn't be able to give your book the prompt attention I'm sure it deserves."

That encounter remains vivid in my memory because it was the first and certainly the most complex of all the bids for readings or blurbs or free advice that are epidemic at the conclusion of Guild panels.

I considered it a routine courtesy when Leo Rosten responded to the Janeway introduction by repeating my name and asking, "Now why do I know your name, Mr. Offit? What is it you've written?"

With such a collegial invitation, I overlooked the possibility that his *Look* magazine colleague may have mentioned me. I told Mr. Rosten that my novel *He Had It Made* was set in the borscht belt. "And most of it deals with waiters, busboys, the chef, baker, and merchants who keep the borscht flowing."

Leo Rosten nodded knowingly and amended, "*Fressers* and *gonifs, alter kockers* and *bulbeniks*." He obviously knew as much about the dining room guests and more about their illustrious peerage than I. Although I recognized the appetites expressed by the overeating *fressers* and *gonifs* and the crotchety, fussy old men dismissed as *alter kockers,* I had to wait for the publication of Rosten's *The Joys of Yiddish* to discover that a *bulbenik* is "one who is inept, clumsy, all thumbs, who fouls things up."

Leon Edel succeeded Elizabeth Janeway as president of the Guild. After a single term the Apostle John of Henry James decided he was spending too much time teaching in Hawaii to lead the charge for the more than three thousand writers who were members of the Guild. The *New York Times* reporter, editor, critic Herbert Mitgang, who qualified as a playwright, novelist, and biographer, swept into office with the Guild's annual version of a plebiscite. On the ticket, too, were Eliot Asimov, Gordon Parks, Peter Prescott, Barbara Tuchman, and me. Margaret Cousins and Ann Birstein were cochairs of the Nominating Committee.

I knew Asimov as the author of *Man on Spikes* and a former semipro baseball player whom the *Chicago Tribune* book reviewer Robert Cromie had introduced as "the one writer in America who knows the answer to all baseball questions." (When I suggested that perhaps Roger Angell shared that title with Asimov, Cromie responded, "Ah, but Angell is an editor, too.")

I was also acquainted with Ann Birstein, whose novel I read after her husband, Alfred Kazin, confronted me at a PEN gathering with a challenge I've responded to ever since: "What kind of friend are you if you don't buy and read a friend's novel?" I did, and I considered *Summer Situations* an entertaining tour de force, Krafft-Ebing as viewed by Noel Coward in the dunes of Cape Cod.

I was acquainted, too, with Gordon Parks and Barbara Tuchman, but I was meeting Peter Prescott for the first time. Prescott had moved on from *Look,* for which he wrote a widely read book column, to *Newsweek,* where his criticisms were among the most respected in the land. Balding but with magisterial bearing, Prescott's voice and diction were so authoritative when he first spoke to me, it required restraint not to stand at parade rest, if not attention. We sat side by side in the dining room of the St. Moritz, and just before Herb Mitgang tapped the gavel, I mentioned to Peter that I thought it brave and daring of a critic to join a council of writers.

"And why would that be?" he asked.

"Look around the room," I said and then recited the names of some of the writers I recognized. "Do you think a year will pass without half of this Council publishing a book? What happens if you write a qualified review, or worse yet ignore a book by a Council member?"

Peter responded with just a trace of hesitation. "I would hope members of our Council would have better manners."

By the time we met again, Prescott incurred just that sort of wrath from the very member who nominated us. Ann Birstein was annoyed at him for not reviewing *Summer Situations.* I tried to distract Ann by engaging her with my genuine enthusiasm for her fiction. Then I sat next to Peter, shielding him, too, from the inquiries of another member who baited with the question "What exactly determines the selection of books you review?"

Although Peter Prescott and I served together on various Guild, Foundation, and Fund committees, that issue rarely surfaced again. Not that it would have diminished his confidence in his own taste or his determination to contribute to the community of writers. Prescott went on to become president of the Authors Guild Foundation and later the League Fund. Ann Birstein continued to write fiction and memoirs and founded the Barnard Writers on Writing Program, in which she once again "nominated" me to participate—but not Peter Prescott.

I was asked to join the board of the Authors League Fund in 1972 not long after my election to the Guild's Council. The Fund is related to the League because it includes representatives of both the Authors and Dramatists Guilds. But the Fund is an independent entity responsible for its own financing and management.

With a generous gift from the novelist James Michener (*Tales of the South Pacific, Hawaii,* et al.), the Fund has served as a source of financial aid for writers down on their luck. The supports, defined as "loans" to distinguish them from grants for writing projects and charity, are rarely repaid. But that's consistent with the intention defined by Michener. Most of the applicants are flat broke and more than a few qualify as what we call "a Michener case," the aged or ailing writer for whom Michener was especially concerned.

Soon after I joined the Fund I was quietly scouting for candidates who were broke and in need of a grub or medical stake. Old pals like Barry Beckham recommended novelists, essayists, poets, and historians too proud to apply to the Fund without coaxing. Barry and I were both surprised by the number of writers and playwrights whom we considered world-beaters but who were unable to pay their own medical bills and were unlikely to bail themselves out with future royalties.

Through the years the Fund was served nobly by a number of unacknowledged doers of good deeds. Among them the poets Daniel Hoffman and Karen Swenson, actress Marian Seldes, playwrights Robert Anderson, Tina Howe, and Marsha Norman, novelists Ira Levin and Kit Reed, historian Paula Giddings, and author-illustrator of books for young readers, Pat Cummings.

After Herb Mitgang retired from the Fund's presidency, Peter Prescott took his place. Prescott's annual Fund appeal letter was so moving, there were trepidations that because he was soliciting from the Guild's constituency, the Fund contributions would significantly reduce gifts to the Foundation and Guild.

Lettie Cottin Pogrebin, who was the president of the Guild during the time this testy issue was raised, suggested a sensible and diplomatic solution—the Prescott direct-mail masterpieces would not be posted until a month after the Guild/Foundation had made its pitch.

The vice president–treasurer of the Fund, George "Jerry" Goodman, who had a series of bestsellers on subjects of finance and investment, and for a number of years wrote and conducted the PBS television series *Adam Smith's Money World,* deftly managed the Fund's money. Sarah Heller, the poet who moonlighted as executive director, and Isabel Howe, devoted friend and colleague, sensitively responded to the applications and made the selection to be submitted to the anonymous loan committee. Madeleine L'Engle, Paula Giddings, and Pat Cummings, secretary of the Guild who succeeded Peter as president of the Fund, provided the links to the Guild and the continuation of the Michener-Mitgang legacy. For me it has been the most congenial and satisfying of assignments, old home week among bards with halos.

Toni Morrison, an editor at Random House, was already a contender in the literary derby, according to the handicappers who reviewed her first novel, *The Bluest Eye,* when, in the fall of 1973, she and I were appointed as a team to represent the Council on the Guild's nominating committee along with three other Guild members. Our selection was announced at a Council lunch meeting conducted in the Dramatists Guild's high-ceilinged studio upstairs from Sardi's. The room had formerly served as the office for the Schubert Organization and was distinguished by two great metal doors engraved with figures of prancing women. Years later, I learned the gates were designed to create a version of a strongbox, because in the days when the Schuberts reigned on Broadway all box office receipts were received and tabulated there.

Reviewing the selections for our Nominating Committee required neither security nor a decorator's splendor. Toni and I started our "tally" as soon as the meeting adjourned. We ambled crosstown toward Toni's office at East 50th Street and my hangout at *Intellectual Digest* on East 57th.

A robust young woman who seemed all smiles and regal dignity, Toni's vivacity, her willingness to talk and share opinions, ideas, and intimacies, delighted me. She assumed my job at *ID* was as much an intrusion on my desire to write as was her responsibility as an editor. We talked about our families. I had the feeling that unlike many of the male writers I knew, Toni considered her children as much a source of wonder as my sons, Ken and Mike, were to me.

When I told her about Avi going to medical school to pay our future bills, she grimaced but said affectionately, "Good for her. She must believe you're worth it."

Neither of us knew much about the Guild members who had been selected to serve with us. Toni was aware of Sam Sinclair Baker. Was he an editor as well as a writer? I knew that Judy Blume was the author of *Are You There God? It's Me, Margaret* and was a hero of young adult lit because she refused to yield to censors. Toni liked that. She, too, was looking forward to meeting Judy Blume.

Before I left her at the entrance to the Random House office building, we agreed to swap novels and meet again at her office to set up our slate. I promptly sent my new friend a copy of *Only a Girl Like You*—and soon after received a copy of *The Bluest Eye*. I read: "Quiet as it's kept, there were no marigolds in the fall of 1941. We thought, at the time, that it was because Pecola was having her father's baby, that the marigolds did not grow." From the first lines to the concluding paragraph, "I talk about how I did not plant the seeds too deeply, how it was the fault of the earth, the land, of our town . . ." the novel was a complex, virtuoso performance. I suspected I was in the presence of a formidable new voice in American fiction, but it was difficult to associate that solemn, biblical style with the agreeable, effervescent editor who was my most recent "friend."

At our meeting in Toni's office several weeks later, she had nothing more to say about my novel than that she received it. Given my impression of Toni Morrison's poetic prose, I was tempted to ask her to keep the title page with my flattering inscription to her and toss my adolescent romance back to me. We shared sandwiches, coffee, and again warm and lively conversation.

I asked Toni if she was empowered to make independent editorial decisions—could she publish any book she wanted without soliciting opinions from other members of the staff? Her response was a skeptical smile that suggested the question was naïve. Of course she could, she told me, with a wink in her voice. "But Bob Bernstein keeps a very close watch over everything that goes on here."

Although there were three other members of our committee, it was kind of routine at the Guild for the Council representatives to draw up the list of officers and new candidates for the Guild Council.

Toni and I agreed before we'd even unwrapped our sandwiches that we'd go with the current lineup of officers.

Our discussion of candidates to the Council was swift. Toni introduced the name of novelist and short story writer Toni Cade Bambara, for whom she expressed admiration. I felt rewarded with this tip and went along. Phil Hamburger, Louis Snyder, and Howard Taubman had established their credentials with engagement in Guild programs. Nancy Milford and Diane Wakowski—a biographer and a poet—were among the other writers we considered our candidates.

We were both friends and fans of John A. Williams. Toni told me John had a rough go with the American Academy in Rome years ago and PEN had not responded with appropriate support.

It was the first I'd heard of it, but it explained why John had declined invitations to join PEN. Toni, too, expressed misgivings about PEN. I took a shot at plugging the good deeds of the American Center by praising the progressive leadership of its two most recent presidents, Charles Bracelen Flood and Tom Fleming. I also tried to make the point that writers' organizations frequently changed "personality" with new administrations. It wasn't fair to hold the current leadership of PEN responsible for decisions made years ago. Toni seemed to find my analysis naïve or too political.

During the course of the next twenty years, she continued to write acclaimed novels, winning the National Book Critics Circle Award and the Pulitzer Prize, but as far as I knew, Toni Morrison didn't accept invitations to join the PEN board or participate in its programs.

She was, however, responsive to the Guild and appeared on several of our panels, including one to discuss author-editor relationships. It was the high compliment of my run as chair of the Guild's program committee when Toni told a crowd in the room at the St. Moritz we'd rented for the seminar that she sometimes wondered why she took off valuable time from writing to talk about writing. "I guess it's because Sidney makes these invitations seem like fun and *so* important."

After she won the Nobel Prize for Literature in 1993, Toni Morrison was swamped with invitations. I saw her only at several

PEN events that she attended while continuing to decline membership on PEN's board. Tina Brown hosted a PEN benefit at Grand
Central Station where Toni joined the dais of Nobel laureates.
When I approached her at the end of the evening she smiled at me.
I thought she was about to say, "Where have you been? I've missed
you." We were photographed together and then she reprimanded
me like a disappointed teacher: "You still have time for this after
all these years? You should be home writing, Sidney."

Robert Caro is sufficiently talented to serve as an innovative administrator while continuing to write classic works of biography. He'd
just won the Pulitzer Prize for his seminal biography of Robert Mo-
ses and launched his study of Lyndon Johnson for a projected
three-volume biography when he accepted the presidency of the
Guild in 1979. At his inaugural, Caro spoke of meeting writers during his cross-country travels for research. "Time and time again
when I spoke to writers I was impressed to hear how the Authors
Guild had helped them."

   Several months into his term, Bob launched a major effort to win
for American writers a Public Lending Right that would provide fees
for authors from books borrowed from public libraries. He invited
Lord Willis, the British author and playwright, who was one of the
leaders of the campaign to achieve such benefits for writers in the
UK, to speak at a Guild meeting. We learned from the British experience that success in such a venture is determined by inexhaustible
persistence as well as political timing.

   When he retired from the Guild presidency, Robert Caro, who
was very much aware of the demands of the assignment as well as the
complexity of leadership talents required to lead the Guild harmoni-
ously, enlisted Anne Edwards as his successor. A biographer and
film writer as familiar with West Coast as with East Coast scribblers,
she accepted, then quietly but efficiently kept us on track. Among
the achievements of her run was a gracious and hospitable response
to the Writers Union, an organization some members of the Guild
Council considered competitive, with a potential for diluting the

Guild's effectiveness. When the Nation Institute sponsored a Writers Congress to discuss the formation of the Union, Anne Edwards tempered criticism with the wise conclusion that Guild Council members should participate if so inclined. "There are certainly enough problems and concerns for writers to go around."

It was agreed at the end of Anne's second term that Robert Massie, former Rhodes scholar and author of the Pulitzer Prize biography *Peter the Great,* would be an excellent candidate as president of the Guild. As the representative of the nominating committee, I offered the scepter to Bob. He was grateful but at the moment engaged in treating the writer's contagion, an "overdue book." We decided I should approach Madeleine L'Engle, a true-blue member of the Guild Council, to hold the fort for two years.

I'd met Madeleine L'Engle years earlier at a children's book fair in Cleveland. On our way to a dinner party the evening before we were scheduled to speak to an audience of young readers, Madeleine, Maia Wojciechowska, Lloyd Alexander, and I were jammed into a station wagon along with several of our librarian hosts. It was my suggestion that we entertain ourselves during the long trip with comic impressions of writers for children, an impulsive idea that turned out to be right on the money.

Maia, a born skeptic and satirist, delighted in mocking our image. Lloyd provided a takeoff of the historian-scholar creating make-believe worlds. I played the retarded adult mumbling fantasies of gumdrops and cuddly bears. Madeleine, who had been a professional actress, performed the I-take-myself-too-seriously author of kiddie-lit with such exaggerated gusto we insisted on encores.

Eventually I discovered that Madeleine (*A Wrinkle in Time*), Lloyd (*The High King*), and Maia (*Shadow of a Bull*) had each won the Newberry Award for novels considered the outstanding contribution for their year to children's literature. It made no difference that I was the least distinguished of our party; the improvs in the station wagon provided our bond.

Soon after we returned to New York, Madeleine invited Avi and me for a piano recital at the spacious West Side apartment she and her handsome husband, Hugh Franklin, shared with their family.

The only other guests were Eli Wallach and Anne Jackson, enduring icons of film and stage. Eli and Anne were old friends of Madeleine and Hugh, dating back to their shared adventures at summer stock. It was a lively evening and I learned why Arthur Miller identified Eli Wallach as "the happiest good actor I've ever known."

I reciprocated by asking Madeleine's son Bion to join Ken, Mike, and me in the grandstand at Yankee Stadium. Bion's favorite home team was competing for the league leadership with the representatives of my "native land," the Baltimore Orioles. The complexities of rooting for different teams were negotiated between orgies of popcorn, hot dogs, and soft drinks. The Yankees dropped a close one to the Birds. I'm not certain to whom to attribute the definitive crack, "It could only happen because of *A Wrinkle in Time.*"

Among all the writers of my acquaintance I think Madeleine L'Engle had the most committed religious-spiritual belief. She expressed it with as much humor as poetry. During lunch one day when we were meeting to discuss Guild-Fund business, we both confessed to having very limited interest in or talent for numbers. I told Madeleine I recognized my deficit when I was in elementary school, the third grade. "I just couldn't understand why or how when you multiplied any number, say six, by zero, you were left with nothing." Madeleine agreed she felt exactly the same way until she realized the reason. "Zero is the devil," Madeleine told me. "Mess with the devil and you wind up with absolutely nothing every time."

During her two-year term as Guild president, Madeleine presided over the transition of our professional staff. Peter Heggie died, after thirty years of service, and Helen Stephenson, his assistant, agreed to cover until we were certain about his successor. Madeleine also rallied Garson Kanin, the president of the Authors League, to moderate a panel, "Writing in 1986," focusing on the effects of conglomeration in publishing. At the conclusion of the discussion, Garson, Madeleine, and I rode down in the elevator with Brendan Gill, a *New Yorker* staff writer, who had also served on the panel.

"I hope we weren't too pessimistic," Garson said wistfully. The author of the Broadway hit *Bells Are Ringing* and some of the

Tracy-Hepburn screen triumphs, Garson was an enthusiast in good company.

"We were just fine, splendid," Brendan Gill reassured him. "I don't believe we provided a single excuse *not* to write."

More than excuses not to write was provided by the Tax Reform Act of 1986, with its onerous capitalization requirements that would have made it mandatory for writers to capitalize business expenses over the earning lives of their work instead of deducting them annually as they were incurred. Bob Massie inherited the campaign to revoke this law when, true to his word, he assumed the leadership of the Guild after Madeleine's two-year tenure.

For the four years of his presidency, it was all double drill and no canteen for Bob Massie. As an historian and biographer, he understood the profound effect the tax ruling would have on long-term research projects. It threatened to discourage if not entirely prohibit the writing of major historical and biographical texts. To amend the law, Massie rallied a galaxy of American historians and biographers to trek to Washington and present our case to the lawmakers. Along the way it was necessary, too, for the Guild to hire a lobbyist. A coincidence enabled me to serve again as the "nominator."

The chain of events began when Bob Caro introduced me to a new friend of his, Stanley Cohen, who was celebrating his rental of the house directly across the street from our apartment on East 69th Street. Sitting by the window in the high-ceilinged room that had previously been occupied by the Shah of Iran's delegate to the United Nations, I was introduced to a dashing young lady whom Stanley Cohen presented as his friend in Washington. She seemed impatient, restless, not at all interested in sitting with a person whose name she didn't recognize. I supposed she was a reporter who covered the capital beat but when I asked, "What paper do you work for?" she responded, "Paper? I'm a lobbyist." By the end of the evening Liz Robbins, with my recommendation, was on her way to meet Bob Massie.

The deadly duo of a Pulitzer laureate and a Washington Houdini arranged for meetings with almost all of the twenty members of the Senate Finance Committee and thirty-six members of the House Ways and Means Committee. Among the writers who were most recognized and therefore helpful in this effort were David McCullough, Tony Lukas, David Halberstam, Tom Clancy, George Goodman (aka Adam Smith), and Barbara Tuchman.

It wasn't until the beginning of his second term that Massie's campaign concluded with a landmark triumph for writers and the Authors Guild. Just before midnight on Friday, October 21, 1989, the Senate and House passed the Technical Tax Correction bill, signed by President Reagan, exempting writers from the Uniform Capitalization net of the new tax law.

The enormous commitments of time and effort by Robert Massie were appreciated by so many members of the Guild, he set an intimidating precedent for a successor. As a member of the nominating committee responsible for getting Massie involved in this no-pay, time-consuming, historic good deed, I became his willing confidant, and once again a member of the committee to find a candidate to be his "heir."

After a summer and autumn of discussions that included chats with David McCullough, who was in Martha's Vineyard, Tony Lukas in East Hampton, Judy Blume at Key West, and a return engagement with Frances FitzGerald, whom I approached so often for PEN and the Guild, I began to feel like a rejected suitor, our friend and lively coconspirator Susan Cheever suggested we ask Erica Jong to serve as president of the now more than six-thousand-member Guild, and she accepted.

The Erica Jong I remembered fondly was a regular at PEN cocktail parties. I recalled a demure young poet filled with passion for English literature and flattered to be in the company of such a variety of professional writers.

But it wasn't long into Erica's reign (1991–1992) before the fireworks began to sizzle and crack. Less than a year after she became our president, Erica called a special meeting of the Council at her apartment on the Upper East Side that concluded with a committee to evaluate the Guild's accounts and management. An assembly of such talent would be the envy of any government commission publisher's list.

This group of Guild guardians assumed the responsibility to effect changes as graciously and quietly as possible. Herb Mitgang was our leader. Herb was joined by Roger Angell, a revered conscience of the Guild as well as *The New Yorker*; Jean Strouse, as deft with the nuances of numbers as with the meter of words; Harry Saint, a former Wall Street wizard with a lone novel to his credit that sold to the movies for a million bucks; and Paula Giddings, a historian-biographer who wrote *When and How I Enter* and the brilliant biography *Sword Among the Lions, Ida B. Wells*.

Six months later the staff was reorganized and at Bob Massie's suggestion our former director, who had been a major contributor to the campaign for tax relief, was awarded a full year's severance pay. That passed without a hitch but meant that Erica Jong's successor would not only have to mend the staff but deal with a major shortfall.

There was no obvious candidate. The script seemed to call for no less a diplomat-healer than Franklin Delano Roosevelt or—Eleanor! Unfortunately both were occupied with other Olympians of the Elysian Fields. Jean Strouse took on the tough assignment of heading the Nominating Committee. When she consulted me, I suggested we ask Mary Pope Osborne, a member of the Council and author of plays, novels, and books for young readers.

Because I was already acquainted with Mary, Jean thought I should speak to her before the formal invitation and try to set it up. I did. Mary was hesitant. She was deeply involved in preliminary research for a new project, but her voice and manner expressed such devotion to the Guild it was clear she found it difficult—perhaps impossible—to discourage the invitation. We followed up with reassuring calls to Mary by Roger Angell and Jean. By the winter of 1993 the Authors Guild had another president qualifying for our Mount Rushmore.

Mary Pope Osborne is tall and graceful, with fashionably curly, frizzy blond hair and a voice and smile that could knock 'em dead on Broadway or the Houses of Parliament. Her four years as president of the Guild were distinguished by balanced books and the introduction of the first full-time staff of attorneys to monitor First Amendment, copyright, and tax issues in addition to offering free consultations to the now seven thousand members. It was Mary who signed up lawyer Robin Davis Miller and, later, attorneys Paul Aiken and Kay Murray, who—working together—graduated Guild services to the broadest and most effective level in the League's eighty-year history.

Another of the complex legacies Mary Pope Osborne inherited from the Erica Jong whirlwind was an annual benefit. To her credit, Erica rallied bestselling writers from Great Britain, as well as writers, agents, editors, and publishers of the United States to support a fundraiser for our Guild Foundation, the educational arm of the Guild. Erica's show was on our road.

Mary Pope Osborne had no hesitation or difficulty keeping it running. By the next year Garrison Keillor, the sage of Lake Wobegon, enlisted as our host, guaranteeing an evening of fun and wit, as well as the sharing of Garrison's enthusiasm and gift for articulating the Guild's egalitarian premise. "Once a member of the Guild, we are all equals," Garrison proclaimed from the benefit podium. "Our Guild represents us all, poets, bestselling writers, scribblers in the night."

With Garrison as our Sol Hurok, the Guild Foundation benefits featured a billboard of the nation's most sophisticated literary personalities. George Plimpton scripted and read a mock rejection letter to Ernest Hemingway from a publisher. The most sweetly brilliant of his generation's humorists, Christopher Buckley not only agreed to pitch in with an original monologue but also consented to serve on our board as a special present to me, whom he adopted as his "Uncle Sid."

If the Guild's constitution provided for the coronation of a queen, Mary Pope Osborne would have been our enlightened monarch forever. Even this constituency of skeptics, atheists, agnostics, and deists agreed Mary was our leader by divine right. But after two terms—four years—Mary retired from the Guild's presidency to pick up the writing project that went on to become the Magic Tree House series of books for young readers. Among the more than sixty million copies now circulating throughout the world are several signed to devoted fans—Anna, Caroline, Tristan, Lily, and Wyatt—our grandchildren! I cherish them as "souvenirs" celebrating four decades of what I think of as Rex Stout's legacy.

This legacy continued to thrive with the leadership of Tony Lukas, Scott Turow, Letty Cottin Pogrebin, Nick Taylor, and, later, Roy Blount Jr. They have been supported by an all-star cast including Rachel Veil, David Levering Lewis, Nicky Weinstock, Jim Gleick, John R. MacArthur, Susan Cheever, James B. Stewart, Clarissa Pinkola Estes, Peter Petrie, James Duffy, and our indispensable executive director Paul Aiken, who in collaboration with Jan Constantine are our laureates of "contract, contract, contract . . . copyright, copyright, copyright!"

On Monday, April 3, 2006, at the Metropolitan Club in New York, the Authors Guild Foundation held its fourteenth annual benefit in celebration of writers and writing. We honored Ruebén Martínez, the owner and founder of Librería Martínez Books in Santa Ana, California. Mr. Martínez, an energetic and dedicated advocate for Latino writers and literature, cofounded the Latino Book Festival and has built Librería Martínez Books into one of the most successful Spanish-language bookstores in the country.

Roy Blount Jr., the newly elected president of the Guild, was the host for the evening. (Roy's memoir, *Be Sweet,* has a subtitle, *A Conditional Love Story,* but there is nothing conditional about Roy's generous support of the Guild.)

The presentation of the award to Señor Martínez was by Guild Council member Oscar Hijuelos, author of the Pulitzer Prize novel *The Mambo Kings Play Songs of Love.* It was a sellout house, a triumph spiced by our hero Paul Aiken's reflections on the Guild's founding and history. The tunes may be different, the lyrics more complex, but the Authors Guild "band" continues, true to the legacy of Rex Stout, to play on and on.

VI

Book—ends: Twenty-first Century

32

A Nobel Laureate for Medicine and a
Philosopher of Bullshit, JHU, Circa 1948

1948–2007

Soon after Martin Rodbell, JHU, B.A. 1949, received the 1994 Nobel
Prize for Medicine, his classmate and best friend, Dan Levin, rallied a
group of Hopkins undergraduates of that era to celebrate Marty's
achievement with a black-tie dinner at the Faculty Club in Baltimore.
"I'd like you and Russ Baker to speak. Just brief remarks. Marty's a
modest fellow and nothing we're going to say will be in a league with
the Nobel Prize, so keep it light, humorous."

Dan's invitation was about as intimidating as a formula for an
after-dinner speech could be. Keep it light? Humorous? About the
Nobel Prize for Medicine?

The best I could come up with was a brief gig acknowledging as
seriously as I could that I'd been selected to salute Marty because
Dan Levin knew I was one of the very few guests who understood
and could explain the science that led to Marty Rodbell's expenses-paid
round trip to Stockholm.

I went on to confess that this was all the more remarkable because I'd received a D, barely passing our biology survey course, 1947. After defining the award as designated by the Nobel committee as a prize for the Physiology of Medicine, I cribbed from the newspaper report and explained that Marty and his colleague, Alfred Gilman, shared the Nobel for their discovery of cell signalers called G-proteins. I don't remember where I went from there, but I vaguely recall educating the house with various sounds, melodies, and chirps that I assured them were signals from G-proteins.

Russ Baker followed, sketching his experience with a Hopkins physics class. Russ told us he had defied the odds and managed to earn an A in the first exam, a multiple-choice quiz. There followed a period of delusional confidence until the final exam, when Russ said his grade was so low it disappeared beneath all microscopic sights. He was called for a conference with the professor, who was right in there with the leading physicists of the day. "We made a deal," the winner of the 1979 Pulitzer Prize for distinguished commentary and the 1983 Pulitzer Prize for biography confessed. "He would pass me with a D but only if I promised never to take another course in any of the sciences."

The pleasures of that evening were so bonding that soon after, Marty wrote me a warm and intimate letter in response to reading my *Memoir of the Bookie's Son*. He remarked about the resemblance of his father to mine as a Baltimore street guy: ". . . in constant brawls with drifters along the docks . . . a professional boxer who got his nose broken several times . . . Jack Sharkey's trainer . . . but after he married my mother he went straight and owned a pool parlor on Pennsylvania Avenue. Eventually he became a grocer, and I grew up in West Baltimore over a grocery store . . . I'm sure you can now understand why I love your father's personality . . . Now, at last, I have your father as a treasure on my bookshelf."

Harry Frankfurt was a philosophy major at Hopkins, class of 1949. An intense young scholar with more good looks than he gave himself credit for, Harry seemed to walk through his years at Homewood wrestling with ideas and a fiercely moral view of what it all meant. Although he was not a member of the *News-Letter* staff, Harry and I were sufficiently acquainted for me, as editor, to ask him to write a piece about Cardinal Mindszenty, who was emerging as a press-ordained hero of the Hungarian Revolution.

"As anti-communists, it is certainly true that we must fight communism," the future philosophy professor wrote in the March 11, 1949, edition of the campus weekly. "But as democrats, we cannot betray ourselves to a mistaken alliance with decadent bourbonism and a feudal Church . . ."

In 2003, the Princeton University Press published a sixty-seven-page book consisting of Harry's essay "On Bullshit." It sold more than four hundred thousand copies and was translated into twenty-five languages. (But not, as far as I know, Hungarian.)

The October 22, 2006, magazine section of *The New York Times* featured a one-page interview with Harry. The focus was on his latest book, a sequel to "On Bullshit" less sensationally titled "On Truth." Harry's remarks about his books and readers' response were reminiscent of the candid, high-minded student I remembered from our years at Johns Hopkins a half century ago. But the answer to the question "Can you tell about your childhood briefly?" passing quietly in type, was to me the most provocative of Harry's reflections. "I was raised in Brooklyn and in Baltimore," Harry said. "My father was a bookkeeper. When I was thirty-six years old, my mother told me I was adopted."

That statement evoked my memory of visiting Harry's family home in the suburbs of Baltimore—was it on Hicks Avenue?—in 1949. I remembered my feeling that Harry was uneasy in the presence of his parents. Like my relationship to Marty Rodbell, it required the passing of half a century for me to discover "clues" as to where two of the most brilliant undergraduates of our era were "coming from."

33

Nathan Lane, *The Boy Friend,* and H. L. Mencken's Book-ends

2003

My fortunate encounter with Nathan Lane was in Sag Harbor in August 2003—not pedigree Hampton but a favorite migration pause for playwrights and actors going back and forth from Broadway. My evening with Avi began at six with the goal of arriving at the Bay Street Theatre at eight for the opening night of the revival of *The Boy Friend,* directed by Julie Andrews, who had debuted in the Sandy Wilson musical in 1954.

It was during the summer month I was preoccupied with structuring this book—should I compensate for its lack of a developing narrative? I was reminded of my dilemma when early in that evening at a party hosted by Arnie Cooper, a psychoanalyst, and his wife, the classical pianist Katherine Addleman, I talked with Ted Solotaroff, whose memoir *First Love* I had just read with admiration. I complimented Ted on his seamless blend of story (a failed marriage) with evocation of time, place, and literary history.

I had no such device to provide even a chronological progression to my series of sketches and reminiscences. Perhaps I was "written out," as Kurt Vonnegut said of himself while continuing to write brilliantly. Kurt said it to me again at the party. I was certain that the eighty-year-old master was still making words bite and tickle. I was much less certain if I ever had or would.

At eight-fifteen the curtain went up for the first act of *The Boy Friend.* Theme: girls need boyfriends. Resolution: girls get boyfriends. Everything in between was charming, vibrant, full of all the romantic promise of "A little room in Bloomsbury / Just a little place for you and me." It reminded me that I had a beginning, lots in between, but no ending, no "book-end."

Filled with warm nostalgia for the first time we had seen the show fifty years ago, and the illusion that our legs were still moving to the beat of the Charleston, Avi and I joined the celebration of opening night at B. Smith's bayside restaurant. Even our evening had structure; it began and ended with a party.

We were greeted by William Pickens III in a double-breasted seersucker jacket, looking every bit the aristocratic gentleman of the world. He immediately introduced us to Barbara B. Smith, a former model who along with her husband owned this gem of Sag Harbor. A stunning beauty with a warm smile recalling Lena Horne, Ms. Smith seemed so pleased to greet us I had the feeling I frequently have in Bill Pickens's company that I'm basking in the affections felt for the "mayor" of his Sag Harbor community.

The evening was gray and humid with the weather report threatening rain, but Bill led us to the open deck and told me Nathan Lane was not more than five feet from where we were standing. It was a leap in memory and style from *The Boy Friend, My Fair Lady,* and *The Sound of Music* to *Guys and Dolls* and *The Producers.* I considered how to start a conversation with him.

Unlike the spontaneous conversations of my lifetime—specifically motivated only when on assignment for a publication—I was hoping something might come of this chat that would help me wrap up my pages of friendships, encounters, and adventures at work and play. It seemed unlikely, but the guy who played Nathan Detroit deserved a little action from a bookie's son.

Dressed in a jacket, white shirt, and tie, with a shy, grateful smile, neither his style nor demeanor suggested the bombastic hustlers Nathan Lane so vividly brought to life on stage.

From conversation with Norman Mailer at a PEN reception forty years ago, I'd learned not to approach a well-known person merely with words of admiration. " 'I love your book. You're my favorite writer,' " Norman had mimicked. "What can you say to that except 'thank you' or 'more, more, more.' Then, if you don't keep the conversation going the next thing you know your former fan concludes you're a snob or a sap."

When I observed Lane's conversation with two young ladies was running dry, I approached him and launched into the Mailer observation. "I learned from Norman Mailer years ago . . ." I began, confident Norman would forgive me using his name as reference. Nathan Lane responded with a textured, musical laugh. Encouraged I said, "So, my opening line to you, Mr. Lane, is what's your vote on impeaching Bush?"

"I'll sign up right now," he said.

I told him there had been an ad in the morning *Times* soliciting enlistments for the campaign. The only name associated with Citizens for Impeachment was Lawrence Lader, identified as "President." I described Larry to Nathan Lane as one of those courtly, well turned-out seniors you'd never suspect of being a radical.

Our conversation drifted back to speculations about where Bush derived his strong support. I qualified the arrogance of the label but mentioned that as a Bawlamer boy I'd received a clue long ago: "the booboisie."

Lane's expression shifted from indulgent amusement to the excitement of a free-association cue. "That's from H. L. Mencken!" he said. "Mencken was my hero. I was absolutely captivated by the character in *Inherit the Wind*," he went on. "I read everything about Mencken I could get my hands on. I was impressed by the originality of his language—his ideas. I wrote my high school term paper about Mencken and actually got to meet an editor who had worked with him. It was a major shock when the editor—what was his name? And how can I forget the name of the magazine—the one Mencken and George Jean Nathan founded after *Smart Set*?"

It had been fifty-five years and three hundred–plus pages since my encounter with Henry L. Mencken. I don't recall ever talking about him during the thirty-five years the Hamptons had been our summer retreat. Belonging to that same era was *The Boy Friend,* the first musical Avi and I ever saw and the gold standard of frantic, vivacious, "Won't You Charleston with Me?" musical extravaganza. Julie Andrews was the songbird of our honeymoon.

So here we were after a triumphant Julie Andrews encore, talking to Nathan Lane, the actor who brought a Damon Runyon character back alive in *Guys and Dolls,* the Nathan Lane who would certainly not be on the wrong side of the pari-mutuel window cutting it up with a bookie's son. And his best bet, my best bet, was one and the same Henry L. Mencken.

"What was the name of that magazine? And that editor—Mencken's managing editor?" Lane repeated. Observing a great performer in modest distress is on a par with standing by when those with less histrionic talents are suffering death by torture. But I couldn't help Nathan Lane because I was momentarily stunned myself. It seemed to me such a coincidence that this young man—Nathan Lane was forty-seven, the age of our elder son—even knew about the magazine, much less the member of Mencken's staff. As soon as my head cleared I told him, "The name of the magazine was *The American Mercury.*"

"Yes, of course," Lane said, relieved but unwilling to settle until he recalled the name of the editor who had indicted Mencken. Was it possible that he had actually spoken to the one person from the Mencken era who was still hanging around Mercury Publications in 1952, the one person who was doing chores for the magazines and mystery reprints that were all that was left of Mencken's legacy?

With the exception of Gloria and Mike Levitas and Avi, I knew no one in the world, or for that matter hadn't known anyone for a long, long time, who would recognize the name, but here I was on the deck of a swank eatery in Sag Harbor overlooking the bay, still hearing snappy refrains about "that perfect thing called a boy friend," and talking to one of the great stars of current musical entertainment—and my passport for the evening was—I said it, "Charlie Angoff."

"Charles Angoff," Nathan Lane repeated with all the gusto of

Max Bialystock announcing the discovery of *Springtime for Hitler.*
"Charles Angoff. Yes, he worked with Mencken. He'd been his managing editor for years." Lane switched into the slightly accented voice
of Angoff, " 'Mencken, that anti-Semite!' Angoff told me Mencken
was anti-Semitic. He went on and on about him. I was disappointed,
shocked. I didn't know what to make of it.

"I admired Mencken so much. It was hard to believe but then
there was this recent biography—was it by Terry Teachout?—anyway,
he said even worse. He wrote about Mencken's reluctance to support
America's war with Germany during World War II. I think he even
said Mencken was uncritical of Hitler. What was I to think? All that
beautiful language. I've always been fascinated by language, by style,
and Mencken had so much of it. He was on the right side, too, of so
many social issues." Nathan Lane sighed and shrugged. His eyes expressed the despair of a young man whose adopted parent has failed
him.

I made a feeble effort to put it all in some kind of perspective.
"Well, you know, it was a different time. . . . We have to remember,
too, that Mencken met regularly with a number of Jewish friends
who were members of his chamber music group. And for all Charlie
Angoff's complaints, Mencken did hire him—a foreign-born Jewish
kid right out of Harvard—and promoted him to managing editor of
his magazine." I was going to go on about his relationship with his
publisher Alfred Knopf, but we were interrupted.

Tony Roberts, Woody Allen's sidekick in *Annie Hall,* had lit up
the Bay Street stage that evening with his takeoff on the British
would-be philanderer Lord Brockurst. Roberts arrived at the party no
doubt prepared to parry praise, and there was Nathan Lane, a visiting
star and peer. They fell into each other's arms.

I stood by wondering if I should remind Tony Roberts of how
often we'd met in the elevator of the Park Avenue building where he
and my son Mike and his family lived. Or should I hang around a
little longer so I could try to further promote my hometown Dr.
Johnson by telling Nathan Lane how gracious Mencken had been to
me when I was a schoolboy. He'd advised me on my collection of first
editions and instructed me never to relight a cigar. I thought about it,

but said no more. Grateful that Nathan Lane had provided me with a concluding book-end if I ever wrote a history, autobiography, memoir, or chat book that opened with my encounter with Henry L. Mencken, Avi and I moved on to cheer Julie Andrews.

Later that evening, as I walked our Maltese, Remy, under the darkening Hampton sky, I lit my cigar for the month, an H. Upmann 2000, Habana #2, and my thoughts about Baltimore, circa 1945, drifted upward with the smoke.

Oh all to end.
—Samuel Beckett,
Stirring Still

Acknowledgments

In many ways this book is an acknowledgment of people who have made it possible for me to get through life with good cheer. Sometimes there are long lists of them. Those old enough will recognize the names and even keep an eye out for their own. The younger generation may, without losing a point on their GPA, skim those paragraphs where I have, in my own way, said thank-you to the grand crowd that has made every day an adventure. They have walked and talked and kibitzed with me when I didn't even know I was down; they have given me work and words and made sure I did not pass many days, like old Boswell, in the exorcism of melancholy, dissipation, and the "the fretful gloom of idleness."

I consider myself fortunate, too, to have had the generous support of family and friends who often shared names, dates, permissions, and esoteric facts from their computers.

Granddaughters Anna, Caroline, and Tristan have enlightened me with information from their "Internet machines" even as we spoke on the telephone. My son Mike, who this past year has been a columnist on worldly goods for *Departures* ("smart advice for smart people"), frequently relieved my bewilderments with answers and wit. Friends at the Authors Guild, Sarah Heller, Isabel Howe, and Julia Berney, checked out verses, history, and points of order. Michael Roberts's gracious assistant at PEN American Center, Ana Bozicevic-Bowling, provided references from PEN's archives and informed me of events via postal mail and telephone.

I discovered Cynthia Barnhart's transcription services ten years ago, and for a modest fee she has patiently and efficiently transferred the pages produced by my Royal typewriter to a disc.

It may be irony, but I prefer to consider it a testimony to enduring love that Avodah K. Offit, M.D., author of the first e-mail novel *Virtual Love*, Simon & Schuster, 1994, continues to compensate for my determination to deny both e-mail and the computer by editing for me with only occasional sighs of incredulity when I retype a whole page.

Thomas Dunne and Sally Richardson have been my friends, editors, and publishers in various roles for more than thirty years, a rare run in the literary derby. I appreciate, too, their colleague Katie Gilligan, associate editor Thomas Dunne Books/St. Martin's Press who, along with John Morrone, has helped me dot the *i*'s and cross the *t*'s without spell check.

—Sidney Offit
January 2008

Index